My Journey: The Life and Times

of

Dr. Emily Moore

Civil rights Activist, Physical Educator, Philanthropist

and Hall of Famer

By:

Ayanna L. Moore

"I claim the last name Moore, and I say if you are a Moore -- then we are related because history has done some things to our people. All of them that I have met outside of my immediate family have been educated, and respectable. The Moore's are all over, not afraid to move, travel and go to strange places. Let me tell you something. Them Moore's, they do things."

- Dr. Emily Moore

Acknowledgements of Dr. Emily Moore

This book is dedicated to my mother and father who made my life possible. My beloved mothers' constant support and encouragement always motivated me through her famous quote, "Just try and do your best." To my Aunt Marie Gillespie for her matriarchal spirit and love that she always shared with her family and friends. To my brothers, Edward, Ronald, Richard, and Gary that always kept me honest, and forever saw me as their little sister. To my sister Marion, who has seen me through many trials and tribulations, always still being in support. Special thoughts and love to Ruby and Maxine Brown. Special love to my college roommate, sorority sister, and confidant Marcia Hazelton. To Maxine and Charlene Gillespie. Also, Arlene McKeithan and a whole bunch of other people whom I have met and who have helped me throughout my journey here on earth. It is to all of them that I give my love and dedicate my legacy.

Luta Continua – It's a lifetime struggle.

Sincerely,

Emily Moore

Author Acknowledgements

I would like to thank God/higher power(s) of the Universe for the blessings bestowed upon me thus far. I thank my parents, Anne-Marie, and Darrin for making sure my siblings and I were never in need. To my close friends and family Ashley, Chareese, Jonathan, Justin and Ni'Gea. To Danara, my mentor and Nadira, the reason I hold myself to be a woman of example. To Twelvette, you cared for me during Covid, in my heart there is always love. To Fineapple, I thank you and I love you for the insight you've brought into my life.

To the Velt Villians, those Rough Riders. There is so much joy and pain that coursed us through the One Square Mile we know as home. As the last class of what was the original Roosevelt Junior-Senior High School building, we a legacy of adults who did not make a deal of what we did not have but made do with what we didWe are now architects, business owners, care professionals, constructors, doctors, educators, law enforcement, mechanics, musicians and always hustlers! I am proud of you all. Shouts to the Gully side where I composed most of this book.

The History Professors at Morgan State University, Dr. Brett Berliner, Miss. Gloria Marrow, and Dr. Brandi Brimmer (no longer at Morgan), this is something like my redemption song for all those Cs. I hope you all read this one day. Lastly, the former chair of the History department Dr. Palma who said they saw something in me as I sat in that chair, as my fate of graduation laid in the stroke of her pen, I am forever grateful.

If the character Albus Dumbledore from Harry Potter were a principle from Roosevelt High School, he would have said, "There is always help in Roosevelt, if you ask." Thank you to those who have contributed their stories that helped solidify Dr. Moore's Journey.

Finally, I want to thank Dr. Emily Moore! As you said, *Life is a struggle,* and we must keep moving! I appreciate you giving me this opportunity. Thank you for trusting me to complete this lifetime project of yours. I have heard your stories for years, but I only had you for two months as a new student in Roosevelt in 2006. The faith, legacy, and support that you have poured into the Roosevelt community is to be remembered for years to come, and now the future generations can read about your life and glory! In your eighties, you are the hardest-working person I know, and I continue to see recognition and blessings unfold around you.

May God Bless you all, and as my grandfather James Deans would say, *"may the train run easy."*

Ayanna L. Moore

CONTENTS

Forward 6

the Island CALLED PAUMANAUK 8

Moore Family History: Andrew Walker Become Andrew Moore (1849-1932) 61

The Journey Begins: Emily Moore 77

Cleveland Elementary: The American Constitution & Honorable Judge Moxey Rigby 85

Black Adolescence and the rise of Civil Rights Era: It was not fair 92

A Book and two Rackets: the Rise of Emily Moore 108

Morgan chose me: Morgan State College 125

Malcolm X comes to Morgan 148

"Over my dead body": The Northwood Demonstrations 160

Summers Sorrows: Without struggle, there would be no sense of victory 185

Summer of 1963: The Moore's Move to Roosevelt 188

Service to the world and the people: Peace Corps 212

Amerikkka on Fire: The Race RIOTS AND The Rise of 'Black Power' 225

Emily Moore the educator 1968-1972 243

Long Island's OUSTED "Firebrand" 255

Unapologetically Black 276

The Alliance Junior Tennis Development Program 301

Rough Riders to Velt Villianz: A Rough Rider for Life 328

'Moore' or Less.. 380

EMILY MOORE VS THE ROOSEVELT BOARD OF EDUCATION
.... 405

Retirement or New Beginnings 414

Rough Rider Remarks.. 439

Bibliography 448

FORWARD

If you know Dr. Emily Moore, her life mission has always been *to fight for the youth, because the youth are the future.* Dr. Moore has selflessly dedicated her life to educating and helping others get further in their lives with messages of encouraging progression of education, and socialization. She recognized the struggle of every generation since the 1960's, and in the same notion, it's the reason she continues to be active on the Roosevelt School District as a trustee in 2024, as she seeks to ensure that the children of Roosevelt are getting the services needed, to be provided to them by through their school district. As an Author, the effort it took to compose and colaorate with Dr. Moore on completing her autobiography has given a clearer meaning of what it means to be consistent, staying determined, and most of all, delivering on what is to mean what you say and say what you mean.

For over 60 years, Dr. Moore has been a champion advocate for youth of New York as she has provided consistancy, determination, and professional development as a physical educator and tennis coach. As a public entity, Dr. Moore has never been afraid to carve her own path, and take on battles for what is right and wrong on the behalf of the youth. When it come to civil rights, and the welfare of children people can trust that Dr. Emily Moore will show up everytime. At eighty-three years old, Emily thanks God for the blessings she received to aquire so many memories sand acomplishments, and than her mother for always telling her to *"Do her best,"* with every effort. Dr. Moore is from a generation that experienced segregation in both the North and south. She has fought against racial inequality, and witnessed the changes of the Civil Rights Movement, and what it represents and means if we give up fighting for our rights in today's society since she was a young girl.

Anyone who knows Dr. Moore, knows that she will tell those around her to write down the things that are happening in their life as she questions, *"who do you want to tell your history? You? Or What someone thinks they know?"* Dr. Moore has lived a vigorous life full of adventures, usually the person behind the camera, or the scenes but leading the way at the same time. She has thousands of photos from events that she has attended during her lifetime, but barely pictures of herself alongside the prominent figures mentioned in her life. Dr. Moore's collection of books, flyers, and photos of African/Black American history, sports history, and various other topics are extensive. Most of all, in the fulfillment of this project, Dr. Moore wished that she had the habit of taking pictures during her life journey way before the demonstrations at Northwood Theater.

To understand Dr. Moore as a person, the History of Long Island, with focuse on the history of Freeport and Roosevelt is provided. Dr. Moore, wanted to ensure that the history of Long Island, and its relation of enslavement and segregation as she knew and experienced it, not the envisionment of what people have always thought in the broad history of Long Island, New York. This section of work will be followed by the family history of Dr. Emily Moore, beginning with the Emancipation of her great-grandfather Andrew Walker.

THE ISLAND CALLED PAUMANAUK

In ancient times, Long Island was called Matouac by some, Paumanok by others. Matouac means a "young man," or "the young warriors," referring to the younger tribes of the western half of the island. Paumanok is a term in the Renneiu language indicating "land of tribute," in reference to Long Island's role as a main source for the Quahog and Conch shells used in the manufacture of sewan or wampum, often used to pay tribute or taxes to another tribe (Prtichard, 2002).

When Italian Explorer Giovanni Verrazano sailed the Atlantic Ocean in pursuit of Asia in 1524, he became one of the first documented Europeans to explore the island called *The Island of Shells* by the Natives of the land. During his exploration, he wrote about his encounters with the native populations. Verrazano learned that the native tribes called the land Paumanauk, Sweanhacky, and Montauwack, all relatively meaning the Island of Shells (Prtichard, 2002).[1] The tribes identified themselves under two main confederacies: the Paumanauk to the East and the Montauwack to the West. The natives of the land honored the shores for its bountiful supply and variation of clams, mussels, oysters, and other sea life that washed upon its shores. The native tribes of the Paumanauk

---

[1] Due to different dialects of the time, these Native American names will have a variation in spelling according to references.

Confederacy were the Shinnecock, Setauket's, Montauks, and Manhassets. The native tribes of the Montauwack Confederacy were the Massapeaquans (Marsapeques) and the Merrick and the Mantinecock tribes (Victor G. Becker, 2022). The Lenape, Maspeth, and Canarsie tribes inhabited the furthest to the east and mainland. Though Verrazano did not choose to settle on the land that hosted various bays along the coastal shores he told of the information he experienced and witnessed.

When English explorer Henry Hudson conducted a sea voyage for the Dutch in 1609, he came across Paumanauk and the mainland as well. His exploration lead to the migration of Dutch migrants to the area and proclaim the lands as a colony, naming it New Netherland/ Amsterdam. During settlement, they called Paumanauk, *Lange Eylant*, eventually merging to the English vernacular, *Long Island.* As the Dutch continued to settle on Long Island, as they eventually migrated from the sandy shores into the densely wooded areas that were deemed uninhabitable for an extended period. New Amsterdam was renamed New York in 1665 after England's Duke of York, who later became King James II of England. The Paumanauk Confederacy lands became Nassau

County, Montauwack lands became Suffolk County, the lands of the Lenape, Maspeth, and Rockaway tribes became Queens County. Lastly, the lands of the Canarsie tribe, which was the hardest to concur, would become Kings County, also known as the Borough of Brooklyn in the 21st Century.

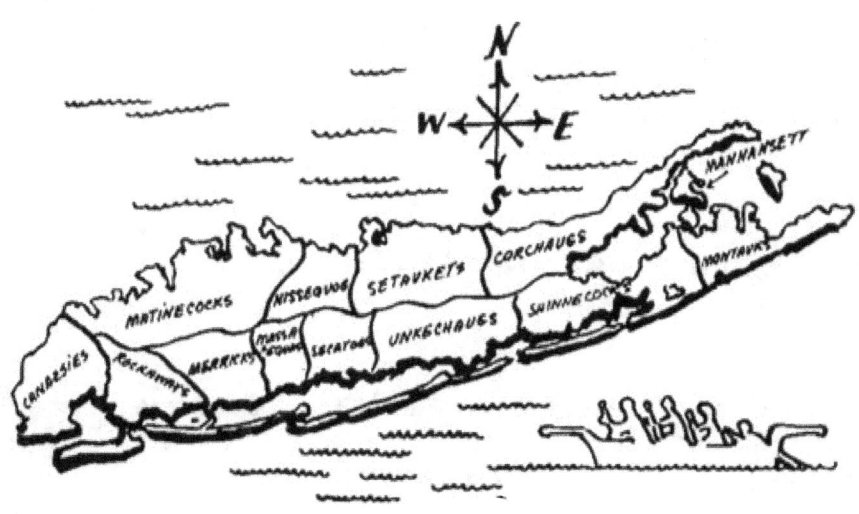

MAP 1 GEOGRAPHICAL MAP OF LONG ISLAND DEPICTING NATIVE AMERICAN TERRITORIES. (MARTINE, 1992)

It was the Lenape Native American tribe that helped the English and Dutch settlers navigate between the North and South shores of Nassau County. European exploration memoirs of North America reference the Lenape tribe as 'Wood Nymphs' and 'Fairies' by the English, and Leprechauns by the Irish because of their small stature, and good intentions as they helped the explorers as they became lost in the wooded areas. In 1643, an area Nassau County was purchased from the Natives through an unfair treaty. Due to its location in the middle of the Nassau County land, it received the name Hemel-Hempstead, *Hemel* means Town Center in the Dutch language. After the mass genocide and pushing out of the Native Americans during the Colonial Era the area south of Hemel-Hempstead was named The South Woods.

New York and the Atlantic Slave Trade

The act of War and the unwritten rules that followed once allowed the enslavement of enemies, and their families as reward. The enslaved populations of Africa and Islamic countries of the Mediterranean Sea allowed for the enslaved to have opportunities to buy their freedom, to marry into the families they served, all n alignment with their religious and social beliefs. European seen the act of slavery as an exploitive endeavor as the explored of the continent of Africa, changing the definition of what it was to be a slave in the development of Colonial America. In the 1400s, King Phillip II of Spain received African prisoners of war from voyagers who traveled through Africa and the Mediterranean Sea into the Gulf of Guinea. As explorations and conquering continued, so did the exchanges of African people as gifts. The Atlantic Slave Trade was officiated in 1518 by King Charles I of England when he authorized Spain to ship captured African people directly to North America, South America, and the Islands of the Caribbean Sea for servitude. In 1650, King Charles II of England authorized the charter for the Royal African Company, the first Voyage line catered to the capturing of African people. Since then, the history and practice of treating Africans as human chattel has left a long history of brutalization, exploitation, forced assimilation and the rhetorical theories of mental, emotional, and physical capabilities and incapability's of the black and brown populations of the world

New York became the epicenter for the slave trade in the 1600s. The Manhattan area of Wall Street, Pearl Street and Water Street housed the main enslaved auction centers of the African people (Olly J. M., 2021). Though New York served as a trade epicenter, most people of the New York metropolitan areas only owned 1 to 15 slaves. In comparison, Suffolk County, Long Island had the largest enslaved populations of Native Americans and

Africans within the northern colonies (Olly J. M., 2021). The earliest presence plantations in the Suffolk County area had enslaved Africans sent from of Caribbean Island Barbados in 1655. Records indicate that the enslaved during that time were from the Bight of Biafra, the Gold Coast, and the Bight of Benin regions of Africa (Hofstra University Library Special Collections Department, unknown). Most Black families that are native to Long Island are of Native American and African descent and in present day, on Long Island, the Native American reservation populations reflect a mixture of African and Native American people.

The Quakers, Pilgrims, and Puritans practiced slavery differently than the later English settlers at the beginning of the Colonial Era. The Quakers and Pilgrims were once indentured servants, rejected citizens, criminals and social-economically poor people who all experienced the same subjection and punishments as Black people in their European counties. There forth, they lived with a shared experience in labor and restriction, allowing for a notion of what freedom was to the colonial settlers. Black men who served their indenture were able to buy land, create profit, enlist in the colonial army, and live as a family with their spouse and children.

This enabled a population of freed Black and Brown people to grow in Long Island and within the populated city regions ("Dutch West Company", 2014).

When the Dutch West India Company began in 1621, the enslaved were able to buy their freedom in exchange for labor or annual payment through indentured servitude. The clause to this rule was that even though they were emancipated, their children remained property of the Dutch West India Company until they too were bought or emancipated. As English settlers arrived by the masses with preconceived racial restrictions and treatment practiced in the United Kingdom and Caribbean territories, there was a change in the social, political, and economic structures created prior to their arrival. The differences in the religious and moral backgrounds of the settlers brought a variation of economic, social, and political treatment of the enslaved within the customs and progression of the Peculiar Institution.[2] This was a huge contrast between the comparison of North and South cultures of slavery.

In 1712, a slave revolt occurred in New York, this resulted in

---

[2] The name that was given to slavery during the time of reflection of slavery leading to the abolition movement. (The Peculiar Insitution)

the implementation of *Black Codes* upon the freed people of New York bringing drastic social and economic changes. These restrictions included prohibiting the meeting of groups larger than three; owning firearms; trading; being entertained in a private home; owning or inheriting property; and traveling without passes, all laws to be met with physical punishment (Olsen, 1944). All white citizens were able to enforce the social law of Black Codes, eventually leading to the rise of the Ku Klux Klan, who were disgruntled former slave owners, scorned and scared of retaliation.

In control of my destiny: Black Nationalism

The American Colonization Society was founded in 1812 with the mission to regulate and diminish the presence of born-free and emancipated Black people in the United States of America. To white enslavers, the presence of freed Black people posed a threat to the institution of slavery enacted throughout the states. The Quaker and Puritan religious groups greatly contributed to the cause by using their moral advocations for the return of Black people to Africa. Also, the introduction of mechanical technology such as the Cotton Gin to agriculture, made the need for excessive populations of enslaved people obsolete. With the freedom to control their destinies due to emancipations by legal Will and good judgement, Black people were becoming economically and socially astute, and often purchased freedom for their counterparts.

Notably, Paul Cuffee and Martin Delany, though from two different periods, were pioneers of Black nationalism and black emigration. The men were known for their contributions to the organizing and carrying forward of helping Black people travel to Africa in pursuit of a different and better life after enslavement.[3] Cuffee was a naturally born free man who worked as a naval merchant from Massachusetts. Cuffee had vast knowledge of naval navigation and experiences with various countries through his travels. Historically, he is known to have been the first Black man to enter the White House through the front door in 1812.[4] Cuffee had a tremendous affluence of wealth and presence in the North as an Afro-Native American man in his era. In his older age, he dedicated

---

[3] Though there were mixed views about Emigration by the black people of the United States, the country Liberia became an independent state in 1847 for black Americans to relocate by the American Colonization Society.

[4] During the War of 1812, there was an embargo on any British goods. Cuffee was not aware of the war when he returned to the United States after his extensive travels. It led him to have to communicate directly with President James Madison, unprecedented and unfathomed for a black man during his time. Madison sanctioned the return of Cuffee's property and merchandise.

himself to taking freed black people with his own money to Sierra Leone, Africa. (Paul Cuffee (1759-1817), n.d.)

The Abolitionist Movement

The Abolitionist Movement began in the 1830s as groups of people from religious backgrounds who used their wealth and privilege to help freedom seekers. European and Spanish exploration brought religious missionaries used The Bible to convince black and brown people that by serving the white man, with loyalty and faithfulness, they would go to heaven. Teaching them their circumstances and abuses were in result of punishment from God to the people of Ham. Abolitionists spoke of how enslavement was inhumane, and that planters manipulated The Word of The Bible to convince the world that the practice of enslavement was a morally just. The newspaper *The Leader* by William Lloyd Garrison would serve as the voice of anti-slavery rhetoric that would become known throughout the now United States of America. In fear of further slave rebellions, slaveholders fought to keep the words of abolitionism from traveling deep into the southern states. Despite the efforts, abolitionist found ways to secretly meet with groups of the enslaved at night.

The Underground Railroad was the name given to a network of various routes indicating dedicated and reliable homes, stores and transportation methods supplied by abolitionist. These discrete routes and hideouts ventured from southern states such as Alabama Mississippi and Texas; extending North to New York, New Hampshire and Canada, and west to Indiana and Ohio. Freedom seekers endured an unknowing and uncertain adventure to gain freedom. Many freedom seekers joined the Maroon Societies with Native American populations in Canada that remained uncharted territory for Colonizers and Antebellum-era Americans.

On Long Island, The Underground Railroad passages can be traced to the towns of New Cassel (Westbury) and Jericho, north of Hemel-Hempstead. Abolitionists traveled across the United States to preach in churches and along the streets of the United States to maintain and spread the mission of abolition. White elites and religious figures such as William Lloyd Garrison, Harriet Beecher, Susan B. Anthony, and regular upper-class citizens took part in the abolition movement, but it did not negate their prejudices about the

Black and Brown position and population within economic, political and social societies. In New York, the tradition of racism and classism mesh together as white citizens had their limitations to how freed populations maneuvered with their Black Codes.

Partial Views: The Elderly

In the North, the views of enslavement and emancipation amongst the Black population varied due to the nature of enslavement experienced by Quaker and Puritan religions, coupled with the ages of the enslaved. By 1783 most Quakers on Long Island freed their enslaved, during the early phases of the abolition movement. A prime example of elderly Black people contemplating their freedom in New York came from Jupiter Harmon, who lived as an enslaved man. Harmon once lived in Queen's Village, now the Lloyd Harbor section of Huntington, a town in Suffolk County. Hamon belonged to the family of Joseph Lloyd, a generational slaveholder family that resettled into New York from Massachusetts.[5] By the 1780s, Harmon was an elderly man, in

---

[5] The surname Lloyd has been used to name many roads and buildings within Long Island.

retrospect of the abolitionist movement he supported the ideal of the emancipation of the younger generation of black people. Freedom was important for the black people of the United States of America but he felt that for the elderly people, their survival depended on the safety of being owned by a person, who would have obligations to care for them than face of destitution due to their age and inabilities.

Runaway ads from Hempstead

The New-York Gazette: and the Weekly Mercury, Nov 10, 1783

RUNA-AWAY on Tuesday night the 4th instant, from the subscriber at Hampstead, in Queen's County, Long-Island, a negro man slave named ANTHONY, about 35 years old, of a middling stature, a black complexion, very talkative, speaks good English, and pretends to be a preacher, and sometimes officiates in that capacity among the Blacks. Had on when he went away a bearskin great coat and the rest of the claths [clothes] cheifly[chiefly] of the same kind, and partly worn, and may very likely have changed his clothes. Any person who will apprehend said Negro man and delivers him to the subscriber's master may have him again, shall receive a reward of FIVE DOLLARS, if taken in Queen's County; and TEN DOLLARS if taken elsewhere to be paid by me.
N.B. All masters of vessels, and others, are hereby forbid to carry

him off, & C.S. Clowes

(Graham Russell, 1994)

The education of Black and Brown people was forbidden under any circumstance during the era of slavery, but it did not stop enslaved people from learning, and on many occasions, it did not deter planters' mistresses, and children from teaching a black adults and children to read and write. Jupiter Hamon is known as one of the forebears of African American literature for his 1761 published work *"An Evening Thought, Salvation by Christ with Penitential Hamon Cries."* The lengthy poem reflected on how he and the enslaved found a great personal meaning for their life struggles through God. It was an act of defiance, it challenged the meaning of power and position of the slaveholder in the lives of the enslaved. Hamon's notoriety even gained him a chance to have correspondence with Phillis Wheatly, the first African American woman to have literary work was published throughout the World (Olly J. M., 2021). In an address to the African Society of New York in 1786, Hamon told the society that he did not wish to be free as Hamon's emphasized that his concerns were for the elderly enslaved population as they were now too feeble to take on a new world (Olly J. M., 2021) In theory, Hamon may have had a different view and stance on being enslaved if he was younger. The State of New York legally began gradual abolishment in 1799 but the law had a clause for Black people already enslaved.[6]

Relations between the enslavers and the enslaved

The bonds between the enslaved, enslavers and freed people of the North and South did create friend and family-style relationship dynamics between populations. In 1820, Comus Fanning, a free black man, brought 21.75 acres from Sylvester Dering on Shelter Island in the waters of the Long Island Sound. It was the largest known property owned by a Black man during that time. Fanning practiced traditional wealth practices, passing down his land to his wife and children in his Will and Testament. When Fanning's wife passed away, their elderly daughter Julia inherited the land and though she had married, her husband's financial affairs left her in debt. Unfortunately, American real estate and financial businesses devalued the property assets of black-owned properties. The unfair

---

[6] If any Black person was born after July of 1799 was a person of free status; but if male was not 28, or woman 25 on said date and year would be enslaved until said age (Landy, When did slavery end in New York?, n.d.).

selling value resulted in the Fanning's daughter to eventually become homeless.

The Sylvester Family, the same family that owned Jupiter Hamon before the Lloyd family, hired elderly Julia Fanning as a domestic worker, but not with the expectations of her fulfilling domestic duties because she was no longer physically able. The Sylvester family provided her with money, and shelter, so she could live her remaining days with dignity. This act was not uncommon, as generational slaveholders shared sentimental familial ties to the enslaved. Many sons and daughters of plantation owners were used to being fed, raised, watched, and being taught life skills from the now elderly enslaved people since childhood. Julia Fanning moved to Sag Harbor, Long Island with the Sylvester family, where she died around the age of 93 in 1906. Fanning is buried on Sylvester Manor's property. The land once owned by Julia Fanning is now Dering Harbor of Shelter Island. (Comus Fanning, Dido and Julia Dyd Havens Johnson, n.d.)

Domestic Slave Trade and the Fugitive Slave Act

The practice of the Domestic Slave Trading in the South furthered continuous disruption, dismantling, dissemination, and elimination of generations of Black families for generations. The passing of the Fugitive Slave Act in 1850 made it even harder for free Black people as bounty hunters often confiscated and destroyed emancipation documents (Movement, n.d.). For example, *Twelve Years a Slave: Narrative of Solomon Northup, a Citizen of New York, Kidnapped in Washington City in 1841, and rescued in 1853, from a Cotton Plantation near the Red River in Louisiana (1853),* provided first person account of what happened to Black people that were illegally captured and sold into slavery. Solomon Northup (1807 - 1858), was born free in New York but captured by fugitive slave hunters. The bounty set on black people with the Fugitive Slave Act, white men would capture any Black person they could and sell them regardless of their legal freedom papers and education. For twelve years, Throup served in slavery until a white friend from the North came across Throup and finally led the fight to recover him, Throup's narrative was published in 1853.

Illegal trading that occurred in the United States of America became a public scandal when the Spanish voyager ship *Amistad* was seized along the shores of Montauk, Long Island by the United States naval brig *Washington* in 1839 (The National Archives, n.d.). The Amistad came from Sierra Leone, Africa with intentions to dock in the country Cuba. During the voyage, captured Africans overtook the crew aboard the ship. Unfortunately for the Africans, one of the crewmates was able to redirect the ship back towards the Americas, eventually reaching Montauk, Long Island. The white shipmates that were captured in the ship seizure were released, and the Africans were arrested and jailed in Connecticut (The National Archives, n.d.). During the investigation, the captives and the captain's journals told of the events that took place along the long voyage, detailing the "seasoning" of the captured African people. *Seasoning* was the emotional, mental, physical, and sexual abuse of men, women, and children to "break in" their resistance. The Journal described the throwing of chained people of all ages into the sea by the masses, along with other practices that occurred during these voyages were commonly enacted. The depiction of moment in history is portrayed through a United States-produced film named *The Amistad* that was released in 1997.

The 1839 case of the Amistad captives reignited the Abolitionist Movement as the debate over what to do with the African people who were aboard *The Amistad* reached the United States Supreme Court. The seizure of the Amistad created a new space for political debate in the United States for the future of the South as abolitionists advocated that the captured should be able to live as free people in the North rather than be sent to their demise in Cuba, or into slavery in the South. Future President John Quincy Adams (1761-1848), then a lawyer; represented in defense of the African captives in February of 1841. Adams debated that the ship crew of the Amistad had performed illegal abductions from African soil. Adams further argued that since the African's were free people prior to capture, and their arrival into the United States was on free soil, it constituted them to remain freed people if they survived jail. Quincy won the Supreme Court case in favor of the Africans being able to remain Emancipated in the United States, with the choice to return to Africa. The last known illegal slave ship to enter the United States was the *Clotilda* in 1860 in Mobile, Alabama, three years before the Emancipation Proclamation, fifty-four years after the abolishment of the international trade of slaves in the United States (Allison Keyes, 2019).

Black Abolitionism

The Free Black people that became abolitionist worked discreetly due to the dangers their involvement imposed for them and their family, in comparison to their white northern counterparts. In 1808, the United States of America made the Atlantic Slave Trade illegal but slave trading was still active in other parts of the world. Twenty years after the Haitian Revolution (1791-1804), Nat Turner (1800-1831) a runaway slave, and white abolitionist John Brown (1800-1859) lead nightly revolts against plantation owners throughout Virginia from the 1820s into the 1830s. New York abolished slavery in 1827, but revolts continued to impose increased and stricter regulations of Black Codes (Landy, n.d.)

Frederick Douglass (1818-1895) was a man born into slavery in the state of Maryland but escaped to freedom in New York within a day in 1838. He would then publish his narrative in 1848 *Narrative in the Life of Frederick Douglass,* allowing the world to see from the other side of the veil of slavery once again. Frederick Douglass would become a famous orator within the abolitionist movement, who often attended church with Tubman and Sojourner Truth in

New York. Douglass grew to become one of the most influential figures of his time as he continued to publish and orate speeches against slavery. Douglass would disband the myths and hateful stereotypes from slave-owners as he debated that Black people had the intellectual capability to become independent Americans as a freed population. When John Brown came to Douglass about the raid on Harpers Ferry, Virginia, he denied the opportunity to join him, calling it suicide. Frederick Douglas would continue to be a voice for the equality of black people during his days as a Statesman and would be the only African American to attend the First Women's Rights Convention in Seneca Falls, New York (Noelle Trent, unknown). Douglass visited Westbury in April of 1849, staying with the Post Family. Spoke at the New Light Baptist Church, now known as Westbury AME Zion Church on Grand Boulevard (Olly J. M., 2021). In 1857, Douglass traveled to Rochester, New York to speak at an address for the West India Emancipation. In this speech penned one of Emily's favorite quotes:

> *If there is no struggle there is no progress. Those who profess to favor freedom and yet deprecate agitation are men who want crops without plowing up the ground; they want rain without thunder and lightning. They want the ocean without the awful roar of its many waters.* (Douglass, 1857)

Thirty years after her experience, in 1861 a former enslaved woman named Harriet Jacobs published *Incidents in the Life of a Slave Girl, Harriet Jacobs* written under the pseudonym Linda Brent. This narrative is now considered an American Classic by literary figures. Harriet Jacobs (1813-1897) was born into slavery in the state of North Carolina where she spent much of her life on the run from her place of enslavement because of her master's father-in-law's continuous sexual advances. For seven years, she hid and lived solely in a crawl space under her grandmother's cabin in North Carolina. Throughout that time Brent had to watch her children grow without her. Once she was able to escape, she lived constantly on the run from her perpetrator after she reached New York in 1835, until she gained her official emancipation papers.

For over a decade she tried to get her narrative published, she even sought help from Harriet Beecher Stowe, but she denied her. Many elitist white women of that time did not sympathize with the life of an enslaved woman. Nonetheless, with tireless effort, Jacobs sought to get her book published. Denial was not a surprise, but a disappointment to her just as it had been to black abolitionist Sojourner Truth. Truth was born into slavery in New York and had to escape her master even though the ban on slavery was enacted (History.com Editors, 2009). Even though the white abolitionist women helped work towards the freedom of Black people, the women still did not view Black women as a figure within society because there were no Black women invited to the First Women's Suffrage Convention at Seneca Falls in July 1848, even though Frederick Douglass was in attendance. In 1851, Truth would reflect her feelings in *"Am I not a Woman?"* about Black women not seen as women who deserved the right to vote, contesting that she had borne as endured pain more than the average white man and woman in the United States.

> That man over there says that women need to be helped into carriages, and lifted over ditches, and to have the best place everywhere. Nobody ever helps me into carriages, or over mud-puddles, or gives me any best place! And ain't I a woman? Look at me! Look at my arm! I have ploughed and planted, and gathered into barns, and no man could head me! And ain't I a woman? I could work as much and eat as much as a man – when I could get it – and bear the lash as well! And ain't I a woman? I have borne thirteen children, and seen most all sold off to slavery, and when I cried out with my mother's grief, none but Jesus heard me! And ain't I a woman? (Truth, 1851)

During her time in New York, Jacobs worked as a nanny, and an abolitionist. Once her narrative was published, she used her status to help raise money to improve the conditions of newly freed people (Jacobs, 2001).

Turmoil over states' rights of upholding brought the United States to a Civil War from 1861 to 1865. The Southern states of the United States became the Confederate States of America in opposition to the abolishment of slavery and the Northern states became the Union States lead by President Abraham Lincoln (National Park Services, n.d.). In 1863, U.S. president Abraham Lincoln enacted the Emancipation Proclamation, though the war would still last for two more years with the final victory battle for the Union occurred in Texas in 1865.

Harriet Tubman (1820-1913) was born into slavery in Maryland. Despite the fainting spells that occurred since she was a teenager, she escaped to the North as an adult, but continuously returned south to led freedom seekers North in the thick of the night. Tubman became known as *The Conductor* of the Underground Railroad. Tubman was known to be a supporter John Brown's raid at Harpers Ferry in 1859, but did not partake in the event. Even with a bounty on her life, Tubman join the Union Army as a spy in the Civil War. Tubman lead over ten missions of enemy takeovers during her time in the war. Tubman settled in New York, continued as an abolitionist, and joined the women's suffrage movement, continuing to advocate for justice until her death, when Tubman died of old age she was known as *"The Moses of Her People."*

The Reconstruction Era

The Reconstruction Era began when the Civil War ended in 1865 with the Union Army of the North winning against the Confederate Army. The once enslaved were now a freed Black population, now faced with a new promise to life, liberty, and the pursuit of happiness afforded by the United States Constitution. The committee in charge of the reconstruction progress was called the Freedman's Bureau, with Frederick Douglass serving as the president of the Savings Bank of the Bureau (Noelle Trent, unknown). During this era, Black people were able to take the skills they had their whole life to create communities that boasted churches, businesses, schools, grocery markets, and medical offices. In St. Helena, South Carolina, the Reconstruction Era would technically begin in 1861 as white planters and slave owners abandoned their lands, leaving thousands of Black people to fend for themselves during the Civil War. The Penn Center was founded in 1861 and served as a hub of learning for black people across America and the Caribbean as many were sent there to learn to read and write, along with trade and domestic knowledge.[7] As far as higher education, black people were able to seek higher education due to historically black colleges and Universities (HBCUs) such as Lincoln, Howard, Spelman, Morehouse, and Morgan Colleges being founded across the South during this Era.

In 1870, Black men in America were granted the right to vote with the Voting Rights Act. During this time, seven Black men were elected to Congress for the first time with the prospect of finally providing the political voice that the freed population was denied for centuries. White officials mocked the Black newly elected officials, biased to the fact that these newly elected officials naturally lacked the broad knowledge of reading, writing, and rhetoric of facilitating laws and politics due to their previous lives as slaves. Even if there was access to education, high caliber schooling was afforded only white people with significant monetary status

> "...during Reconstruction, some 2,000 African Americans occupied positions ranging from members of Congress to state legislators, sheriffs, city councilmen and others. This unprecedented experiment in biracial democracy aroused intense opposition from adherents of white supremacy, at that time concentrated in the Democratic Party, who sought to undermine Reconstruction through outright violence and a campaign of vilification that portrayed black officials as ignorant, corrupt and unfit for public service." (Foner, 2020)

---

[7] The Penn Center served as the central hub for civil rights leaders of the south, MLK wrote his "I Have A Dream" speech on the grounds of The Penn Center.

As for the black politicians, they did not let their lack of education demise their missions because the representatives knew how the freed population wanted to lead their new lives, providing various resources and jobs. Naturally, the newly freed population outnumbered whites, prompting fear of retaliation but the Black population of America just wanted to have the chance to achieve their versions of the American Dream. As Black people learned a new way of life and gained property, there was a rise in black wealth in the South, as they used the skills that were forced upon them to gain employment and start businesses. Soon enough, their wealth would be displayed within their communities, taking away from white economic profiteers.

For White citizens, the inauguration of Black people into Congress impeded the meaning economic, social, and political fabric of what they wanted the United States of America to be for them. After the Civil War, white planters and socialites of the South faced a devastating series of loss and damages to their land and properties during Union occupation, including the loss of the enslaved people who made them wealthy[8] There was a fit of jealousy from the southern whites as they felt there would soon be a loss in power for white men in the United States. To no avail, black politicians were pushed out of political positions and voting processes altogether once again by 1890.

Jim Crow laws were established in 1896 with the case Plessy Vs. Ferguson making it harder for Black people to have adequate and equal access to voting tolls due provisional test enacted by town and state. The white supremacist group the Ku Klux Klan would be founded and spread amongst the masses of whites as they took on the self-designated "responsibility of keeping Black people in line" through beatings, kidnappings, mass lynching, and sexual abuses and torture of men, women, and children. Systematic voter suppression of Black people and its effects remained at the forefront of economic, political, and social stunting of Black neighborhoods across the United States Along with acts of violence. Most notable was the practice of burning prominent and small Black towns like Oscarville, Georgia (Now Lake Lanier, GA) in 1912, and the "Black

---

[8] The Emancipation of the last plantation is now a national holiday called Juneteenth, June 19, 1865. (The Editors of Enclyclopedia Britannica, 2022)

Wall Street," of Tulsa, Oklahoma in 1921. (Crowe & Lewis, 2021).

Klan activities increased during political periods, and eventually, the

rules of Jim Crow stripped Black Americans of their voting rights in

the south. Overall, the injustice and maltreatment suffered by Black

people through the actions of white citizens and local law

enforcement evoked over 400,000 Black people to migrate to

Northern and Western regions of the United States of America in

pursuit of happiness, liberty, and justice for all.

Freeport, Long Island

On Long Island, the Village of Hempstead served as the epicenter of Nassau County. By 1651, the Great South Woods, south of Hempstead, was split into two towns: *Raynor South* and *Rumpoint*. The name Raynor South was the namesake of Edward Raynor, a wealthy English migrant that settled in the South Shore region around 1650. According to Freeport history and property maps of Freeport, many Raynor family members moved to the area within a short time period. This prompted citizens of the area to call it Raynor, Raynor South, and/or Raynor town. An 1873 map of Freeport displayed that various families with the last name Raynor owned properties throughout the Raynor South and north into Rumpoint. In the 17th Century Raynor South became a work and tourist destination because of the various beaches along the shore and maritime trade. Eventually wealthy socialites began to build lavish Victorian-styled summer homes. The increased population lead to the renaming and incorporating of Raynor South as The Village of Freeport in 1853. The building of the Woodclef Canal in 1897 and other warehouses would create an increased need for laborers, attracting Italian and Irish migrants, along with an influx of black families from Southern states that migrated North known as the Great Migration (McGovern).

Roosevelt, Long Island

Rumpoint, north of Freeport received its first name because it once housed to two taverns, making the small town known for its import and exportation of Rum and other spirits. Rumpoint gained its second namesake 'Greenwich Point' due to the dense woodlands that provided wood for housing and paper making, and vast farming lands that were maintained in the area. In 1885, future President Theodore Roosevelt, and native New Yorker moved to the town of Oyster Bay on the North Shore of Nassau County after he built his mansion known as *Sagamore Hill.* Due to Roosevelt's wartime notoriety and political status, views on alcohol and the affects it had on society, and Long Island residency, the name Rumpoint was no longer a socially and politically astute name to have for a town in encouraged the name change to Greenwich. In 1901, Theodore Roosevelt became the 26th President of the United States. In the same year, a post office was established on the corner of Babylon Turnpike and Nassau Road under the name Greenwich. Eventually, citizens chose to rename the town Roosevelt because of his strong ties to Long Island (The History of Roosevelt).

The only roads of the one square mile village that was laid in brick were Babylon Turnpike, Nassau Road, Centennial and Washington Avenues. Gas lamps illuminated the main roads, with each street connected to give access between the North and South Shores, East to Suffolk, and West towards New York City. The town had to depend upon an old-fashioned stagecoach to connect it with the outside world (unknown, The History of Roosevelt). Summer and residential homes were raised in Roosevelt at the same time they were being built in Freeport. The introduction of the railroad system into Long Island created a population boost from New Yorkers who once lived in the overpopulated city areas to various Long Island towns.

Black on Long Island: Redlining of properties and schools

MAP 2 PROPERTY MAP OF BENNINGTON PARK IN 1906. THE STAR INDICATES THE PROPERTY OF MOSES JARVIS. (FREEPORT MEMORIAL LIBRARY, 1906)

Red Lining, the racial segregation of housing areas also consisted of

racially biased banking loaning procedures resulted in various

enclaves of migrant and black families to grow in certain sections of

New York. In 1902, the Bennington Park area was developed to

house low-economic black and migrant families. The presence of

Black families in Freeport have been dated back to 1883 with the property census of Moses (1852-1917) and Henrietta Jarvis (1856-1950), along with their children living in the Bennington Park Section. According to Freeport Library records, Moses Jarvis grew up in Hempstead, and lost one of his legs as a boy in either a fall or an accident involving the Long Island Railroad. A property map of Freeport from 1902 showed that Moses Jarvis owned land in Bennington Park, before that other property records indicated that he also owned land in Hempstead and Huntington in Suffolk County.

Moses Jarvis was known for his scavenger business, farming, and even renting his horses to funeral businesses for processions. The Jarvis family was also known to have contributed lands to the founding of the Bethel African Methodist Episcopal Church in 1902, the sixth-oldest institution that straddles the borderlines of Freeport and Roosevelt (Library, Bethel African Methodist Episcopal Church, 2019). Information about the Jarvis family can be traced through local periodicals, as two of the Jarvis children suffered Paris Green poisoning along with a few other people of color around town (unknown, Long Island Notes, 1883).[9] Though it has never been

---

[9] Paris green is the inorganic color pigment used to provide green for paints and dyes. Toxic, used as pesticides during the time era.

confirmed, it's possible that the poisoning could have been racially related. Due to different news accounts of the incident, it is uncertain if the children survived the poisoning. (Ritchie, 1883). One of the Jarvis daughters owned her own professional cleaning business. Their daughter became the first Black woman to be employed by the Freeport bank. One of their sons was also known for his scavenger business, which was busy well into the 1930s. During his time as a business owner, he was able to employ both Black and white citizens (Crew, Kreig, Feeney, & Rushton, 2018). (NYS Historic Newspapers)

The Jarvis family was well recognized and respected in the community of Freeport, but it did not stop others from using systematic oppression against them to gain what was rightfully theirs. In 1914, the Jarvis family was ordered to move from their land because of a deal with a former lawyer that went shady; the lawyer and his brother by the last name Seaman (descendants of the Seaman family that resided in Hempstead) claimed that they were now the owners of the Jarvis land (Unknown, Demand Property Back , 1914). Both White and black people of the Freeport community did not like this because the Jarvis family were known as lifetime residents who contributed greatly to the town of Freeport.

Moses Jarvis died when he was 66 years old, but the couple still had young children at the time (Nassau County Review, 2 February 1917). The widowed Henrietta Jarvis never remarried and raised their children on her own. Fortunately, the Jarvis family was able to keep the land. Mrs. Jarvis passed at the age of 94 in 1950, and there was a newspaper article written in her honor (unknown, Aged Freeport Mother Triumphed Against the Odds, 1950).

There are no exact records of when Black people settled into Roosevelt, and there is a lack of records for Roosevelt because it was treated as a separate community from the Town of Hempstead. Mrs. A Denton, an early member of Roosevelt since 1905, is documented stating "One Black family lived in Roosevelt in the wooded area in the Southeast of the village." Denton noted that the children of this family grew up and built homes near their parents' house. Most of the Black males worked for road maintenance contractors who owned many homes in Freeport. Overall, there was a small but isolated Black community in Roosevelt (James & LaGumina, 1980).

As Black communities grew in the towns of Hempstead, Roosevelt, and Freeport, the children of Roosevelt had the choice to attend Hempstead or Freeport schools, since Roosevelt did not have a middle or high school. Since Roosevelt is located between

Hempstead and Freeport, many parents chose Hempstead because of its higher Black population, it was promoted that it would be better if children did go to school with their kind to avoid emotional and physical scrutiny. Freeport never had a segregated school system even though segregation was blindly practiced throughout the town. In 1913, Freeport High School graduated its first Black student Moxey Rigby (1892 – 1962), a native of the Caribbean whose family had moved to the Bennington Park area when he was a teenager. Rigby would later become a judge, and the first Black man to serve on the judicial courts of Nassau County (New York Law School , 2018). During Rigby's time, the Black population of Freeport was not high enough to stir the need for segregated schooling.

PHOTO 1 MOXEY RIGBY SENIOR CLASS PHOTO. RIGBY LOCATED SECOND ROW, SECOND FROM LEFT. (SENIOR CLASS. 1913. FREEPORT HIGH SCHOOL . 1914)

By 1922, there were two schools in Roosevelt named School #1 and School #2. School #1 was located on Washington Avenue but was destroyed in a fire; it was rebuilt with the name the Theodore Roosevelt School.[10] The Centennial Avenue and Underhill Avenue Schools would be erected in 1930. [11] Roosevelt had no middle school and high school, therefore students beyond the sixth grade went to either Freeport or Hempstead School districts. After World War II, the Black population began to relocate from the five boroughs into the Suburbs, just as their white counterparts. Real estate brokers began to guide Black families to the Bennington Park section of Freeport, the Village of Hempstead, and outer-lying hamlets Roosevelt and Uniondale (James & LaGumina, 1980). In 1931, Cleveland Avenue School was raised in Freeport to educate the rising Black populations that would come out of the Bennington Park Area. A newspaper article noted how some residents of Freeport opposed the erection of the school because it was unsafe for children to have to cross the Long Island Railroad tracks with no guidance to attend school (Unknown, Decribes

---

[10] Now Washington Rose Elementary School
[11] Now Ulysses Byas Elementary school.

Freeport Election as Crude, 1922) Historically, the erection of schools and communities that served black populations would be located along train lines because the lands were found unfavorable due to the noises and dangers of passing trains, a primary example would be Vicksburg High School in Vicksburg, Mississippi. The school closed its doors in 1963, as various allegations of racial discrimination and treatment differences were received by the student's parents from the staff and educators of the school.

According to an untitled newspaper article clipping, Theodore Roosevelt School (now Ulysses Byas) was a predominantly black primary and elementary school that was so overcrowded that the school had to conduct kindergarten classes in the gym. At one point the school rented the basement of the Roosevelt Jewish Center (now Roosevelt Youth Center) for other grades. Rose-Washington Elementary (Washington Rose) had a 50% Black and 50% Jewish population; Centennial Avenue Elementary was a 100% White school and Black students who lived close to Centennial Avenue Elementary had to attend Northeast Primary School in Freeport, almost a mile further to attend school. A local newspaper stated, *"Integration is one thing, but the board obviously does not allow*

Negro children to attend the Centennial Avenue School under any circumstances," regarding the integration of the Roosevelt School District as Roosevelt consists of a square mile radius sits between Hempstead, with a higher Black population, and Freeport a higher White population. In September of 1956, the Roosevelt Junior-Senior High School was opened, to transition students from Roosevelt into the new district, Freeport only allowed students to register if older sisters, brothers, and parents had attended their schools. In 1961, Freeport would continue to integrate Black and White students into their new high school building once it opened. In September 1962, the Roosevelt Junior-Senior High School opened its doors, the mascot: Theodore Roosevelt and the Rough Riders. The first class to graduate from Roosevelt High School was in 1964 (The History of Roosevelt).

The first Long Island Ku Klux Klan chapter

In 1920, the first Ku Klux Klan chapter of Long Island was established in Freeport. The founding was in response to the presence of migrant workers of different religious groups such as the Jewish and Irish-Catholics. (Barr, 2015). According to a Newsday Article, the low population of Black Americans on Long Island back then did not pose a significant threat to what the white Americans envisioned for their suburban lifestyles. The Black population of L.I. mostly served the white community of Long Island as domestic servants or labor force (Beherens, 2009). Members and supporters from all over the United States came to the first annual KKK parade that occurred in 1920 in Mineola, L.I., approximately a fifteen-minute drive from Freeport today. Members did not hide their faces during parades, even wearing no hoods at all (Paquette, 1996). Long Island at one point was known to have the highest percentage of women members within the Northeastern region of the United States. According to historian Dr. Neil Buffett, statistically for every seven white Long Islanders, one was a part of the Klan (Barr, 2015).

The lack of public record takes away from the fact that Long Island has been home to generational white segregationists since the 1920s. At one point it was said that the Long Island Ku Klux Klan was formed "to counterweight the dullness of life on rural Long Island," in synopsis: innocent people have been terrorized in the name of boredom and white superiority complex (Beherens, 2009). By 1924, fire departments across Long Island pleaded with the KKK chapters to refrain from conducting cross-burnings during a specific season to prevent greater bushfires and damages; not because it was wrong. Fortunately, the general presence of racism and the Ku Klux Klan could not be presented broadly and boldly amongst the liberal society of New York City, making it hard to remain active. The Long Island KKK members would continue to have run-ins with law enforcement during the Prohibition Era for their involvement as alcohol 'bootleggers' and smugglers, a violation of the Prohibition Act that was enacted by President Theodore Roosevelt (Olly J. , unkown).

Dr. Neil Buffet wrote,

> It seemed that the theatrics of it all really attracted the older
> generations of Klansmen that lived and resettled in Long Island...
> [that] "there is a lack of known members of the KKK from Long

Island on paper, even though the openness of their membership was uncanny. (Beherens, 2009)

FIGURE 1 FLYER FOR ANNUAL KLAN PARADE CALLED KLORERO, JULY 1926. (OLLY J. , UNKOWN)

PATCHOGUE KLAN PARADES.

Elks Clear Way for Gowned Marchers – Legion Has a Concert
Special to The New York Times
August 2, 1925

New York Times Articles about the Ku Klux Klan on Long Island
Provided by Longwood Central School District

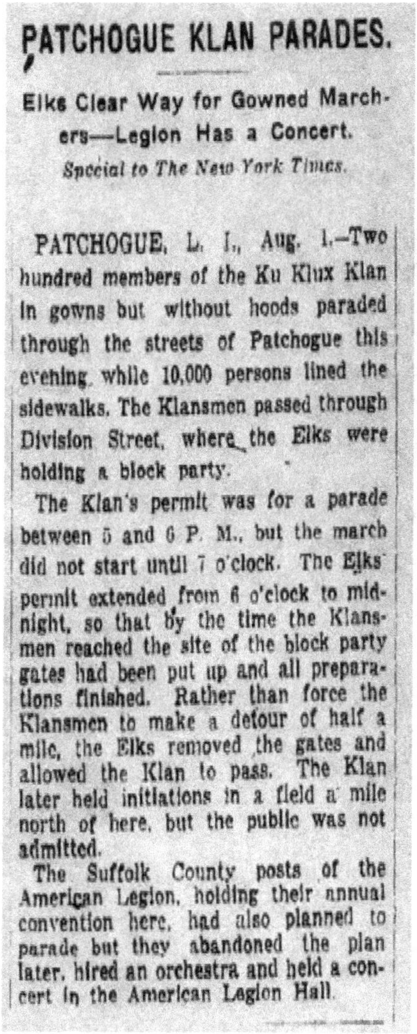

PATCHOGUE KLAN PARADES.

Elks Clear Way for Gowned Marchers—Legion Has a Concert.

Special to The New York Times.

PATCHOGUE, L. I., Aug. 1.—Two hundred members of the Ku Klux Klan in gowns but without hoods paraded through the streets of Patchogue this evening, while 10,000 persons lined the sidewalks. The Klansmen passed through Division Street, where the Elks were holding a block party.

The Klan's permit was for a parade between 5 and 6 P. M., but the march did not start until 7 o'clock. The Elks permit extended from 6 o'clock to midnight, so that by the time the Klansmen reached the site of the block party gates had been put up and all preparations finished. Rather than force the Klansmen to make a detour of half a mile, the Elks removed the gates and allowed the Klan to pass. The Klan later held initiations in a field a mile north of here, but the public was not admitted.

The Suffolk County posts of the American Legion, holding their annual convention here, had also planned to parade but they abandoned the plan later, hired an orchestra and held a concert in the American Legion Hall.

FIGURE 2 NEWSPAPER ARTICLE ABOUT KLAN PARADES IN PATCHOUGUE, SUFFOLK COUNTY, N.Y. (NY TIMES, 1925)

Patchogue, L. I., Aug 1.- Two hundred members of the Ku Klux Klan in gowns but without hoods paraded through the streets of Patchogue this evening, while 10,000 persons lined the sidewalks. The Klansmen passed through Division Street, where the Elks were holding a block party.

The Klan's permit was for a parade between 5 and 6 P.M., but the march did not start until 7 O'clock to Midnight, so that by the time the Klansmen reached the site of the block party gates had been put up and all preparations finished. Rather than force the Klansmen to make a detour of half a mile, the Elks removed the gates and allowed the Klan to pass. The Klan later held initiations in a field a mile north of here, but the public was not admitted.

The Suffolk County post of the American Legion, holding their annual convention here, had also planned to parade but abandoned the plan later, hired an orchestra and held a concert in the American Legion Hall

WOMEN AND GIRLS PARADE WITH KLAN

Women And Girls Parade With Klan - Longwood Central School District

3,000 Members, in Regalia but Unmasked, Take Part in March at Mineola.

NEW YORK HAS DELEGATION

Demonstration Attracts Many From Surrounding Towns—Coins Thrown Into Flags.

Special to The New York Times.

MINEOLA, L. I., July 5.—The Ku Klux Klan, 3,000 strong, paraded through Mineola this afternoon. Delegations from many up-State counties and from almost every village in Nassau County and many in Suffolk were in the line. New York City was represented by a delegation of several hundred.

The parade started promptly at 2 o'clock from the Mineola Fair Grounds, where the Klan is holding its annual State Klorero. There were five bands and two fife and drum corps in the line. Every marcher, and there were men, women and children in the parade, wore the Klan regalia, but none was masked. There were many floats and two large American flags were carried horizontally by lines of women and into each were thrown many coins by the crowd that lined the sidewalks.

Women and Girls Parade with Klan

3,000 Members, in Regalia but Unmasked, Take Part in March at Mineola.

NEW YORK HAS DELEGATION

Demonstration Attracts Many from Surrounding Towns – Coins Thrown into Flags.

Special to The New York Times.

Mineola, L. I. July 5- The Ku Klux Klan 3,000 Strong, paraded through Mineola this afternoon. Delegations from many up-state counties and from almost every village in Nassau County and many in Suffolk were in the line. New York City was represented by a delegation of several hundred.

The Parade started promptly at 2 o'clock from the Mineola Fairgrounds. Where the Klan is holding its annual state Klorero. There were five bands and two fife and drum corps in the line. Every marcher, and there were men. Women and children in the parade, wore the Klan regalia, but none was masked. There were many floats, and two large American flags were carried horizontally by the lines of women and into each were thrown many coins by the crowd that lined the sidewalks.

FIGURE 3 NEWPAPER ARTICLE ABOUT THE SIGNIFICANT PRESENCE OF WOMEN AT THE KLAN PARADE. (FIRST PUBLIC APPERANCE OF WOMEN OF THE K.K.K ON LONG ISLAND, 1924)

The heavy migration of Black people to Roosevelt led to a response from the local Ku Klux Klan, a meeting was held where the rhetoric was against the Jewish immigrants and Black Americans. It was reported that a chapter of the KKK was active at 59 Babylon Turnpike, land that is now the home of the AME Zion Church. They were effective in keeping the Black population out of Roosevelt through their initial presence alone. One known Cross burning occurred in Roosevelt on July 4, 1928.

PHOTO 3 ROOSEVELT CHAPTER OF THE KU KLUX KLAN DURING THE KLAN PARADE. (BEHERENS, 2009)

1960s Long Island: Pushed Out and Commercially Zoned

In the United States, small Black communities became the targets of "slum removal," commercial zoning and infrastructure builds resulting in the which destruction of thriving Black neighborhoods. In options of relocation and real estate properties, Black people were given properties that were in unfavorable residential properties. These homes were commonly located near noisy commercial areas, on unfertile land, along dangerous roadways, and train tracks. For instance, Bennington Park was founded on lands not too far from the Brooklyn Sanitation Water Reservoir, and area unfavorable to white citizens for purchase. The Village of Freeport recognized that Bennington Park needed to be upgraded in 1942, twenty years before the commercialization of its land in the 1960s. For decades, property owners and town officials did not want to encourage the settlement of Black and immigrant populations. Landlords of Bennington Park ignored the community pleas for land and housing upgrade approvals. It was not until longtime Black residents of Freeport sought to redevelop the

Bennington Park area homes in the late 1950s that the town of

Freeport developed/ and or evoked their long-awaited plans for the

area. By then, properties were in condemnable conditions, creating

an easy recommendation for demolition of the homes.

To Recommend Improvements in Buildings there: Landlords Queried on Living Conditions in Their Holdings, January 1942 from periodical The Leader: Nassau County

Having established the need for improving conditions in Bennington Park, the Freeport Housing Authority now is calling individual property owners for hearings with a view to recommending specific improvements to rectify conditions in their holdings.

Two persons were heard last Thursday night. They were Mrs. Rose Schindler, owner of the houses at 58 and 62 Henry Street, and Peter Lago, who represented his wife, Felicia, who owns four former Camp Upton shacks at 59, 61, and 63 Liberty Avenue, there being a rear house at the last address. T.A. Tomaselli, counsel to the commission and Lawrence L. Luther, manager of the sanitary department, who long has been urging the cleaning up of the park, inspected these buildings before the hearing.

Mr. Tomaselli reported the conditions in the various houses as follows:

No Sanitary Facilities

Fifty-eight Henry Street [is] owned by Mrs. Schindler – six apartments of one, two or three rooms, occupied by nine known persons. One apartment has sanitary facilities, but there are common sanitary facilities and sink with cold water on the second floor for the tenants of the five other apartments. There are no bathing facilities, and no central heating plant, each family having to heat its own rooms with kerosene or old-style coal stoves.

To Recommend Improvements In Buildings There

Landlords Queried On Living Conditions In Their Holdings

Having established the need for improving conditions in Bennington Park, the Freeport Housing Authority now is calling individual property owners for hearings with a view to recommending specific improvements to rectify conditions in their holdings.

Two persons were heard last Thursday night. They were Mrs. Rose Schindler, owner of houses at 58 and 62 Henry street,

his wife, Feliccia, who owns four former Camp Upton shacks at 59, 61 and 63 Liberty avenue, there being a rear house at the last address.

T. A. Tomaselli, counsel to the commission, and Lawrence L. Luther, manager of the Sanitary Department, who long has been urging the cleaning up of Park, inspected these buildings before the hearing.

Mr. Tomaselli reported the conditions in the various houses as follows:

No Sanitary Facilities

Fifty-eight Henry street, owned by Mrs. Schindler—six apartments of one, two or three rooms, occupied by nine known persons. One apartment has sanitary facilities, but there are common sanitary facilities and a sink with cold water on the second floor for the tenants of the five other apartments. There are no bathing facilities and no central heating plant, each family having to heat its own rooms with

FIGURE 4 THE LEADER:NASSAU COUNTY ARTICLE ABOUT THE CONDITIONS OF BENNINGTON PARK HOMES (AUTHORITY ACTS TO CLEAN BENNINGTON PARK, 1942) (AUTHORITY ACTS TO CLEAN BENNINGTON PARK, 1942)

PHOTO 4 11 BENNINGTON AVE, FREEPORT, N.Y. 1961. (LANE, 1961)

As for the residents of Bennington Park, there were only a few
Black people who had owned their homes at the time who were
eligible to protest the buying out and commercialization of the land.
After property owners sold their properties, the former residents of
Bennington Park either moved further into Freeport or neighboring
towns like Roosevelt, Hempstead, and Uniondale. In the 1960s, the
concept of "apartment projects" was developed and began to house
low-income families on a larger scale across America. A small
number of homes of Bennington Park were allowed upgrades, and
housing complexes named the Moxey Apartments, also known as

the Bennington Projects in the 1970's and 1980s by local residents were built around the same time of commercial reconstruction to not completely make a group of people destitute of living arrangements. The Moxey Apartments were built down the street from Cleveland Avenue School, named after Moxey Rigby, who served as the chair of the Freeport Housing Authority (FHA). Bennington Projects

FIGURE 5 HISTORICAL MARKER OF BENNINGTON PARK (WILLIAM G. POMEROY FOUNDATION)

MOORE FAMILY HISTORY: ANDREW WALKER BECOME ANDREW MOORE (1849-1932)

Lineage of Emily Moore's family can be traced back to her great-great-grandfather Andrew Moore, and his brother John Walker (Priester, 1987). The men were of African and Native American heritage born into enslavement in North Carolina. They were owned by a man with the last name Walker. Andrew grew up with and became close with one of the Walker sons because of age and his position as a houseboy. Andrew was taught how to read and write in secrecy. According to family record, when the Walker brothers were emancipated, Andrew was seventeen years old. Like many newly emancipated Black people, Andrew decided to shed himself of the past and changed his last name to Moore, as John kept their original namesake Walker. The brothers migrated from their plantation and relocated to the territory that is now Quincy, Florida.

The 1860s census of Liberty County, Florida verified that the brothers once owned a great parcel of land brought from William H. Gunn, Sr. The means of how the brothers acquired the lands were not mentioned but there are two theories since it was the Reconstruction Era and Gunn, Sr. was an elderly man.The first theory is that the brothers may have sharecropped Gunn, Sr's land for a short time before they acquired land from him. The second theory is that the men could have gained monetary compensation from the Freedman's Bureau to start farmlands during the Reconstruction Era and brought their land from Gunn, Sr. The nature of relationship and interaction with Gunn, Sr. is unknown. Gunn, Sr. had also delegated nearby lands to Isaac Creel from Aiken, South Carolina, possibly before the arrival of John and Andrew. Creel may have purchased lands under the same circumstances. To an extent, its understandably conceived that there was a fair bond between Gunn, Creel and the brothers as it is known that Gunn Sr. wrote Issac Creel's Will and Testament. The brothers and Creel family would remain neighbors for at least 10 years. During this time, Andrew met and asked to court Issacs's daughter Rachel Creel (1853-1936), a native of Charleston, South Carolina and the pair married in 1872. While together the Moore's were an economically dynamic duo during and after the Reconstruction Era. Andrew was a successful farmer, and served as a minister, preaching at the African Methodist Episcopal Church (A.M.E) in his area. Andrew also created the first school in Quincy that served both Black and poor white populations. Rachel was known in Quincy and surrounding areas as a midwife and taught others how to do midwifery. According to the Moore family history, Rachel is described as a soft-haired but fussy woman, with a strong disciplinarian demeanor. The pair had four children while in Quincy. Lewis Moore, Emily's grandfather is one of the children that was born during that time, but overall, the union produced fourteen children. The Moore family left Quincy, relocating to Estiffanugla, Florida (later known as Bristol, Florida) due to racial violence and threats due to their success.

In Bristol, Andrew prospered as farmer and entrepreneur, alongside Rachel in midwifery, as she delivered babies of both Black and white families. The family farm was composed of more than ten acres, growing various crops that included white and sweet potatoes, a staple food of white and black Americans. The land was extremely fertile due to its location near a body of water, timber grew on the land which served as the most profitable and continuous source of revenue. The timber was also used to build fencing and shelter for Andrew's farm animals which had chickens, geese, goats, horses, and mules. The Moore family even had a bee farm; therefore, they became one of the primary sources of honey in the area. In 1902, When the United States Postal Service started a route in Quincy, Andrew served as the postmaster for Bristol and surrounding towns, he then became one of the first residents of Quincy to own an automobile.

The Moore family was known to spread their wealth and knowledge to their children and into the community of Quincy. The Moore children continued farming, midwifery, and the towns postal services, continuing their parents' legacy as they became elderly. The Moore family employed both Black and white citizens as farmers and store workers. Once again, as the Moore family's popularity and economic status excelled, they were met with opposition from white civilians and threats from the Ku Klux Klan. Andrew decided to leave Bristol to escape the various mass lynchings and burnings that were occurring amongst the surrounding Black communities. Before the Moore family departed from Quincy, Andrew's son Louis / Lewis (born 1877) married Laura Gee, whose origin was not mentioned. Lewis assumed his father's role within the clergy, serving as minister and presiding elder at the A.M.E church in the Bristol area. The pair would have six children: Elana, Andrew, Ancel, Rachel, Lillian, and Eddie (Edward); Emily's father.

The Moore family migrated once again to the state of Ohio during the Great Migration or the Second Diaspora Era.[12] Andrew went to Ohio, to avoid the congestion that would come from Black people migrating north and depicted that it would make finding work hard for him and his sons. His daughters went to historically Black colleges and universities such as Wilberforce in Ohio. It seemed that wherever Lewis traveled, he had to keep his bible and a gun. Their success as a Black family caused them to relocate the Moore family once again to Pittsburgh, Pennsylvania. This time, Lewis moved first and returned to bring his sons to obtain jobs and proper shelter. Lewis then returned to retrieve his wife and daughters. Lewis would serve as a camp meeting preacher in Johnston, PA. In Pittsburgh, PA, he also worked as a coal miner and served as a preacher at the Buena Vista church. Though Edward gained his education in Florida, his younger siblings completed their secondary education in Pittsburgh, Philadelphia.

---

[12] A time where half of a million black Americans relocated North and to various other areas of the United States and Canada from the South during the beginning of Emancipation and the continuous racial violence's associated with the burdens of being black in former slave holding states (Christensen, 2007)

PHOTO 5 LEWIS MOORE, GREAT GRANDFATHER

(PATERNAL)

PHOTO 6 RACHEL CREEL, GREAT GRANDMOTHER (PATERNAL)

PHOTO 8 MOMMA GEE, GRANDMOTHER, PATERNAL

PHOTO 7 AUNT UNIDENTIFIED RELATION

Raleigh " Felder" Moore (1888-1966) was one of the younger children of Andrew and Rachel Moore, he has a day named after him in Florida in honor of his contributions to the Communities of Florida.

Office of the Mayor of Fort Lauderdale
Proclamation

Wheras, Raleigh Felder Moore was a planter of Broward County
And the founder of the first Black newspaper for people of color,
" The Whole Trouble News", and
WHERAS, Raleigh Felder Moore was a businessman with a
Vision to help people, provide work, education, and information; and

Wheras, Raleigh Felder Moore, an activist in the community
And entrpreneuer, also was a realtor, the owner/operator of a confectionaryice
cream parlor, the owner of a shoe shop and a newspaper
And
WHERAS, Raliegh Felder Moore was a man that contributed to his community and
believed that God gave him a gift to help people; and

WHERAS, Raleigh Felder Moore, as the family patriarch. Started
Moore's family reunion, and

WHERAS, the legendary Raleigh Felder Moore's legacy to Broward County,
his family, and friends as on of Fort Lauderdale's most outstanding
pioneeres will live on in the Historical Musuem of Fort Lauderdale, Florida

NOW, THEREFORE, WE, as City Comminssioners of the
City of Fort Lauderdale, Florida do hereby
Proclaim July 6, 2006 as:

ROBERT FELDER MOORE DAY

In the City of Fort Lauderdale and urge all citizens to join us in
recognizing the many contributions of this outstanding individual.

DATED this, the 6th day of July 2006

Carlton B. Moore
Comissioner, District III
Fort Lauderdale, Florida

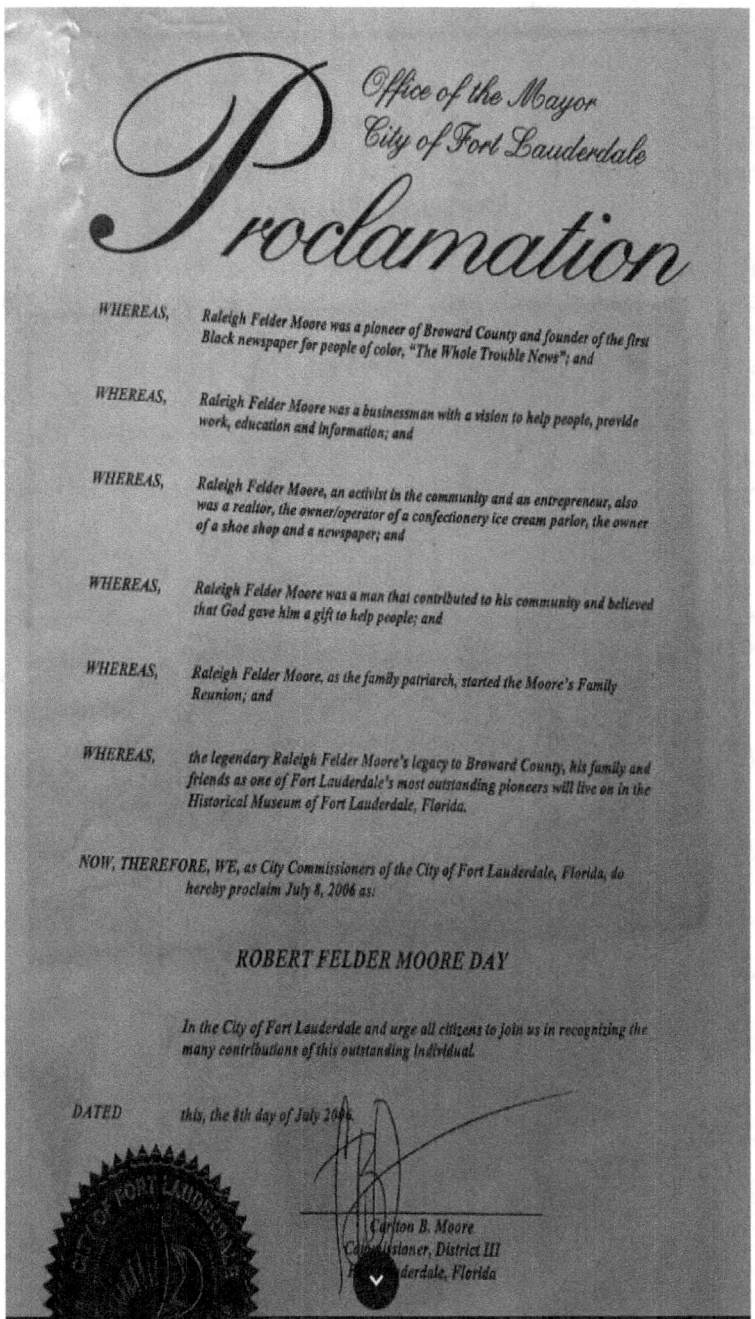

Office of the Mayor
City of Fort Lauderdale

Proclamation

WHEREAS,   Raleigh Felder Moore was a pioneer of Broward County and founder of the first Black newspaper for people of color, "The Whole Trouble News"; and

WHEREAS,   Raleigh Felder Moore was a businessman with a vision to help people, provide work, education and information; and

WHEREAS,   Raleigh Felder Moore, an activist in the community and an entrepreneur, also was a realtor, the owner/operator of a confectionery ice cream parlor, the owner of a shoe shop and a newspaper; and

WHEREAS,   Raleigh Felder Moore was a man that contributed to his community and believed that God gave him a gift to help people; and

WHEREAS,   Raleigh Felder Moore, as the family patriarch, started the Moore's Family Reunion; and

WHEREAS,   the legendary Raleigh Felder Moore's legacy to Broward County, his family and friends as one of Fort Lauderdale's most outstanding pioneers will live on in the Historical Museum of Fort Lauderdale, Florida.

NOW, THEREFORE, WE, as City Commissioners of the City of Fort Lauderdale, Florida, do hereby proclaim July 8, 2006 as:

ROBERT FELDER MOORE DAY

In the City of Fort Lauderdale and urge all citizens to join us in recognizing the many contributions of this outstanding individual.

DATED   this, the 8th day of July 2006.

Carlton B. Moore
Commissioner, District III
Ft. Lauderdale, Florida

FIGURE 6 PROCALAMATION BY FT. LAUDERDALE FLORIDA INDICATING RALEIGH MOORE DAY. (OFFICE OF THE MAYOR FOR THE CITY OF FORT LAUDERDALE, 2006)

A Weekly Paper for Colored Citizens of Broward County

Fort Lauderdale, Florida, January 12,1940

The Whole Trouble Today

WHAT SHOULD BE THE BASIC EDUCATION PRINCIPLES OF EDUCATION IS OUR TROUBLES TODAY.

To many who place their children in our schools, strng temptations will come because they desire them to secure what the world regards as the most essetial education, to this I would say my friends, bring your children to the simplicity of the word, and they will be safe, for God's book is the foudation of all true knowledge, and the highest education they can receive my friends is to learn how to add to their faith virture; and to viture knowledge; and to knowledge temperance; and to temperance patiences; and to patiene godliness; and to godliness brotherly kindness; and to brotherly kindness charity… what may bring life, both temporal and eternally; is of God, he is the lfie ad to tell the whole story my friend, if we would live, we must choose to know him, to obey him, to truly know Christ is life eternal. And in choosing an education that truly elevates, you will witness the fact, that one must study that which leads to the fuller understanding of God and Christ, children may be trained for the service of sin or the service of righteousness, will you remember Soloman sats, train up a child in the way he should go; and This language is positive, the training that Soloman enjoins is to direct, educate, develop, but in order for parents to do this work, they must themselves understand the way-the child should go, and for Christ sake my friends, let the aim of your educatin be shaped by the inducement of the better world; parents are entitled to a degree of love and respect which is due to no other person, God himself, who have placed upon them a responsibility for the soulds committed to their charge, has ordained that during the earlier years of life, parents shall stand in place of God for their children.

Now let your heart be our limit dear friends, and good contion be your gide, and you can't go wrong.

By RALEIGH MOORE

A WEEKLY NEWSPAPER FOR COLORED CITIZENS OF BROWARD COUNTY

FORT LAUDERDALE, FLORIDA, JANUARY 12, 1940

THE WHOLE TROUBLE TODAY

WHAT SHOULD BE THE BASIC PRINCIPLES OF EDUCATION IS OUR WHOLE TROUBLE TODAY

To many who place their children in our schools, strong tempations will come because they desire them to secure what the world regards as the most essetial education, to this. I would say my frends, bring your children to the simplicity of the word, and they will be safe, for God's book is the foundation of all true knowledge, and the highest education they can receive my frends is to learn how to add to their faith virtue; and to virtue knowledge; and to knowledge temperance; and to temperance patience; and to patience godliness; and to gardliness brotherly kindness; and to brotherly kindness charity . . . what may bring life, both temporal and eternally; is of God, he is the life, and to tel the whole story my frends, if we would live, we must choose to know him, to obey him, to truly know Christ is life eternal. And in choosing an education that truly elevates, you will witness the fact, that one must study that which leads to the fuller understanding of God and Christ, children may be trained for the service of sin or the service of righteousness, will you remember Solomon says, train up a child in the way he should go; and This language is positive, the training that Solomon enjoins is to direct, educate, develop, but in order for parent to do this work, they must themselves understand the way the child should go, and for Christ sake my frends, let the aim of your education be shaped by the inducement of the better world; parents are entitled to a degree of love and respect which is due to no other person, God himself, who have placed upon them a responsibility for the souls committeed to their charge, has ordained that during the earlier years of life, parents shall stand in place of God for their children.

Now let your heart be your limit dear frends, and good contion be your gide, and you can't go wrong.

By RALEIGH MOORE.

FIGURE 7   ARTICLE BY RALEIGH MOORE , ABOUT WHAT THE BASIC PRINCIPLES OF EDUCATION IS OUR WHOLE TROUBLE TODAY. (MOORE R. , 1940)

Edward B. Moore, Sr. (1920-1985)

PHOTO 9 EDWARD MOORE JR, , FATHER. (PRIESTER, 1987)

Edward Moore Jr., also known as "Nick," was born in 1920. Even though Emily is not sure about the whole encounter, her father got into a fight with a white man who was physically abusing his sister within a relationship. Edward was even stabbed during the incident but got the best of the man. Luckily for Edward, police relations in the North differed dramatically during the time of her father's young adulthood in comparison to the Southern region of the United States. The officers around town had known Edward to be a jobholder who did not cause trouble. Emily was told that the

Police approached Edward, giving him the ultimatum to either go to jail or leave town and not return. Edward agreed to leave because he and the police officers knew that the white community would not be happy if he was not incarcerated or "taught a lesson" that was physically gruesome and usually followed by death. Initially, Edward would move to Harlem, New York, the black mecca of the United States at the time, and work in his cousin's butcher shop. When Edward and Fannie married, they lived in Queens, NY for a brief period before and after Emily's birth.

As far as relocation to Freeport, New York, his response, according to Emily, *"He thought it was F-R-E-E!"* During their first years living in Freeport, Edward gained employment as a shoemaker but eventually Edward made a career working for the Gruman Aircraft Company factory that was located on the Freeport and Baldwin boarder, even producing aircraft parts during World War II. Though Emily joked about what kind of wealthy they may have been if her father continued shoe making, Edward was well-known and respected at his job until his retirement. [13] Edward passed away in February 1985.

---

[13] Grumman Aircrafts plant, Baldwin, N.Y., built in 1926.

Fannie-Mae Mims- Moore (1915 – 1999)

PHOTO 10 FANNIE-MAE MIMMS-MOORE , MOTHER. (PRIESTER, 1987)

Fannie-Mae Mims was a native of Aiken, South Carolina. Fannie had fifteen brothers and sisters but relocated to New York with her older sisters Emily, and Marie to escape the racial violence of the South and build a better life for themselves. The sisters came to Freeport and worked as domestic workers amongst various other talents. Fannie-Mae worked on and off for a long time, being a dedicated mother to seven children it made working difficult according to Emily. Fannie-Mae was known to be an advocated for education who worked tirelessly to raise her children. She was a devout member of her church, and provided various services to her community. Fannie-Mae was born into a Baptist family, coming from a line of Clergy, but it was not until Emily's sister Marion joined the Church of God in Freeport around 1960 that she would dedicate the rest of her life in service to the church. Fannie-Mae served as a dedicated deaconess and matriarch at the Church of God in Freeport, New York for over 40 years until her passing in 1999.

Fannie and Edward married in September 1935 and began their life together in Queens, New York but moved to Long Island before they had Emily. They made the Bennington Park area of Freeport their home for over two decades until finally settling in Roosevelt until their final days. The Moore Siblings are Dolores (deceased), Edward Jr. (deceased), Marion, Emily, Richard, Ronnie, & Gary. Emily's sister Marion provided the story about how their parents met,

> *Well, it was -- one of those situations where you had to be in the right place and right time. Even though my mom was up here in New York to live a new life, she was still the quiet type. She stayed to herself and her sister besides working. Well, my father, when he moved here, he had the opportunity to work with a shoemaker here in Freeport, right by the railroad tracks. Back in the day, shoemaking was a great skill to have, and a rare one at that. If he had taken that more seriously, who knows how we would have ended up. Anyways, my father was working in the shoemaker's shop, and he would see my mother pass by the shop very often.*

Not too sure where she was going, but she did. One day my father finally got up the nerve to say something to her, and the rest is history. Otherwise, she would not have been dating anyone possibly, she was quiet in that way.

PHOTO 11 FANNIE-MAE AND EDWARD MOORE TOGETHER AT AN UNDISCLOSED LOCATION IN THE 1970'S. (COURTESY OF MARION MOORE)

The First Quarter 1941-1961

The Journey Begins: Emily Moore

PHOTO 12 EMILY AT 13 OR 14 YEARS OF AGE IN HER HOMEROOM
CLASS PHOTO. (NEW YORK HERITAGE: DIGITAL COLLECTIONS, 1956)

Emily Moore was born on December 19, 1941, at the Nassau
County Community Medical Center in East Meadow, New York.
Emily was born four days after the United States entered World War
II, after the bombing of the Naval Military base at Pearl Harbor,
Hawaii by the Japanese. Fannie-Mae told Emily that during her time,
pregnant women were kept in the hospital for the last month of their
pregnancy. Fannie-Mae remembered having to consistently run back
and forth, and up and down stairs to the bomb shelter in the
basement to hide in protection during bomb alerts for about two

weeks before delivering Emily. It may explain why Emily could never just sit down! Emily's mother often told her that she lived two lives due to the similarities in appearance to her sister, Fannie's firstborn who died in infancy.

Fannie Mae was incredibly close with two of her sisters, Marie (Mims) Gillespie, and Emily Mims who remained in the South after Fannie and Marie migrated North. Unfortunately, for Aunt Emily Mims, she was not able to conceive children. According to the story told by Fannie, young Emily was supposed to have been adopted when she was born by her aunt Emily. The arrangement did not play as planned, as Emily was named after her Godmother instead when Fannie Mae changed her mind when it was time for young Emily to go. Emily credits her aunt Emily for exposing her to collegiate academia, as she accompanied her aunt to Columbia University to apply for her master's degree as a child. Emily Moore spoke of the ordeal during a video interview with Carol Gilliam, a longtime friend, and retired African American Heritage Collection librarian of the Roosevelt Public Library in 2016.

> I was named after my aunt Emily, my Godmother, she was educated. When I was to be born, my aunt Marie was going to adopt me because she could not give birth. Fannie told her that if she had

another girl after Marion, she would allow her to have her. My mother said, one day I was packed up, and ready to go south, and Fannie told her sister 'You can't take my baby!' Emily laughed, "So I never left, but my mother and I were always close to my aunt, she decided to stay in the North.*

After Emily was born, the Moore family moved to Freeport, from Queens, by invitation from Emily's Aunt Marie, the matriarch of the Mims family. Aunt Marie had invited them to live at her two-family style home at 74 Woodside Avenue on the border of Freeport and Roosevelt. As the Moore family continued to grow, her aunt Marie gifted a two-story home located at 114 Sunrise Highway in Bennington Park to Fannie and Edward to raise their family. Aunt Marie wanted Fannie to remain as close as she could since they came up to New York from the South together. On the Sunrise Highway Property, Emily played with her brother Edward Jr. and sister Marion often, though the neighborhood kids often came to play with Emily and her siblings in their yard. They spent their time figuring out new kinds of games and playing sports, using a basket as a hoop. In a time before the inventions of newer games, Emily said, *"Anything to keep us occupied and out of trouble."* As the children played, Fannie-Mae always looked out the window for her children and the children of the neighborhood. The ethics of

Bennington Park was that *the village raised everyone*. This is what Marion Moore had to say about growing up in Bennington Park with her family, and her Aunt Marie's family.

> *Coming up as a child, my aunt had a house that we stayed at in Freeport. My aunt and her husband owned the home, but my parents rented it from them. Right where staples are now. We always had a big yard, and we always played in it. Our property ran in a way that gave us the largest backyard on the block. With six children, you did not play inside, and the house was not that big. Big enough for our family but not enough for the chaos. We played in the yard, a dirty yard, with no grass. The grass may have grown in the front yard. Knowing my uncle, it probably did, but a neighborhood full of kids running through it would surely kill it. My uncle, my mother's brother-in-law, kept the properties up, and brought a house on 72 Woodside Avenue, that house always had grass, and everything looked nice. [...] We helped around with the property, but we mainly used our yard as an athletic field, kickball, and basketball on the dirt. Put up a little something to shoot into. We played softball, not baseball! We used a softball, so we did not break windows. We did everything that did not cost much, to keep us busy and the neighborhood joined would come to our property to play. The kids had their yards of course, but ours was the biggest. That is what we did, we were outside children. We were only inside if the weather was bad.*

Marion Moore, 2022

PHOTO 13 (L) FANNIE-MAE AND (R) MARIE, YEAR UNKNOWN, POSSIBLY 1980'S OR 1990'S. (COURTESY OF MARION MOORE)

Emily Moore, the adolescent

Out of all her siblings, Emily was known as the most outspoken of them. Emily described all her siblings as "*eager to learn,*" but she was "*one of those people who went to people's houses and didn't mind helping out because I was always looking for something to learn about, that is how you learn best, by doing it*". Emily described herself as a curious child, interested in listening to stories from the people in her church, and other family members. She enjoyed hearing about Black people thriving, being resilient during the process of making great things happen for themselves and making it north from Jim Crow segregation. Emily felt that her family was full of strong women who set examples of what Emily should accept and strive for in life, as they were a host of caretakers, educators, organizers, and leaders in various ways. Emily gave respect and gratitude to all the neighborhood friends and adults who would engage in informational conversations with her at a very young age.

Emily always sought knowledge, and Fannie-Mae made sure that her children stayed on top of the world news and education.

Fannie-Mae, a southern woman of her time, did not know how to read well, which was typical culturally for Black people of the South to have at-most a seventh-grade level of education due to segregation and poverty. It remained an unknown fact until the Moore children became older. Marion spoke of the day she realized her mother could not read well because she received a letter that chastised her actions in school, and her mother did not react. Nonetheless, Fannie wanted better for her children, advocating for each of her children to value their education and to do their best in the world. When Emily reached a certain age, her mother would send her to the bank with $10 every Friday to save for college. Even further, Fannie-Mae mandated that the whole family would listen to the news on the radio and the 6 PM news together every night when they purchased a television. Emily would often take her father's newspapers and practice how to read.

> That is how I was learning about what was going on in the world. It is how I learned about colonialism and the practices of apartheid in South Africa and the transition of how the Independent Democratic of the Congo defeated Belgium's control! I learned about Patrice Lumumba, the first prime minister of the newly independent country (at the time) and his assassination. My father once told my mother, "Fannie, your daughter talks to everyone that comes past this house! And he was right, I did.

Growing up in the Bennington Park, Emily remembered it as a community of Black-owned businesses, churches, and organizations that kept the citizens of the town busy. Specifically, Emily remembered a grocery store that was run by the Brown family, a Black family. Across the street there was once a meat market/deli and an animal hospital that is still in operation today. In the summer, on July 4th, Emily's father took the family to the Freeport Stadium Racetrack to watch the fireworks and watch the races every year. The land is now BJ's Wholesale Club.

Marion also spoke about the former Freeport:

> Bennington Park had one of the first Black communities of Long Island. If we were asked where we were from, we did not even say Freeport necessarily, we would say we were from Bennington Park, Freeport. I mean they knew anyhow because it was the only section of Freeport where Black people lived. It was the only section we could live in for many years. Then we started moving out. The Black people started to move and buy homes was Amityville, and then later we started going into Uniondale, Parts of Freeport. There was a lot of land and stores in the Bennington Park area. It pretty much was a commercialized area, and the people who were white, and had money did not want to buy any homes in that area. It was not residential enough, too many cars coming in, and we were right on Sunrise highway. We had to teach children from little not to go into the Street, to keep them safe. If a ball goes out there, well Sunrise Highway has always had the same kind of traffic. Well…not as much, because back then not a lot of people had cars, but it was still a dangerous area.

CLEVELAND ELEMENTARY: THE AMERICAN CONSTITUTION & HONORABLE JUDGE MOXEY RIGBY

PHOTO 14 CLEVELAND ELEMENTARY SCHOOL,1931. (CLEAVELAND AVENUE SCHOOL, 2017)

As Emily grew into age, she learned about organized educational and vocational institutions founded by prominent and elite Black Americans, such as Mary McCleod Bethune, Booker T. Washington, and Mary Terrell. These schools educated both Black youth and adults. Unfortunately, for Black people of the North, these institutions were only in Southern states due to the perimeters of the

Reconstruction Act.[14] One of Emily's earliest and fondest moments of her mother was when Fannie walked Emily to Cleveland Elementary School on her first day of school. Emily's favorite time of the year is fall, revealing that she has always loved how the summer transitioned into a calm and cool fall. She always admired the beauty of the transitioning of trees' green leaves into colors of yellow, orange, and red for the winter. As Emily and her mother walked to the school building, Emily recalled how all the elders and mothers took their children on their first walks to school, all stressing the importance of street safety and stranger danger to their young ones as they walked the streets from their homes to the school. The most important lecture was to stay out of trouble when they were walking the streets of Freeport because their parents knew that anything could result in extreme reactions. Emily described the path to her school as they would walk east towards Merrick Road. The journey could have been proven dangerous for Emily and other children because it included the crossing of the four-lane Sunrise Highway. Marion spoke of how if the children did not want to cross

---

[14] Prominent Black American figures of the 20th century, responsible for providing freed people and future generations of black Americans educational and vocational training during the times of Jim Crow segregation.

the highway, they would go through the woods and across the brook that still runs through the wooded area. Marion recalled feeling that it seemed like such a long journey back when they were younger.

During her first days, Emily felt that Cleveland Elementary was huge, and viewed the principal to be almost as tall as the entry door. As an elementary student, Emily remembered learning parts of the United States Constitution and the Declaration of Independence, but as she learned she realized the words of the Constitution would not be just to people of her skin color. The quote *"We hold these truths to be self-evident, that all men are created equal, that they are endowed by their Creator with certain unalienable Rights, that among these are Life, Liberty and the pursuit of Happiness,"* Emily made sure she memorized first. As Emily would get into debates about race and segregation in her later years, she would recite the quote when she felt the situation was necessary during her plight for Civil Rights. Emily attended school in the Freeport School District for the rest of her primary and secondary studies. Though it was a predominantly white setting, Emily felt that she received an adequate education, despite not having Black teachers. Emily said that she could not recall direct discrimination during her schooling at

Cleveland Elementary, but she was not blind to the racial and economic biases of certain white teachers as they taught and interacted with certain Black students.

As far as what Emily found special for the Black Cleveland students were the visits from the late Honorable Judge Moxie A. Rigby. Hon. Rigby often visited and always had words of encouragement for the children at Cleveland Elementary. Emily loved the fact that Hon. Rigby played with the children during their recreational activities. Particularly for Emily, she played table tennis with Hon. Rigby, mainly noticing how her table tennis skills improved with each match she played against him. The matches encouraged her to continue to play table tennis, leading Emily to join the team at Freeport High School table tennis team in the future. Emily was able to witness Judge Rigby swearing in as a Nassau County's first black judge.

PHOTO 15 MOXEY RIGBY. (NEW YORK LAW SCHOOL , 2018)

Judge Rigby would come up to the school with a table tennis set and challenge us to games against him and encourage us to play between each other. He would push us to play our hardest and it left us with a feeling that even though some may have lost if we put our best foot forward, we would continue to grow.

- *Emily Moore*

Senior 50 yd. Dash—1st., Faye Henwood, Archer; 2nd., Marilyn Heller, Seaman; 3rd., Pat Phillips, Columbus; 4th., Emily Moore, Cleveland.
Cub Broad Jump—1st., Jean Jawor.

FIGURE 8 UNIDENTIFIED NEWSPAPER ARTICLE SIGNIFY EMILY'S PARTICIPATION AS A RUNNER FOR CLEAVELAND ELEMENTARY (UNKNOWN)

Cleveland Elementary School was shut down in 1963 due to racial allegations of teachers' treatment of their Black students. The Cleveland Elementary School grounds became the home of a BMW dealership/garage located on the corner of Merrick and Albany Avenues. The athletic field belonged to the elementary school and then specifically to the district of Freeport since 1949, remaining north of the dealership and is still used by the Freeport school district and its community (The Leader: Freeport's official Newspaper, 1949). Currently, in the year 2022, the town is trying to convert the Cleveland Avenue field into an Amazon Company warehouse, though there are residents of Roosevelt-Freeport who are in objection and fighting against this development. (Business: Cleveland Avenue Controversy Deepens, 2021) The village government denies the authority of the 1949 document where the Long Island State Park Commission granted the easement of the land for the Cleveland Avenue School and claims the legal right to revoke the easement and sell the land (Business: Cleveland Avenue Controversy Deepens, 2021).

PHOTO 16 AIIREAL VIEW OF CLEAVELAND ELEMENTARY ATHLETIC FIELD., 1970.
(COURTESY OF GOOGLE IMAGES)

Black Adolescence and the Rise of Civil Rights Era: It Was Not Fair

PHOTO 17 EMILY MOORE AT 15 YEAR OLD IN HOMEROOM . (FREEPORT HIGH SCHOOL, 1957)

When Emily was around ten years old, she and other neighborhood children saw a terrible car accident that took the life of one of her classmates. According to Emily, the car jumped the curve and made an impact on the young boy. Emily remembered that the driver, a white woman, blamed the crash on her nervousness about seeing the little black boy on the corner. At Emily's young age, she knew that what the woman said was nowhere near justifiable but knew that her skin color allowed her to not receive prosecution. This moment showed Emily firsthand that there was no limit to what were able to get away with when it came to the law and Black people. Emily must have been well respected and seen as a strong figure among her peers since she was asked to read the obituary at the young boy's funeral, "*Despite my emotions, I remember calmly reading his obituary, calmly getting through it.*" This moment lived in her mind and heart forever, because it exposed her to the meaning for what black lives meant to the public. It was at this moment that sparked the fight for justice and equality against segregation and racism within.

Emily understood that her racial struggles were different from the Black Americans who lived in the Deep South. Though New York's social-economic prejudices remained present, it just was not as loud and boastful as in the South. On Long Island, historically the North Shore region of Nassau County, and Suffolk County have been known for their prejudices, as with Hempstead, Roosevelt, and Freeport, where the Black population of the Island mostly resided. In New York City, it was generally known that you were not welcomed by the crowds that frequented a location. In the mountainous and farmland regions of upstate New York, where Confederate flags continue to fly high on the various homes and lands, hence many black people traditionally remained in Albany and Troy, New York. Culturally, these were established areas and places on Long Island where Black people like Emily simply knew not to voyage.

Emily's earliest participation in civil rights activism was the demonstrations against Woolworth's Five and Dime diners in Freeport alongside other local shops in the late 1950s. Emily did not disclose whom she went to the demonstrations with as she admitted that she did not disclose her whereabouts with her parents during the time. Emily remembered feeling jolted with energy by the Anti-racism and equality propaganda, as well as the opposition demonstrated from those who wanted to preserve the segregation of public spaces. For Emily, that event solidified her calling to be a Civil Rights activist. An interview with Dr. Julian Bond in the 2000s, captured him briefly speaking about the sit-ins within the North stating, *"... yes, there had been sit-ins in the late 1950s, run largely by the NAACP, but they never caught on"* (Bond, 2010).

The Death of Emmett Till: The bullet that loaded the Movement.

> *When people saw what happened to my son, men stood up who had never stood up before. People became vocal who had never vocalized before. – Mamie Till " ((PBS), 1990's)*

The death of Emmett Till is remembered as one of the most publicly known heinous acts and tragedies committed against a child in the face of racism before the rise of the Civil Rights movement. In the summer of 1955, when Emily and Emmett were both 14 years old, Till was murdered in Mississippi by four white men. Till was from Chicago, Illinois but the evils that racism withheld in the South held no bias towards age and origin. Till was accused of speaking inappropriately and whistling at a white woman in a store. Later that night, this young boy was taken from his uncle's house, tortured, shot, mutilated, tied to an industrial fan, and dumped into the Tallahatchie River, where his body would resurface days later. It was a nightmare for every Black American, snatched out of their homes into the darkness of the night to meet their demise. Losing a child, but a child in that way devastated women throughout the world.

Emily remembered hearing the news, greatly saddened by it, and angered her as well stating:

> I felt for his mother. When JET Magazine, one of the first Black American magazine. They printed the article for the next month; his mother Mamie Elizabeth Till-Mobley displayed him in an open casket, which has that boy's body was on the front cover. It changed the mindsets of children, the teenagers, and us. It made us stand up!

The world would come to find out that the woman who accused Till lied about the details of the encounter almost 70 years later. As far as immediate actions, the men who were accused of kidnapping Till were taken into custody and set to trial at least three times but were never convicted. Mammie Till-Mobley passed away in 2003. In 2020, there was a ploy from the Black American community asking for the charging of the woman who accused Till of his action, which is still ignored.

"Church was mandatory."

Traditionally, Black American churches served as social hubs for Civil Rights activism throughout the North and the South. Fannie-Mae attended another church before she joined and attended The

Church of God in Freeport alongside Marion in 1959, who became a devoted Christian after graduating from high school.[15] Fannie served as a devoted deaconess of the church for over 30 years and made sure that Emily and her siblings attended church every Sunday when she became a member. They were involved with church and community events throughout the school year and summer. Emily expressed that with her mother "church…it was mandatory!" What Emily loved, maybe just a little more than learning the Stories and Words of God, was the gossip about the grassroots of the Civil Rights movement that was spoken about among the congregation. Emily noted that her church did a great deal of fundraising for the Southern Christian Leadership Conference (SCLC), and the National Association for the Advancement of Colored People (NAACP), two main groups involved in the grassroots of the Civil Rights Movement. According to Emily, even though the church supported the Civil Rights movement a great deal, but not many members of the congregation were active participants in civil rights activities. Emily always understood that no matter the role, everyone

---

[15] The first location of the church was near Sunrise Highway transitioning, its current church building is on Babylon Turnpike in Freeport. The original church has been renamed, but the original building remains on a corner a few blocks away from Freeport's Long Island Railroad Station.

played a part in the unification towards equality. Church of God would hold various fundraising opportunities that would help the community and the Civil Rights movement.

To

Mother Fannie Moore

In Appreciation of your faithfulness and dedicated service

FREEPORT C.O.G

Prayer Group

April 16,1994

FIGURE 9 (COURTESY OF AYANNA MOORE)

To

Sister Fannie Moore

In appreciation of your faithfulness and dedicated service

Freeport C.O.G

Prayer Group

November 12, 1994

FIGURE 10 (COURTSEY OF AYANNA MOORE)

Prayer Pilgrimage at the Lincoln Memorial

FIGURE 11 FLYER FOR THE PRAYER PILGRIM, (THE '60S AT 50, 2019)

As the Civil Rights movement rapidly developed in the mid-1950s, Emily recalled hearing and reading about Rev. Dr. Martin Luther King, Jr., Rosa Parks, and the organization of the Alabama Bus Boycotts with the SCLC, which resulted in the desegregation of Alabama Public Transit and other demonstrative activities throughout the south .[16] In the 1960s, Phillip A. Randolph, Roy Wilkins, Bayard Rustin, and Dr. King came together organized the Prayer Pilgrimage, in conjunction with activists and groups alike. It served as the predecessor to the March on Washington that would later occur in 1963. Emily was sixteen when she attended the Prayer Pilgrimage for Freedom in Washington, D.C. in support of voting rights on May 17, 1957. She found herself able to attend because she joined a committee that was fundraising for the event. During the event, Emily heard the singing of legendary gospel singer Mahalia Jackson, and Marian Anderson, the first Black woman to perform opera at the Constitution Hall in Washington, D.C.

This was also the same event that solidified Dr. King's position a universal symbol of the Civil Rights Movement when he delivered his speech "Give Us the Ballot," advocating that Black Americans deserved to vote without oppression and acts of violence due to the pain and toil that the black people have received in the United States since its beginnings. It was the first time Emily had seen prominent figures of her skin color gathered in one place. Most

---

[16] Martin Luther King Jr. (1929 – 1968) Reverend, Orator, Civil Rights pioneer. He Pinned the " Give me the Ballot", and "I have a Dream, speeches" on equality and voters' rights.

importantly for Emily, in her young age, she was able to witness the connectivity between black and white people, within a space and time. An exemplifying vision of what racial unity and action looked like. The lessons learned during the event made Emily think deeper into what it meant to have true freedom in America versus equality, and what needs to be done to help achieve them both.

Freeport High School: "The teacher called me a pig"

Emily and her siblings were one of the few early Black families to graduate out of the Freeport School district. Citizens of Freeport were familiar with the Moore family within the community and school district. As a student and young lady, Emily was and remained unapologetic about her pride in her culture and her vocal rhetoric against segregation and prejudice. Emily was steadfast in wanting to make a change in how Black American men, women, and children were treated. Emily had decided that her mission was to not allow herself or future generations to remain helpless because of systematic oppression, to the best of her abilities, even before she even knew what she wanted to do for a career. As a young vocal Black woman in a predominantly white town, one would like to think that her activities would lead to mistreatment or seclusion from her fellow peers, but fortunately, her activities did not dampen or affect her social life at school. Emily noted that those who were prejudiced in school took no action towards her. Emily had only one racially related incident in Freeport High School.

> I do not even remember his name, but he was my sister Marion's teacher. We...my friend and I were walking in the hall from the Gym, and I stopped to get water out of the fountain like the other students.

The next thing I know, the teacher is pushing me against the wall face first. He was saying, "You pig, what are you doing drinking out of that fountain?" I thought he was a student. So, as I was turning around, I swung in defense. (Brown, 2001)

Despite Emily's toughness, she admitted she cried on the way home. Emily told her mother about the ordeal and went to the principal's office the same day. As they spoke to principal, Emily explained that she was not the only person who stood in line for water, as it was hot that day, and that she was the only person targeted, as the only Black girl there at that moment. Emily was suspended for the incident and was given until the following Monday to return to school. Emily even cried at the thought of missing school, but not with regret, she was not going to let anyone become physical against her in the name of racism. Emily mentioned that her sister Marion's grades were not affected by the situation in retaliation because she was already known as an "A" student and was favored amongst the teachers. The teacher did not know that the two were sisters until after the event but had an idea to ask Marion about Emily when he realized they had the same last name (Brown, 2001, p. 4). The teacher did not face repercussions for his actions. Emily felt that since that day, throughout the rest of her middle school days, she had faced challenges from staff and students that were meant to break and continually test her resolve. Instead, she let it build her and prepare her for what is outside of Freeport.

The Moore family was always known for their involvement in the community. Emily served as a secretary officer for the A&B youth groups of Freeport and Roosevelt in 1958. She and her sister Marion also served as members of the Freeport Booster Club. The Moore sisters helped run a fundraiser for their spring dance held at the V.F.W. Hall once located at 404 North Main Street.[17] Emily remembers the A&B Youth Group of the Utopia, a program that served the black community of Freeport and Roosevelt. She also recalled being a debutante at 16, a traditional experience that Black American middle-class citizens would use to introduce their children into society as young adults. Emily appreciated that her mother for kept Emily and her siblings active, believing that it heavily influenced and shaped her to be the person she is today. Emily acknowledged that there were tons of events that the Moore siblings took part in, but she specifically remembered the spring

---

[17] This location is now the Spanish Evangelical Church.

dance since it was the first event, she had attended outside of a church setting.

Emily did appreciate that she had white friends who did not mind her skin color and enjoyed her company, as well as accepting her stance and actions towards achieving equality. Nonetheless, Emily never forgot that she was a representation of her family and her people wherever she went. Emily described herself playfully as the only "jiggaboo" amongst her friends as during her teenage years, as she was one of the few Black teens to attend Freeport high school during her time there. As far as friendships, Emily reminisced about how her classmates would bring her to the Elk Club, a white social club once located on Merrick Avenue. While there she was a part of the bowling club, but since this was the same Elk Club that supported the KKK and their parades in the 1920's. It was still a place Emily did not frequent unless she was with her white peers.

The description of Marion Moore in the Spring Dance Souvenir

Journal is as follows:

MARION MOORE

Marion Moore – Always a smile, is good-natured, liked by everyone. "Loves dem bums." Treasurer of GAA (Girls Athletic Association). Top in hockey, volleyball, basketball, and softball. One of five girls to receive a Gold Key the highest girl's athletic award. Desires to become an accountant, studying at Brown's Business school.

PHOTO 18 MARION MOORE PHOTO IN THE SOUVENIER JOURNAL (LIBRARY, SPRING DANCE,

FIGURE 13 SOUVENIR JOURNAL OF THE SPRING DANCE (LIBRARY, SPRING DANCE, 2015)

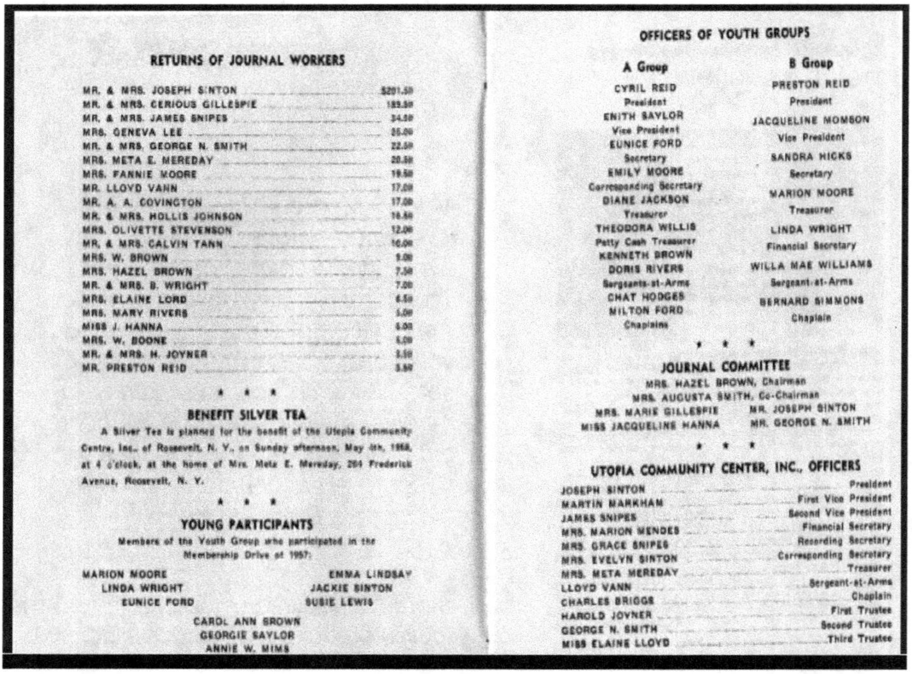

RETURNS OF JOURNAL WORKERS

MR. & MRS. JOSEPH SINTON	$201.50
MR. & MRS. CERIOUS GILLESPIE	189.50
MR. & MRS. JAMES SNIPES	34.50
MRS. GENEVA LEE	35.00
MR. & MRS. GEORGE N. SMITH	22.50
MRS. META E. MEREDAY	20.50
MRS. FANNIE MOORE	19.50
MR. LLOYD VANN	17.00
MR. A. A. COVINGTON	17.00
MR. & MRS. HOLLIS JOHNSON	16.50
MRS. OLIVETTE STEVENSON	12.00
MR. & MRS. CALVIN TANN	10.00
MRS. W. BROWN	9.00
MRS. HAZEL BROWN	7.50
MR. & MRS. B. WRIGHT	7.00
MRS. ELAINE LORD	6.50
MRS. MARY RIVERS	5.00
MISS J. HANNA	5.00
MRS. W. BOONE	5.00
MR. & MRS. H. JOYNER	3.50
MR. PRESTON REID	3.50

* * *

BENEFIT SILVER TEA

A Silver Tea is planned for the benefit of the Utopia Community Centre, Inc., of Roosevelt, N. Y., on Sunday afternoon, May 4th, 1958, at 4 o'clock, at the home of Mrs. Meta E. Mereday, 264 Frederick Avenue, Roosevelt, N. Y.

* * *

YOUNG PARTICIPANTS

Members of the Youth Group who participated in the Membership Drive of 1957:

MARION MOORE
LINDA WRIGHT
EUNICE FORD
EMMA LINDSAY
JACKIE SINTON
SUSIE LEWIS
CAROL ANN BROWN
GEORGIE SAYLOR
ANNIE W. MIMS

OFFICERS OF YOUTH GROUPS

A Group

CYRIL REID, President
ENITH SAYLOR, Vice President
EUNICE FORD, Secretary
EMILY MOORE, Corresponding Secretary
DIANE JACKSON, Treasurer
THEODORA WILLIS, Petty Cash Treasurer
KENNETH BROWN
DORIS RIVERS, Sergeants-at-Arms
CHAT HODGES
MILTON FORD, Chaplains

B Group

PRESTON REID, President
JACQUELINE MOMSON, Vice President
SANDRA HICKS, Secretary
MARION MOORE, Treasurer
LINDA WRIGHT, Financial Secretary
WILLA MAE WILLIAMS, Sergeant-at-Arms
BERNARD SIMMONS, Chaplain

* * *

JOURNAL COMMITTEE

MRS. HAZEL BROWN, Chairman
MRS. AUGUSTA SMITH, Co-Chairman
MRS. MARIE GILLESPIE
MISS JACQUELINE HANNA
MR. JOSEPH SINTON
MR. GEORGE N. SMITH

* * *

UTOPIA COMMUNITY CENTER, INC., OFFICERS

JOSEPH SINTON	President
MARTIN MARKHAM	First Vice President
JAMES SNIPES	Second Vice President
MRS. MARION MENDES	Financial Secretary
MRS. GRACE SNIPES	Recording Secretary
MRS. EVELYN SINTON	Corresponding Secretary
MRS. META MEREDAY	Treasurer
LLOYD VANN	Sergeant-at-Arms
CHARLES BRIGGS	Chaplain
HAROLD JOYNER	First Trustee
GEORGE N. SMITH	Second Trustee
MISS ELAINE LLOYD	Third Trustee

FIGURE 14 SOUVENIER JOURNAL MENTIONING EMILY, FANNIE, AND MARIONS INVOLVMENT WITH THE CENTER AND DANCE

A Book and Two Rackets: The Rise of Emily Moore

Sports was the key, me, and my sister, we trained young and old people. I would go meet and watch my sister practice and play games. I remember one time my father told Marion she could not play in a volleyball game and made the emphasis on us not to go anywhere. I said to my mother, Marion is the captain of the volleyball team, she must go! Marion said,' what they gonna do? All they can do is whoop us! I went to my mom and told her, "She gotta' go, and I am going with her.' So, we went! I remember telling the lady Ms. Clark that I HAD to go to the game with Marion TODAY.

Emily Moore

In the 1950s, Black people continued to challenge and cross racial barriers which included the world of sports and entertainment. Jackie Robinson would integrate major league baseball as he joined the Brooklyn Dodgers. More importantly was Althea Gibson who became the first Black woman to win the Wimbledon Cup in 1957. In 1958, Gibson would also become the first Black woman to win the French Grand Slam. In the same year Gibson published her biography *I always wanted to be somebody*. The biography reflected on moments of her childhood, current life, and her experience as a Black woman in a predominantly white male profession. In this same period, Marion Moore would buy Gibson's book and two rackets, gifting the items to Emily. Marking the day that created Emily Moore, decided to become a tennis player, a physical educator, and ultimately one of the best black female tennis coaches on the East Coast of her time.

As a child, before the introduction of tennis, Emily was not known as an academically advanced student as she entered ninth grade after being left back in two different grades in Elementary school. Emily claims that she simply was not into learning in the classroom as a young child but was more interested in what was happening outside of it. Along with the topic of world news and politics, sports became Emily's primary focus as she learned and taught the fundamentals of games to her peers in the neighborhood. During Emily's 9th grade years, due to her academics, she was not able to take part in any student athletics until she had proven her grades worthy of the allowance to join teams by her guidance counselors. On academic probation, Emily rose to the challenge, completing, and passing the necessary courses needed to qualify for varsity sports. It was the only year Emily did not play a sport for Freeport High School; it was the same year she homed in on Tennis.

In consideration to Black American culture, tennis was viewed as a predominantly white sport, the same way golf was for many decades. In Urban communities, it is not played because were no parks created in those communities to play the sport. Usually, many great athletes practiced a sport they excelled at from a young age, but that was not the same story for Emily. As many black people couldn't afford the associated gear needed, before her gifts from Marion, Emily only played table tennis, and handball, which possibly made her coordination for the sport even greater. Emily and Marion often played with and compete against each other, which helped Emily develop her skills because Marion was also a gifted and competitive athlete. Gibson became one of Emily's athletic inspirations after completing the book and invested her time into practicing the game of tennis.

Emily practiced and practiced, finding people to challenge her skills, and eventually building a small reputation for her athleticism in the sport. As far as competitors and sportsmanship, Emily claims that she always played with the white children because the Black children were too afraid to intermingle with them. In return, she gained great rapport with the white community of Freeport. As

Emily played with her white peers, they went to areas such as the town of Huntington to play tennis. Fortunately, the parents of her peers made sure to keep an eye out for Emily to make sure that nobody bothered her as she played on private and public courts, as she was always the little black girl playing in the sea of white children.

Marion's story on introducing Emily to tennis:

> Well, I taught her many things but in sports, she would eventually go on to surpass me. When you get into something, and you play with it, you do better. I was into tennis before Emily was. I always wanted to learn how to play tennis but there were no courts around my neighborhood, in the Bennington Park section. Nobody tried to help us learn tennis. Nobody really likes to say it, but I will! Tennis is an expensive sport. The rackets are expensive, and you cannot just find one! You can always find a rubber ball, but not a racket. My mother barely worked; at that time, she did not work too much because she stayed home to take care of all the younger siblings, so there was that too. My father supports all of us. It is in our genetics to be athletic; my mother and her sister were track athletes back in South Carolina. I had two older cousins who played college basketball, I never have to see them play, I just heard about it. It seemed like all the women were athletic though.
>
> I had graduated high school; I got my first job and had started working at Freeport High school during the summer every now and then in the offices. I decided to buy two tennis rackets. I brought two because even though you can play by yourself against a wall, you will not really get a feel for it until you are playing against people but of course, we could not afford six tennis rackets between all my siblings. Having a court is key, and even though all these years we have had the backyard space to do it, she never made a court in her backyard. I have a swimming pool; it is semi-ground, but I never was interested in swimming because of my hair. (Emily said the same). In Freeport, the young men used to run down to the reservoir and go swimming. They were not supposed to swim there

because it was for the town water, but it was easier for them to do that because they did not have hair back then, just shortcuts.

G.A.A. OFFICERS—Left to Right: G.O. Rep. L. McDougall, Treas. M. Moore, Vice-Pres. S. Hicks, Pres. K. Canapary, Sec. M. L. Johnson, Advisor D. Clark.

GIRLS' ATHLETIC ASSOCIATION

PHOTO 19 SECOND FROM LEFT IS MARION MOORE, APART OF THE F.H.S GIRLS ATHLETIC ASSOCIATION. (FREEPORT HIGH SCHOOL, 1959)

I started tennis because it was a challenge, (it was not purposely that she intended for Emily to get into tennis) I naturally went for the challenge, which is why I went into accounting. We did not have any life-like examples; there was not one in my community. Now, they are all over the place. Back in my day, I did not know one Black woman or man that was an accountant, and it was the kind of jobs that they had for women. The only one I knew, and was not sure if he was an accountant, was my bookkeeping teacher at Freeport High school in 9th or 10th grade, and I liked it.

- Marion Moore

Emily recalled being able to see Althea Gibson at Forest Hills Park (now Arthur Ashe Park) in the Forest Hill section of Queens, New York. As Emily did not want to take away from the fact that Gibson was an exceptional player when she mentioned that "*Gibson was not as interactive with the fans who looked like her (black) as she was with the white fans*". In her book, Gibson even wrote, "*Someone wrote that the difference between me and Jackie Robinson is that he thrived on his role as a Negro battling for equality, whereas I shy away from it.*" (Wayne Coffey, 2007) Overall, Emily felt that Gibson was always under pressure and in the public eye, wanting to please the public and Emily did not let it make her bitter about her views of Gibson. Emily would later become acquainted with Gibson in her adult years through her work at the Harlem Tennis Center in the 1970s.

Emily on Marion introducing her to tennis,

> *When she [Marion] got the rackets, we would go to Randall and Northeast Parks, which was traditionally a white park, but Randall was the only park with tennis courts at the time. We crossed the bridge, crossed the tracks to play. Marion and I were also the only Black players on a white softball team that traveled all over Long Island. When my sister got heavily involved with the church, she could not play sports or do the extracurricular activities a young teenage woman would normally do, and that was when I realized that people would have things they want to do, and you are not going to be able to count on them. I would walk down to Randall Park, leaving the Black community to the white community, my*

parents would give me a nickel to get home by bus, but all the people would bring me back home because they had cars. Being involved in sports and understanding the things that were happening in the south and long island itself to our people, I knew I was BLACK. I knew I did not have any freedom, no equal opportunity, so it was understood to go to school and stick to your plan.

Senior Year: I was the First Black Red Devil of Freeport

As a student-athlete, Emily was a part of various clubs throughout her high school years: Library Club, Art Club, Hockey, Table Tennis, Table Tennis Honor Team, Basketball, Basketball Honor Team, Softball, Softball Honor Team, and Athletic-Student Leader her senior year. Emily even served as the first Red Devil, the school mascot. The opportunity came about when one of the coaches approached Emily about the position, *"She [a coach] said… Emily! We need some more students of color to be a part of the team, and you are athletic. I want you to be the mascot."* Emily enjoyed her high school experience as an athlete at Freeport and was more than happy to accept the offer to help integrate the team. Even as a proud black woman, coming from a Christian family, Emily was not too sure how her mother would react to hearing the news that Emily would serve as the "Red Devil," but to Emily's surprise, Fannie agreed to allow her to represent as the mascot, but not until after a long discussion, of course. *The Leader* newspaper covered the announcement of her new position as Mascot.

Emily Moore
FHS "Red Devil"

Following a precedent adminis-tered last year. Emily Moore was chosen to serve as the Red Devil for the coming school year. Emily made her debut at the practice football game held with Lafayette High School. The Red Devil, the symbol of Freeport High School, adds spirit to all football games by assisting the cheerleaders.

Following a precedent administered last year, Emily Moore was chosen to serve as the Red Devil for the coming school year. Emily made her debut at the practice football game held with Lafayette High School. The Red Devil, the symbol of Freeport High School, adds spirit to all football games by assisting the cheerleaders

FIGURE 15 NEWSPAPER ARTCLE COVERING EMILY'S SELECTION AS MASCOT. (THE LEADER, 1960)

At the first football game of the season, Emily wanted the community and guests to see that she was a Black woman saying, "*I walked on the field with my mask on, then I took my mask off in front of the crowd and the people began to cheer. I never put the mask back on after that.*" During her time at Freeport High School, Emily admitted to feeling moments of seclusion from students and staff over the years, but it overwhelmed her to see the support displayed for her at that moment. In Emily's yearbook, her peers referred to Emily to be the "Hilda" of her school, meaning that she was considered good-looking among her peers. It also said she was known for having "devilish ways" and being "physically fit" for teaching.

PHOTO 20 EMILY IN THE TOP ROW, HOCKEY TEAM 1959.

PHOTO 21 EMILY FAR LEFT. TABLE TENNIS, 1959

PHOTO 22 EMILY FAR RIGHT, TOP ROW. HOCKEY 1960

PHOTO 23 EMILY, TABLE TENNIS 1960

PHOTO 24 EMILY TOP ROW RIGHT, BASKETBALL 1961.

PHOTO 25 EMILY TOP ROW, RIGHT. HOCKEY, 1961.

PHOTO 26 EMIILY, TOP ROW RIGHT, STUDENT LEADERS, 1961

PHOTO 28 EMILY, MIDDLE, BASKETBALL 1961.

PHOTO 27 F.H.S VARSITY STUNT TEAM. (FREEPORT, 1961)

PHOTO 29 F.H.S. KICK LINE. (FREEPORT, 1961)

PHOTO 30 F.H.S CHEER TEAM WITH EMILY AS THE MASCOT, 1961. (FREEPORT, 1961)

On Thursday, March 9, 1961, the Fifth Annual Library Club Tea was held in the Freeport High Library. In attendance at the tea, besides the almost fifty Library Club members, were Supt. of Schools Dr. John W. Dodd; Principal J. Wesley Southard; Vice - principal Irving Franklin; guidance counselors Mary Didas, Henry Puff, and Lawrence Hamel; and a host of other faculty members. In charge of the tea were Miss Mary McIntosh and Miss Ruth Norris, librarians; and Alan Munro, Library Club President, who gave the opening address. The featured speaker for the tea was Dr. Dodd, who spoke on the importance of books and libraries in our society. Presentations were made by Dr. Dodd to one and two-year members of the Library Club, outstanding awards going to **Alan Munro, Robert Greenblatt, Dale Klar, Emily Moore, Terry Azzara, and Bernice Jacobson.**

On Thursday, May 9, 1961, the Fifth Annual Library Club Tea was held in the Freeport High Library. In attendance at the tea besides the fifty club members, were Supt. Of Schools Dr. John W. Dodd; Principal J. Weasley Southard; Vice-Principal Irving Franklin; guidance counselors Mary Didas, Henry Puff, and Lawerence Hamel; and a host of other faculty members. In charge of the tea were Miss Mary McIntosh and Mis Ruth Norris, librarians; and Alan Munro, Library Club President, who gave the opening address. The featured speaker for the tea was Dr. Dodd, who spoke on the importance of books and libraries in our society. Dr. Dodd to one- and two-year members of the Library Club, outstanding awards going to Alan Munro, Robert Greenblatt, Dale Klar, Emily Moore, Terry Azzara, and Bernice

FIGURE 16 NEWSPAPER ARTICLE ABOUT F.H.S TEA PARTY WHERE EMILY RECEIVED AN AWARD. (THE LEADER, 1961.)

PHOTO 31 F.H.S GIRLS ATHLETIC ASSOCIATION (FREEPORT, 1961)

MOST
ATHLETIC

EMILY
MOORE

MIKE
FRANK

PHOTO 32 F.H.S. MOST ATHLETIC SUPERLATIVES. (FREEPORT, 1961)

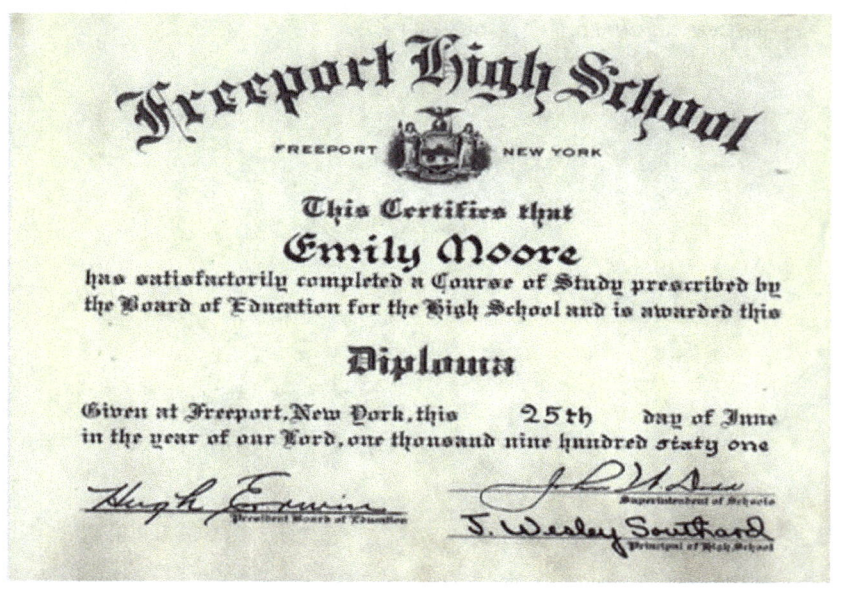

FIGURE 17 HIGH SCHOOL DIPLOMA., JUNE 25, 1961. (FREEPORT, 1961)

Second Quarter: 1961-1967

MORGAN CHOSE ME: MORGAN STATE COLLEGE

PHOTO 33 HOLMES HALL ON MORGAN STATE UNIVERSITY CAMPUS (GILL, THE HISTORY OF MARYLAND'S HISTORICALLY BLACK COLLEGES, 1992)

Emily excelled in high school and took part in various extracurricular activities, making her an ideal collegiate candidate, but Emily viewed that college was not going to help her progression as a civil rights activist. Steadfast in her decision, Emily wanted to at once join among those who chose to fight for the civil rights of black people; she wanted to help the progression and resolve of her culture. It was now time for her to prepare for graduation and step toward her next journey into what she wanted her future to be like. For all her primary and secondary educative years, Emily had only experienced white teachers and predominately white classmates, and though it proved tough at times. Emily was well received among her peers, but other Black seniors, at Freeport and other towns, spoke excitedly of applying and attending historically Black colleges and universities (HBCUs) such as Clark, Hampton, Howard, Morehouse, Morgan, and Spellman.

Though she had no attention to attend college, Emily knew that if she did attend college, it would be an HBCU because she always wanted to experience being surrounded by black intelligence and cultural significance that HBCU facilitates for the black culture. It was said by Emily that Black educators in Hempstead commonly graduated from Morgan and Howard Colleges. Even though Emily's family members attended Lincoln, Wilberforce, and even Columbia Universities, and colleges, but there were no specific family allegiances to an alma mater. Unexpectedly, Emily had the chance to experience the campus in Northeast Baltimore, Maryland.

All my aunts' daughters were educated, and one of them married a Morgan graduate. The youngest Maxine went to Morgan. Maxine would take me to dance school and many other activities. My aunt was sickly, so she asked me to help take Maxine and her things to Morgan. My sister and I had perfect attendance, but after all that, my aunt had done for her and my family, I would never tell her no, so I went. "I only visited one campus that year, and it was because of Maxine. She was the one who had attended Morgan, and I

*helped bring down some of her things with her parents to Baltimore.
I remember I had perfect attendance that year until that moment...
that is how I messed it up! Thanks to Maxine I went to Morgan!"*
(Brown, 2001)

During Emily's visit to Morgan, she was able to see images that promoted the Black community and individual prosperity, and wealth, but most importantly, she felt a sense of belonging and community based upon the equality that was accessible as an HBCU. Emily said, "There *were many people of her skin, of her age, all on a mission, to educate and be educated, and progress the culture."* The sights of different male and female professors with their poise, interactions and styles astounded Emily. Various buildings on campus were named after trailblazing Black Americans such as Harriet Tubman, Benjamin Banneker, Sojourner Truth, and Harriet Woodfield, a Nurse who was honored for saving Morgan residents during a fire at a Morgan campus that was in Lynchburg, Virginia in 1917 (Brown, 2001). When she finished touring the campus and found out how far the campus was from New York, she replied, *"Oh! I can hitchhike from here!"* Little would she know that Morgan College would serve as her front door into the Civil Rights Movement (Brown, 2001). Emily sought an application as she left the campus. Emily gained admittance to Morgan for the graduating class of 1965.

Maryland, as a historically former slave-holding state, practiced Black Codes and Jim Crow laws after the abolition of slavery. Maryland is a state that separates the North and South for the East Coast. The effects of slavery transcended just as they did in the Deep South. Morgan State College was once The Centenary Biblical Institute when it opened its doors during the Reconstruction Era in 1867. It was a men's missionary school that also accepted African American students. Morgan College received its name in 1890; renamed in honor of Black American Reverend Lyttleton Morgan (Gill, University History, 1992). Morgan set up its permanent grounds on the corner of Hillen Avenue and East Cold Spring Roads in Northeast Baltimore. The expansion of Morgan's campus came with opposition from the neighboring town of Laurelville for decades due to the "fear" of Black people moving into their neighborhood, which was less than ¼ of a mile from the campus border. During this period, Morgan's students demonstrated against the seclusion, as legal teams of the NAACP fought within the judicial system and gained permission to expand their lands throughout the years. In

1934, the state of Maryland recognized Morgan College as an HBCU. In the 1980s, Morgan College was renamed Morgan State University after Vera Welcome fought for its renaming to bring history and the prestige results of its education to light, like the surrounding white colleges.[18] Morganites simply call it Morgan.

In 1955, Morgan students engaged in demonstrations that began the desegregation of Read's Drug Store at Lexington Market in downtown Baltimore (Vise, 2011). This was around the same time Emily, as an adolescent, was demonstrating against segregation at Woolworth's eating establishments in Freeport and Hempstead, New York. Dr. Martin Luther King, Jr. also visited Morgan, once before to speak at commencement ceremony with invite from Dr. Martin L. Jenkins, the president of Morgan. Before the arrival of Emily at Morgan College, the involvement of young supporters of the civil rights movement took a nationwide strategic change when the *Greensboro Four* event occurred in February 1960. During this event, four first-year students who attended North Carolina

---

[18] Vera Freeman Welcome – A civil rights and community activist, and politician who served as the senator of Maryland from 1962 until 1982. Born in North Carolina, Welcome came to Baltimore to finish secondary school at Coppin Normal School, now Coppin State University. Welcome graduated from Morgan State College. Represented Baltimore's fourth district (Parish 2007).

Agricultural and Technical Institution (HBCU) protested inside a Woolworth's Five and Dime dining establishment, refusing to leave.

Emily felt the journey that she was going to embark on at Morgan was going to be memorable; she just did not know how. Headlines and media coverage across the United States and foreign countries continued to report on the newer energy that college student participation and organization brought to the Civil Rights movement. Dynamics of demonstrations changed as young adults and teenagers bonded together against racial injustice. Across the South, college students and young adults conduct sit-ins, often met with ridicule and humiliation with food and insults thrown at them by white citizens of all ages. In 1955, Morgan State students participated student-led sit-ins. In 2011, those students were recognized, and received honors for their participation by Morgan State. In addition to the honoring, Morgan displayed the stools and newspaper coverage of the students that participated in the Dine-in sit-ins in the Morgan's Student Center as an exhibit.

John F. Kennedy, James Farmer, and the Congress of Racial Equality

During Emily's first year at Morgan in 1961, John F. Kennedy became the President of the United States. Kennedy's campaign made promises that would confront the issues of racial oppression, segregation, and the injustices of the political and economic system against Black Americans. As his presidency progressed, the War against Communism and the Vietnam War heavily distracted Kennedy. Historian H.W. Hinds wrote about racial tensions steadily increasing in the South and its effects on the progress of Black Americans. Hinds mentioned that the Civil Rights movement leaders and groups such as NAACP, CORE, and SNCC were growing impatient with President Kennedy, concluding that he was not keeping his word about setting up civil rights legislation during his first two years in office (Brands, 2011). Hinds wrote in Kennedy's defense, "The young president was torn between trying to ensure equality for all Americans and trying to keep southern political support while he did it. Kennedy's efforts at war were not going well with the failed invasion of Cuba, given the name The Bay of Pigs on

April 17, 1961 (Brands, 2011).[19] Kennedy tried to keep his promises to the Black Americans by nominating Thurgood Marshall as Circuit Court Judge for the Court of Appeals. The nomination made him the first Black American to ever have the title. Before his appointment, Thurgood Marshall was a legal representative for the NAACP during the Supreme Court trial *Brown vs. Board of Education of Topeka, Arizona* that ruled to desegregate schools. Marshall also helped lead the case that led to the desegregation of the United States Military in the 1950s. Morgan's campus has a Thurgood Marshall Dormitory originally built in the 1990s; rebuilt in 2022.

---

[19] The Bay of Pigs – A failed attempt by the United States to overthrow Fidel Castro, the socialist leader of Cuba, by the Central Intelligence Agency (CIA) and Cuban Exiles. (Office of the Historian, Foreign Service Institute, n.d.)

The Freedom Rides

From 1960 to 1961, James L. Farmer – the founder and leader of the Congress of Racial Equality (CORE), and other members decided to organize a series of interracial bus rides from Northern states into Southern states to combat Jim Crow segregation. Black riders had to exchange their seats with white passengers when they got to the Mason Dixon Line, the demonstration would refuse to switch seats when comanded.[20] CORE named the series of demonstrations "Freedom Rides", and its passengers "Freedom Riders". In May 1961, the FBI intercepted a telegram addressed to Farmer about organized meetings in Birmingham, Alabama; Nashville, Tennessee; Washington D.C., and Baltimore, Maryland that prepared participants for what they were to be met with during their daring and defining acts against southern law enforcement. (James Farmer Part 4 of 7, n.d.) In July 1961, Farmer spoke to the Baltimore chapter of SNCC and CORE. The announcement of his arrival was mentioned in the *Baltimore Afro*

---

[20] Farmer grew up as one of the major young influencers of the Civil Rights movement in the 1960s. Having studied under famous debater and English professor Melvin B. Tolson, at the age of fourteen, as a student at Wiley College, he was a well adept orator and debater. James Farmer passed away in 1999 after retiring as a college professor and an extensive career in Civil Rights politics.

and by the month of August, the first set of Freedom Rider demonstrators rode to Alabama.

Though the Freedom Rides were non-violent demonstrations, Emily decided that she would not partake in the rides because the dangers the situation presented, and she was right. During one of the rides, opponents of their message deliberately headed the bus off the road. As Freedom Riders fleed the bus under attack, it was with no avail, that segregationists assaulted the passengers with various weapons. The Freedom Rides gained major media attention because one of the white passengers of this assault was put in intensive critical care because he was beaten nearly to death during the assault. Media outlets began to broadly cover the Civil Rights movement and the events that would happen, causing a shift in people's participation in demonstrations and how people viewed demonstrators. With sentiment to the Freedom Riders, Rev. Dr. Martin L. King, Jr. told the public to "*Fill the Jails,*" using the method of mass incarceration as the means of desegregation (unknown, The Baltimore Afro-American: "Fill the Jails" King Tells 2,500, 1961). Farmer would resign from CORE in 1966 as its members became more influenced by the militancy of Malcolm X and the Black Panther

Party (BPP) of the 1960s non-violent student groups would face

confliction and controversy as their members begin enacting BPP

theories and ideologies.[21]

---

[21] Ten Point Program – A philosophically militant system that the Black Panther Party operated. A list of principles and rules dedicated to the facilitation and progress of Black culture politically, socially, and economically.

Freshman Year (1961-1962)

Emily only packed one suitcase for her journey to Morgan, emphasizing jokingly that in her time, people packed lightly because bags "did not have wheels." As Emily helped escort her cousin Maxine to Morgan, it was now Maxine and her husband who took Emily to Morgan at the end of the summer. Emily noted that the drive seemed like it was faster during her return trip because she knew where she was going. On the way, they dropped off another friend, Gordon Wright, at Delaware State University for his first year as well. In a moment of reflection Emily humbly mentioned, "*To be honest, I always thought that my sister Marion should have been the one to go to Morgan. She had always been the number one student. She chose to stay home and attend school, so she could help the family*"

Emily chose physical education as her major because she wanted to help train young people to think with more determination and become better versions of themselves. During the fall semester, Emily kept a low profile, claiming it to be the calmest year she had at

Morgan. During orientation week, as an observer of people and surroundings, Emily did not fraternize too much. Emily explained how she wanted to get to know the social climate of the school, the people, and the land of Baltimore better without the pressures of possibilities of social clichés. During her first week, she met and made new associates that would turn out to be lifetime friends and associates. She continued to learn more about Morgan, and what it had to offer as an educational institution and buffer for Black culture. By the end of the week, it was time for her to hear Dr. Martin D. Jenkins, the president of Morgan to deliver his speech to the new first years. There is a part of the president's speech that is traditional at every first-year student orientation and convocation:

> We sat in orientation and the president; Dr. Jenkins said many things during his speech. Mostly what I remembered was the end when he said, "I am here to prepare you for the World" He paused and continued, "Shake the person to your left, and the person to your right...only one of you will make it to graduation," and we all did just that. After he spoke, they showed us videos and slideshows of Ancient Civilizations of Africa and the contributions African Americans have made so far in the United States of America...to American Society.

During Emily's time as a young woman, women were just starting to push the boundaries of their physical abilities in sports. As a lover of sports, of course, she tried out for various sports teams:

cheerleading, basketball, and field hockey teams, serving as a member of all the teams. Emily always made sure that she was an asset to each team, but she wanted to challenge herself as a tennis player. There was no tennis team for women at Morgan, but Emily would come to know at least ten women who played on campus. The lack of a team did nothing but encourage her to reach out to other males to practice, playing recreationally to sharpen her newfound talent. Instead of giving in to adversity, Emily felt that practicing with men made her twice as sharp as a competitor on the tennis court because she learned how to keep up against the strength and speed of her male counterparts.

Dr. Jenkins, August Meier, and Morgan's student-activist population

PHOTO 34 MARTIN D. JENKINS (MARTIN D. JENKINS,
EDUCATOR BORN. 2022)

Archived resources provided by Morgan State to the

African American Registry about Dr. Martin Jenkins captured t

Dr. Jenkins views on desegregation and integration, and how

demonstrations could obscure his overall mission for Morgan

Students during the time when student demonstrations were

consistently happening across the United States:

Many students and professors on campus were deeply involved in the movement.
Dr. Jenkins felt that as an institution of higher learning Morgan State an institution
should have nothing to do with the movement. Many felt as though he was
betraying his race due to the fact, he had so much power and influence but failed
to use it in support of the movement. Dr. Jenkins was a practical and conservative-
minded man. He only wished to enhance the experience of the students without
getting involved in the movement. He felt that the student body was racially
unbalanced, so he sought to find and recruit more white students to attend Morgan

State. Many students and faculty disapproved of this choice, and some even protested the decision on campus. He felt by them interacting with white students they would learn to function in society more effectively (Martin D. Jenkins, Educator Born, 2022)

On the other hand, there were professors and scholars, such as African American studies historian August Meier, who was also a professor and CIG advisor at Morgan, who supported student involvement in the Civil Rights Movement. Meier was one of the few white scholars of that time who wrote on the history, culture, and achievements of Black culture through an opposite lens that praised the greatness of the different African cultures rather than spreading false information in the name of white anthropology, psychology, and sociology. After publishing various scholarly journals and books, he was asked to teach at Morgan by historian Dr. Benjamin A. Quarles, a Black man, and pioneer of African American studies and writing. At this time, Dr. Quarles served as a professor and chair of the History department.[22] Among the various memoirs Meier left behind on this earth, his reflection on Morgan State and its Civil Rights atmosphere is compiled into the book *A White Scholar and the Black Community, 1945-1965: Essays and Reflections.*

---

[22] Dr. Benjamin A. Quarles was known for his Biography of Frederick Douglass, and various eras of Black American history. (authors n.d.)

Meier was a well-known Civil Rights activist and member of the Baltimore chapter of SNCC during his time at Morgan. He served as an adult academic advisor to the Civic Interest Group at Morgan College from 1960 to 1963 (Lewis D. L., 2003). Meier wrote that student involvement on Morgan's campus fluctuated from 1961-62 before the visitation of Civil Rights leader Malcolm X in February 1962. According to Meier, the fluctuation was mainly due to the rhetoric of Dr. Jenkins about their activities, but Meier noted that his stance was one of the mixed signals because Dr. Jenkins did recognize what the Movement and demonstrations meant to the Black American culture, and himself at the same time. Dr. Jenkins made it known that his job at Morgan was to make sure students received an education and remained safe while doing so (Meier, 1992). The rise of other social and student-activist groups meant that there would be meetings along campus, but Dr. Jenkins consciously reminded students to remember that being a participant in demonstrations could result in academic expulsion, judiciary consequences, or even on the worse side of things, a loss of life. Emily mentioned that during one of the speeches, Dr. Jenkins made the notion of letting the student body know that he would not go looking for active meetings either. Meier felt that Dr. Jenkins' approach did result in a slight change in the student dynamics of those who remained present as demonstrators before 1963.

PHOTO 35 AUGUST MEIER. (LEWIS D. L., 2003)

Meier wrote,

> By the Fall of 1962, Morgan's students seemed unusually apathetic on the surface, and supported the small number of people who stayed with CIG, but a lot of the core members of CIG slowly faded away and many of them sought refuge behind Dr. Jenkins's advice of preparing themselves for the world, and not just the United States. Publicly, He (Jenkins) said nothing about the student movement, but in many ways, he was supportive. He informed the movement leaders at Morgan that they were not allowed to meet in the campus buildings, but then added that of course, he was not going to go around and check on this. Usually, we quite freely used the college classrooms and the student government office. He responded differently than his counterparts in the south. (Meier, 1992)

According to Meier, there was a time where Morgan CIG began to bump heads with the leadership of Baltimore chapters of

CORE and SCLC on how they wanted to coordinate and execute their student demonstrations (Meier, August Meier Papers). Emily kept in mind that since students were from all over the United States and countries, they each had different views on what their experience was and meant as a person of color. When it came to the discussion on how to manage oppression there were many conflicts. Various students from the Deep South advocated more counteractions in response to the physical actions of racists, as others wanted to   follow the non-violent ways of peaceful demonstration. As far as Emily was concerned, she wished that everyone could get on the same page to make organizing and executing plans more   successful for the peer group.

Emily the friend, student, and activist

Emily met her lifetime best friend, Dr. Marcia Saxon-Hazelton of Atlantic City, New Jersey (now California) during the fall semester of her first year. The two of them would become lifetime friends as Emily and Marcia would take part in various demonstrations and student events, experiencing many memories together that cannot all be shared. In the spring semester of their first year, Emily and Marcia took part in demonstrations around downtown Baltimore, Laurelville, and Glenn Burnie. Marcia spoke about how they became friends and the trying times they encountered as young civil rights activists.

> We met because we were both physical education majors, so we had the same classes together. We also played on the Basketball and Hockey teams together; we were very active on campus together. We also worked in the refectory (Refac) together, we became so close at Morgan, and we even pledged Delta together! Emily was very active as a civil rights demonstrator, and we did a lot of them together, such as White Tower, White Coffee Pot, anything White!" She laughed and continued, "We picketed the swimming pools, it was all terrible. I was not used to segregation because I grew up in Atlantic City, New Jersey. It was mostly integrated; I went to an integrated middle and high school. Whatever Emily and I did, we just did it with prayer!

Emily reflected on their first experience in Glenn Burnie, Maryland, approximately a thirty-minute drive south of Baltimore:

> We were close to a physical confrontation with the white citizens and feared for my life. I said that day God was watching out for us because it started to rain and storm, it de-escalated the situation because they went home. Not us! We demonstrated in the rain, sleet, and snow for months. We could not go to these restaurants. We could not even go down to the corner of Northwood, eat, or watch movies, right across the street from Morgan! (Moore, 2018)

In 2019, Gloria (Richardson) Marrow, M.A., contributed the memories she had as a history major at Morgan during the time of 1962-1963. Marrow also served as a student advisor during her master's studies at Morgan. Marrow was a junior when Emily came to campus but was a senior when she came to recognize Emily on campus towards the end of 1962. Marrow acknowledged Emily for being a "passionate" demonstrator on and off campus before to the Northwood Demonstrations in February 1963. Marrow would notice Emily around campus trying to get people to attend meetings and demonstrations. Marrow spoke of how students would gather in the Student Christian Center, known as The Chapel, and other classrooms to receive instructions on demonstrations before they ventured to their various locations during their time at Morgan.

Emily grew into a well-voiced asset to the Morgan student body as a student advocate and demonstrator for Civil Rights on her campus. Emily, Marrow, and other students supported the SNCC and CORE even though they were not paying members, which was common. Nationally, that did not stop young demonstrators from standing on street corners, handing out billets with civil rights propaganda on behalf of these groups. Marrow recalled a dining establishment called the White Coffee Pot in Baltimore City, Murphy's Five and Dime, and eventually Northwood Theater in 1963 (Marrow, 2020). She was involved with the Northwood demonstrations, but she was not arrested or received any physical abuse during the events (Marrow, 2020).

Marrow described Emily as an "aggressive" woman but reiterated that it was not violent but the overall passion she held for Civil Rights (Marrow, 2020). Marrow would further find out about Emily and her character as Emily pledged to the Alpha Gamma Chapter of Delta Sigma Theta (DST) at Morgan during her graduate years, as the chapter's graduate advisor. Marrow sincerely mentioned that she is a pyrophyte, or to simply put it, 'Big Sister' to Emily in the Sisterhood of DST. [23] Eventually, Emily's charisma and leadership qualities would bring her negative and positive attention as a student on campus. For one, Emily was approached by Dr. Williams, a philosophy professor, who asked her to change her major to philosophy. Dr. Williams told Emily that he felt that she spoke with determination and conviction and would make a great leader through the program, but respectively she declined his offer. Emily's civil rights activity did create trouble for her at her dormitory

---

[23] Marrow went on to serve as student advisor for the DST chapter from 1963 into the 1970s. After she graduated from Morgan with her B.A. degree, she continued her education at Morgan for her master's degree, completing her studies in 1963. She continued to engage in various civic engagements in Baltimore, such as the Quakers' Movement against the war in Vietnam. She currently serves as Lecturer of History at Morgan. Also, one of the first black and women Catholic priests in Maryland.

for not adhering to the curfew. Emily would miss curfew because she was attending meetings to organize demonstrations, pledging, and attending the demonstrations gathered attention. Dr. Jenkins warned the Morgan student body in an assembly that if they continued to engage in demonstrations and break campus rules, they would have to give up their student housing. Emily remained unchanged by Dr. Jenkins's rhetoric, exclaiming to her peers "If I could not have freedom, what was the point of an education?"

MALCOLM X COMES TO MORGAN

By 1962, the world had been introduced to Malcolm X, who, as a rising member of the nation of Islam, became a voice for the oppressed during the Civil Rights Movement as his rhetoric took on a more aggressive and militant approach. Malcolm X was born Malcolm Little, who, as a young child, saw the murder of his father by the Ku Klux Klan. As a troubled youth and young man, Malcolm would live his life as a street hustler, performing criminal activities to create income. It was during incarceration that Malcolm would convert to Islam, becoming a devout follower and changing his name to El-Hajj Malik El-Shabazz, but to the public he was known as Malcolm X. His time in prison created a way for him to become interested in debate and philosophy, becoming well known for his orations by fellow inmates and correctional officers. Malcolm would evolve as a member of the Nation of Islam after his release from prison. With influence from Marcus Garvey, Malcolm X had a militant approach, which involved Black nationalism, black inclusion and enterprise, self-defense, and self-policing. Eventually, X would host various speeches about Civil Rights and the end of the non-violent approach.

Young Black adults gravitated towards Malcolm X's messages as they had also seen the same and other travesties that Malcolm encountered, in opposition to MLK. They grew up parallel in life of each other as MLK grew up in a two -family, religious household, with an educated background. Malcolm X would represent the raw feelings of the oppressed, those who were children and teens during the rise of King, witnessing the triumphs of non-violent demonstrations and protests.[24] Malcolm X became so popular that many black people converted to Islam, the Nation of Islam and other subsections, which was a white American nightmare, as the United States fought against socialism and communism, and the Vietnam War. At the height of X's popularity, Cassius Clay, a future Black American boxing legend, converted to Islam, changing his name to Muhammad Ali when he was jailed for not accepting his drafting to the war. In Malcolm X's speeches, he remarked that if the United States government could not supply an

---

[24] The ideologies and methods of Marcus Garvey were passed upon Pan-Africanism, the support of everything black in culture, economics, and politics. He advanced for the makings of Black Americans who wanted to relocate to Africa and help rebuild its countries.

equal and just society for Black people, then there would be no peace at the expense of other white citizens. Malcolm X represented and spoke with the fire that lay dormant in the souls of Black people in the world, long before desperation and retaliation. Malcolm X's plan on how to achieve black excellence was through the practice of armed self-defense and discipline, self-policing, and entrepreneurship through Black Nationalism and socioeconomic inclusion. Malcolm X's ideologies crossed into Pan-Africanism and Garveyism. Malcolm X wanted Black Americans to be cohesive and generate a future filled with wealth for the Black community that would last for generations.

In February 1962, Malcolm X came to Baltimore to visit local Nation of Islam faith leaders and followers and speak to people about his stance on the Civil Rights Movement. He also spent time deliberating on building his own Mosque in Baltimore. The Pi Chapter of Omega Psi Phi at Morgan State extended an invitation for Malcolm X to speak on Morgan's campus and have dinner at their fraternity house. In 1995 Robert J. Branham published, *"I was Gone on Debating": Malcolm X prison debates and public confrontations for the publication Argumentation and Advocacy,* highlighting that Malcolm X had an intense energy for participating in the debate program while serving a sentence at Norfolk prison (Branham, 1995). The article referenced various people that he debated along his way as a civil rights leader, including August Meier, a white American Black History professor at Morgan in March 1962. Meier was highly respected by the student body and one of the more active professors on campus when it came to Civil Rights. Meier, on record, was a Baltimore chapter SNCC Member and successfully protested the Southern Historical Society from meeting in segregated hotels when they held conventions in Maryland (Lewis D. L., 1).

PHOTO 37 MALCOLM X AND THE PI CHAPTER OF OMEGA PSI PHI (JEFFERIES, 2020).

Meier received an invitation to the Pi chapter house to meet and eat dinner with Malcolm X before their debate. For Malcolm X, it did not matter the accomplishments, or how Black people and Morgan Students had vouched for Meier, it did not change the fact that he was a white man. During the dinner, Malcolm X at one point referred to Meier as a "white devil." Unbeknownst, Meier felt honored to have made Malcolm X acquaintance even after this personal encounter (Meier, 1992). Meier believed that integration would help advance a culture that was not his own. Malcolm X had no shame in his rhetoric during his speeches and debates; this debate with Meier was no different. During the debate, Malcolm X openly criticized Black Americans who associated themselves with whites, especially regarding the Civil Rights Movement; he also called President Kennedy a *"political hypocrite of the worst order."* (Sandler, 1992) After Meier's time at Morgan, he published *Negro Thought in America, 1880-1915: Racial Ideologies in the Age of Booker T. Washington,* a study on how black people's support was split between integration and focusing on promoting self-help through segregation, an ideology that would once again cause conflict within the civil rights movement.

PHOTO 39 MALCOM X IN DISCUSSION WITH STUDENTS AT MORGAN STATE. (JEFFERIES, 2020)

Branham wrote in conjunction with the reading of August

Meier's, *A White Scholar, and the Black Community, 1945-1965:*

Essays and Reflections.

White scholar August Meier has described the preparations for his debate on integration with Malcolm X, held on the campus of Morgan State on March 28, 1962. Meier had witnessed the debate between Malcolm X and Bayard Rustin at Howard University a few weeks earlier. "Aware of Malcolm's formidable reputation and his strong showing in debating Rustin," he "quickly began to rue" his decision (p. 31). Meier prepared for the debate (of which no complete transcript survives) with the assistance of students from the Omega Psi Phi fraternity (including Stokely Carmichael), who advised him to avoid any appearance of defense against Malcolm X's charges of racial injustice. Meier instead embraced Malcolm X's indictment of the quality of African American life and joined him in condemning gradualism and various false charges made against the Nation of Islam. Although important differences remained between them, Malcolm X's success in prior debates had clearly shaped the discourse in this one. The strategy by which Meier felt he had held his own against Malcolm X was one in which he narrowed the distinctions between their positions, conceding much ground in the hope of saving some (Meier, p. 32). (Branham, 1995, pp. 117-137)

Before the start of the debate, Emily recalled that the lines to the auditorium were massive, but she and Marcia got in line early because they knew the event would be jammed with observers. Fortunately, she was able to sit in the first few rows with Marcia. Meier and Malcolm X debated on whether segregation or integration was the way for true equality to happen for Black Americans. Malcolm X did not believe in integration as the means to equality, unlike Meier. What was on Emily's mind the most was her concern about Malcolm X's safety during his travels, because she knew the strength that he held within the Black and brown community, regardless of religion. Emily, just like the rest, knew that when prominent Black activists were traveling through the South, they became prime targets of racial supremacists. During the question-and-answer session for the students at the end of the debate, Emily was given the chance to ask a question, or more enough make a statement.

I do not think he was expecting for me to say it...but I told him, "No disrespect to the Honorable Elijah Muhammad, but I am not going through six states in the south, that's elimination!" I said, "The racist is going to poison the water, the animals, how are you going to survive in Mississippi? I was surprised because Malcolm X did not have a direct answer for her but emphasized that if there are precautions that his people took to maintain his safety.

As the questions came to an end, Emily was confident that Malcolm X accepted whatever fate he might encounter, in the name of his culture. Emily internalized the moment with the lesson *"You must weigh the consequences and decide whether you are going to stand and speak or let life run you."* When in doubt about events ahead of her, Emily remembered thinking, *"Malcolm X wasn't going to let fear run him, and neither was I!"* Emily enjoyed the debate and acknowledged it as a very defining moment in her civil rights career. For Emily, the debate made her more to side with the militancy of the next wave of Civil Rights leaders and the movement. Emily understood the importance in exercising constitutional rights to keep and bear arms, but she never approved of unnecessary violence and the advocation of killing anyone.

Emily had viewed desegregation as a means of survival, not equality, and still stands on it. She understood that racism was deeply rooted and passed the public eye of integration at that point in her life. What was most important for Emily at this point was having pride, culture, and cultivating knowledge for future generations. On the cover page of Danielle Brown's interview with Emily reads the words of Frederick Douglass, "*If there is no struggle, there is no progress. Those who profess to favor freedom, and yet depreciate agitation, are people who want crops without plowing up the ground.*" Emily accepted that her fight for justice would be vigorous, non-peaceful, and should not be taken lightly.

Summer of 1962

Instead of returning home for the summer of 1962, Emily and Marcia decided to stay in Baltimore to attend summer courses to raise their grade point averages to be considered for sorority recruitment for the next school year. To be interested in a Greek organization is traditionally something you implied with discretion. Emily and her closest friends were all interested, but her choice was not solidified in which organization she wanted to join. Emily finally took a course that she had been avoiding for a while as a physical education major, swimming class. Swimming classes were a requirement that she avoided as a physical education major. It was not that Emily was afraid to swim, or that she did not know how to, it was that she did not want to get her hair wet because of her perm. In Black American hair culture, getting your hair wet when you have had heat and/or chemicals application is a NEGATIVE.

Emily also admitted that she was avoiding Coach Steven A. Brooks, who as her professor, described him as "*small but tough.*" According to Emily, Coach Brooks was regarded on campus as a stern professor, but in the same statement, spoke of Brooks being known among campus as *"one of the finest Black men on campus,"* who dressed *"handsome and cool."* It is safe to say, some ladies had a crush on the young professor, including Emily. Brooks taught physical education science classes for the physical education department. Brooks was the man who brought the sport of swimming to Morgan, the men's swimming team that won an NCAA championship in 1955, and various accolades are among the trophies in Hurt Gymnasium. Factoring in that Emily once stood 5'9 or 5'11 tall during her younger years, Emily made a joke that even though Brooks was a great swimmer, she could not trust he could save her if she were to drown because he was shorter than her! Coach Brooks was known as being "tough, as a coach because he believed in his students, but as a teacher – tougher."

PHOTO 40 COACH BROOKS, BOTTOM, MIDDLE. MORGAN STATE BOYS SWIM TEAM 1955

Emily recalled that Marcia and other friends who remained around campus during the summer showed up to Emily's last swim class and encouraged her as she did the big deep dive. Emily received a "C," but said, *"If you got a 'c' in his class, then it was like getting an 'A'."* Emily also took a Kinesiology course along with Marcia, with Coach Brooks as the professor during a spring semester. Recalling how the women studied all night for a major test but when it was time for the test Emily became too nervous to even start the test!

> *"I just knew I was going to blow him away with that test. I got there and my hands started shaking! I told Marcia 'I can't write' but he saw me because I was in the first row. He told me to put my head down and not worry about it. When I became relaxed, it was halfway through the class! I did the test until the time was up. When he revealed the results, Coach spoke of how even though I had half the time; I still did better than most."*

With the passing of all her classes for the summer, Emily's biggest concern for the next semester was choosing which sorority to pursue and stay on top of her athletics.

"Over my dead body": The Northwood Demonstrations

PHOTO 41 NORTHWOOD THEATER. (CINEMA TREASURES, 2011)

During the fall semester of Emily's junior year, she mainly focused on keeping her grades and her position on Morgan's athletic teams. However, the only thing that got in the way of her schooling was conducting civil rights activities because her involvement with demonstrations during the day and meetings at various hours would bring her trouble with student housing. As the semester unfolded, Emily continued to miss curfew at her dormitory at the Harriet Tubman House, causing conflict between her and the dorm mother. Eventually, Emily had to face Dr. Jenkins's ultimatum that was told various times to the students: to seize their civil rights activities or be kicked out of student housing. Emily decided to move into an apartment across from campus.

Around January 1963, Morgan's students and Emily began to hear rumors that Freedom Fighters were coming to town, igniting student activists to come together to demonstrate against The Hecht Company at Northwood Theater. Historically for Morgan students, there was a battle for integration that continuously backfired with the shopping plaza adjacent to Morgan's campus, known as 'Northwood.' Northwood was a white-only plaza that included a pharmacy, clothing retail, and a movie theater. For generations, due to segregation, and opposition from the town of Laurelville, Morgan students would have to travel to downtown Baltimore to retrieve medication and other personal supplies. In the face of a possible mass demonstration and the threat of expulsion, the challenge remained: how to recruit enough of the student body to form a mass movement? Using 'pep rally' tactics, they enlisted well-known members of the student body—including Miss Morgan State and the president of the student council. The students continued to organize until they felt that they were ready to move forward.

Day one

Researcher Anjali Cadambi published an article about the Northwood demonstrations and Morgan's involvement in 2011, *"On February 4, 1963, CIG leaders met with members of the student government. Together they agreed to adopt mass arrest as a strategy to accompany mass picketing* (Cadambi, 2011)." February 15, 1963, was a Friday afternoon, and Emily's classes were done for the week, supplying time for all-day demonstrations. Emily and a group of about fifty other Morgan students of the general student body, CIG, Greek organizations, sports teams, and student peer groups went over to Northwood Plaza. The groups tried to see *'In Search of the Castaway*s,' a Disney movie advertised as *'Avalanche of Adventure'* starring Maurice Chevalier and Hayley Mills, where they were denied their purchases and entry by the ticket concession, and the then owner of the theater. Emily went up to Northwood Theater as well to request a ticket, *"The movie man said, 'We was not letting no darkies in his movie, over his dead body' and he meant just that!'* (Brown, 2001). Emily walked away from the theater to a nearby payphone. This is her account of the moment where

She decided to join the student protest.

> *Back in the day there were payphones, and in the apartments around campus, there were den/house mothers. I called Marcia who was with her boyfriend at that time, I told her to tell my roommate Pamela, to tell the lady, I am not coming home today!" I hung up the phone and went back. We demonstrated; it was about fifteen of us. We were the first ones to cross the picket line that was set and went inside, then were arrested. They released us later the next morning.*

Emily explained the essence of the campus after their return to campus:

> *When the news of the demonstration reached out, it sent the campus into a frenzy, and soon enough others were gathering to participate and do what was needed to aid the demonstrators.*

The Baltimore City police told the Baltimore Sun the students moved *"almost on cue"* when they decided to enter the building. Emily and approximately fifteen other Morgan students were a part of the first set of student demonstrators to be arrested and taken to the Northwood jail, which still is located on the same land as Morgan's campus (another problem that was protested by students' years prior). They were charged with disorderly conduct, and after spending the night behind bars, each was released the next day on their recognizance after requesting jury trials (Zizori, 2020). With true Rough Rider spirit, Marcia was with Emily at the rest of the demonstrations, including each arrest each day. This is Marcia's memory of the encounter:

> There was a movie, we went to the theater to go in, and they said that they did not let Black people into the movies. We asked, "How could you not let Black people into the movies when you have a college campus right across the street from there? They said no, and we said we would be back, we were going to picket. So, we got a bunch of people and then the police took us to jail. They were saying, we could picket and not go to jail, but that was not the case because we were arrested, Me and Emily were arrested together.

After the second arrest, Emily considered the fact that the police may not be so nice the next time, or if she would even be released during her next arrest, because she was committed to the fight. Furthermore, what kind of targets would they have on their backs? Brown questioned why Emily took part in the first place, knowing the consequences, and her answer was simply, *"Why not? It was what I was about!"* (Brown, 2001). Emily felt that at that point she should tell her parents and decided to write a letter. Emily did not keep them abreast of her activities often, but she knew they would be worried, apparently, Emily never sent the letter. Emily's parents were not fond of her involvement in Civil Rights activities, but they understood that Emily's heart and spirit were already committed to the greater cause. Emily would always explain that she was taking on the fight against segregation for her parents, herself, and future generations, for survival. Emily was already known as a person amongst her peers to speak against wrongdoing, no matter the situation; it was always a part of her character. Throughout the rest of her Civil Rights activities, there would be disagreements, but her parents did not know what to do. They did not interfere with Emily's efforts, her mom prayed, but her father was very adamant that he did not want Emily putting herself in harm's way between the racists and law enforcement every time she attended a demonstration.

> We were acquitted, and we did not get put out of school; that was a Friday. Then Saturday went back and were arrested; they let us out on Sunday. The second time I was arrested, being that I never really told my parents about my activities, I did not want to worry them all the way in New York, so I wrote to them. . .I wrote to my parents. I said 'well the president of the college said he is going to put us out of school, but I said if I cannot have any justice and freedom, then I might as well be in jail. This was more important to me than school at this time.' We spent the night in the jail, and we came to the court the next morning and it was full of Morgan people. The court was packed with students and the community that came out to support us. It was the most wonderful feeling (Brown, 2001).

Unspecified Maryland newspaper article from February of 1963:

Twenty-six are arrested in theater ...

Morgan Students Attempt to Integrate Movie House White Placard carriers marched about, police arrested 26 Negro Morgan State College Students last night when they allegedly refused to move from the entrance of the Northwood Theater. Some seventy students appeared at the shopping center on Havenwood Road off Loch Raven Boulevard about 6:30 P.M. and demonstrated against the theaters racial segregation policies for several houses. Those arrested, all of whom were charged with disorderly conduct, did not picket, police safety hearings are set for 9 A. M today in Northeastern Municipal Court. Plan Overnight say – That group sought merely to enter the theater and they announced intentions of staying in jail overnight.

Meier explained in his memoir, that the CIG and students continued to explore the idea of mass incarceration to achieve their goals. By day four, student-led demonstrations resulted in the Baltimore Police incarcerating over two hundred participants. As the number of arrests continued to rise, it would disrupt community policing and policy because the jails were becoming overrun by demonstrators. Civil Rights leaders sent telegrams to Mayor Philip H. Goodman and Commissioner Schmidt, asking for their help in desegregating the theater (Zizori, 2020). For Mayor Goodman, the demonstrations compounded the attention of racial relations into discussion among the political issues of politicians who were seeking re-election, such as Baltimore's Judge Joseph G. Finnerty and Mayor Philliph H. Goodman. Students were undeterred by threats of jail, and as demonstrators were released, they would return to protest at the theater throughout the weekend. The daily protests resulted in another forty-two arrests on trespassing and disorderly conduct charges filed by the Baltimore City police (Zizori, 2020).

In 2011, a reporter for *Maryland Matters*, William J. Zizori wrote about the history of Morgan State and student demonstrations in his publication *Baltimore's Northwood: Remembrance of Desegregation*. In his work, Zizori covered details that have been lost over time about events during the demonstrations.

> *On Monday, more than three hundred protesters, mostly Morgan's students, showed up outside the theater, and again, as a line of picketers marched outside, others, lining up in an orderly fashion, entered and attempted to buy tickets. The trespass act was read by*

the theater manager. And again, the arrests by the police began, twenty at a time. This time, however, the crowd of alleged trespassers was significantly larger than in the past, and with more than 150 demonstrators arrested — far more than could be accommodated at any one district station, the police department's No. 2 man was called to the scene. The chief inspector decided that the men in custody should be ferried in patrol wagons to the Northeastern District lockup and the women over to the Eastern. Some of those arrested early in the process had been taken downtown to the old Pine Street Station lockup for women and juveniles, once the Western District police station, just outside the city's central business district. By 11 p.m., the chief judge of the old Municipal Court, T. Barton Harrington (once speaker of the House of Delegates), Joseph G. Finnerty, the judge assigned to the district, and Police Commissioner Bernard J. Schmidt all had shown up at the Northeastern station house but refused to answer questions from the press. The protests were clearly overtaxing anything the system had ever seen — or considered — before (Zizori, 2020)

The following Monday, February 18th, the Morgan students were warned once again by President Jenkins about their activities and their consequences. Emily remembered,

The president of the college told us that 'If you go up to Northwood Shopping Center, and you get involved with those Civil Rights people, you will get put out of school,' that's all I remember, but I said to myself, 'Lord I can't get put out of school.'

According to Danielle Brown's research, *"presidents of privately supported Negro colleges were freer to abstain from disciplining the "Sit-In students than those responsible for tax-supported Negro colleges. They were usually met with threats of reprisals from* governors that threatened their funding" (Brown, 2001). Emily remembered Dr. Jenkins was incredibly upset with the students, which was something that seemed out of character for the president, but he was truly concerned for their welfare. The scolding they received from Dr. Jenkins did not deter the Morgan students from returning each day afterward. Emily and other students embraced the fight for the greater good and Dr. Jenkins's warning only fired up students even more. Emily was known for not backing down from a challenge around campus, a person who "talks the talk, but also walks the walk." Between classes that Monday she remembered her peers asking, *"Moore! Are you going up there? What are you going to do?' When school let out on Monday, I went walking up there and got on the line, marching, and singing! We got arrested again, there were so many people that were arrested*" (Brown, 2001).

Marsha reflected:

Dr. Jenkins was going to kick us out of school. He said, if y'all go to jail, y'all are getting kicked out of Morgan. We said we refused to be expelled Morgan, and we going to jail. We had a lot of political folks on our side like Jesse Jackson, and Rev. Al Sharpton who told him (Dr. Jenkins), you are not putting these students out! They are practicing and trying to gain our Civil Rights!

I met another Moore

During the demonstrations, students and faculty from Morgan, Hopkins, and Goucher colleges, clergy of different denominations, and residents demonstrated in the shopping center for about two weeks. On one of these days, Emily met William Lewis Moore, a 35-year-old white American postman from the upstate region of New York who lived in Baltimore. While in the crowd with William, he spoke to Emily and her friends about his plan to walk to Mississippi from Tennessee wearing a *"One Man, One Vote"* sign. Emily explained that she and her friend warned Moore: *"He was going to walk with that sign, and we told him not to do it. I said, "They were going to kill him."* Five days short of his birthday on April 23, 1963, William Lewis Moore was murdered during his journey to hand a letter to the governor in Jackson, Mississippi. He was about fifty miles outside of Mississippi, in Alabama (Johnson M. , 2013).

PHOTO 42 WILLIAM LEWIS MOORE, 1963. (JOHNSON M. , 2013)

They were rough in Mississippi, but I did not read about where he was killed in the newspaper. But I told him... I told the kids too. I was frustrated about what happened, but we were on a mission. You would be surprised when you are on a mission and the spirit that comes with it. They would tell you all the stories that were happening in Mississippi and what was happening in Alabama...everything. The kids were getting arrested, beaten, treated badly, and murdered. In Baltimore, we just felt uncomfortable as our circumstances were being in jail (Brown, 2001).

Students went to Jail: The Integration of Baltimore City Jails

Emily and other demonstrators were escorted to the Northeast Precinct each day from February 15th until the 19th. On the 20th, she noticed that they were not going to the local jail anymore because the demonstrators had filled up the jail to capacity and that's where they remained for a couple of days. The number of arrested demonstrators had forcibly integrated the Northwood and the Baltimore City jail they were taken to. On Monday, February 18, 1963, Judge Finnerty raised the bond from $100 to $600 for each demonstrator, and the NAACP sought out ways to generate bail for the demonstrators. *"When I got arrested, my name was in the paper (Baltimore Afro-American) it said, 'Emily Moore, is here to break up evil,' and I still get the newspaper every week. I like to keep up with Baltimore,"* Emily emphasized. The next day, February 19, there were over sixty demonstrators added to the list of the arrested. With a crowd of about four hundred participants and bystanders, including Emily on the front lines once again, The Baltimore Afro-American headlines read, *"218 Students Arrested, $90,000 Bail set for 150"* (Afro-American T. B., 1963).

The momentum of the demonstrations gathered students from Coppin, John Hopkins, Goucher colleges, and local citizens to join the Morgan students in their quest for desegregation. *The Afro*'s 5-Star edition February 19th article's main piece said, "Only in America, only in a state such as Maryland, could 218 well-behaved students be arrested and jailed for wanting to go to the movies. Yet again, the police were called to arrest the "trespassers," and again, they were hauled off in patrol wagons" (Zizori, 2020).

> *My last time being arrested, we got arrested, and they took us to the big house, one of the city jails. We did not go to the regular local jail like we had before. The police said we were not going to the same place because there was no space, and it would take too long. Looking out the cracks you could see the different things. I said "We are not going to the same place we went to before, then we got to the prison. The Morgan community filled up the prison, and then we saw that there was a black and white area. They had separate jails and everything! So even though we filled it up* (Brown, 2001).

Marsha reflected on the moment as well:

> *We did a lot of demonstrations during this time, and it was terrible how they were trying to treat us. They put us up in the jail, like the dormitory section. All the college kids from Morgan were in the cell. They woke us up at 6 a.m., to tell us to scrub down the cells with a toothbrush! We told them: "you have the wrong people! We are not your ordinary criminals; we are college students here for our rights! They said we do not care; you are in here, so you are going to do what we tell you. Therefore, we started to sing our freedom songs. The inmates came to us, telling us to sing more songs because they liked it. Jesse Jackson, and others found out about us, Ebony and Jet Magazines did coverage on us. Then what happened was students from Goucher, and John Hopkins, the white kids, they joined us. As soon as the white kids came, we were out the next*

day. That is how racism goes. We went back to the college, and 50 years after, we got the honorary doctorate degree from Morgan.

Historically, when it comes to the treatment and judgment of Black Americans and their fight for Civil Rights and Equality, obsessive and deadly force is commonly used by police. As a theme that is common to Black society in 2020, Emily puts herself in a position where police would have felt justified to use force, one of the biggest tests of courage in Emily's life. Emily embraced the concept that she could have a life full of incarceration due to her dedication to the Civil Rights Movement; she felt that she was mentally prepared for it. Emily recalled her interactions with the police, and Emily noted that the Baltimore Police Department did not get violent with them, and they did not become irate with the police; they were simply arrested. Brown asked Emily, "*You were not attacked or anything?*" Emily responded,

> *Not one time, but one time when I got arrested going into the patty wagon, I fell, and I hit my head. I still have the scar until this day on my forehead. He [the police] took me to the hospital and everything. You could tell how naive I was because the man said, "most of all are not from around here," and my big mouth-- I said, "That's right because the students from here are afraid, they are afraid to stand up for their rights! 'It's not fair, it's not right,' those are my favorite words. We cannot even go to restaurants, sit-down and eat without being mistreated, it was ridiculous. They would say New Yorkers were troublemakers (Brown, 2001).*

The Baltimore Sun reported, *"151 were arrested Tuesday, another 130 or so on Wednesday, as the city police riot squad stood by and watched warily."* On Feb 20,1963, *The Baltimore Sun* headline read *"274 Arrested, Crowd Grows in Northwood,"* a photo accompanied (Afro-American B. , 1963). The article entitled, *"Protest of Segregation On 6th Day; Mayor In 2-Hour Talk"* said,

> [...] By mid-afternoon of a second day of behind-the-scenes meetings and conversations involving the police, judiciary, state's attorney's office, CIG members, students, their legal adviser, Bob Watts, and the theater management, Mayor Goodman emerged from City Hall with an announcement to the pickets outside. [...] Over the course of eight days, politicians, and private establishment owners went against the integration of their eating, and entertainment establishments in Baltimore. [...] An Eastern shore senator drafted a bill that would expel any college student that received state-aid that was convicted of trespassing due to participating in demonstrations against racial discrimination. [...] The next morning, Thursday, February 21, spread across four columns of The Sun's local page was a photograph of sheer bedlam at the well-overcrowded women's section of Baltimore City Jail, where women inmates looked down from the upper tiers onto lines of protesters being checked in (Zizori, 2020).

That morning, among the regular inmates of the Baltimore City Jail, there were 343 Northwood protesters, black and white, with most students from Morgan, John Hopkins and Goucher colleges. On February 21, 1963, Mayor Goodman told the protesters that if they stopped demonstrations at the Northwood Theatre, the management would allow Black people into the movies, beginning at

1 p.m. the following Friday, February 22nd, after six days of mass demonstrations, and eight years of attempts. Judge Finnerty had ordered all charges to be dropped against more than three hundred protesters and for their release from jail.

PHOTO 43 WOMEN IN THE JAIL READING THE NEWSPAPER ABOUT THEM BEING INCARCERATED. EMILY IS HOLDING THE TOP RIGHT CORNER OF THE NEWSPAPER. (MORGAN MAGAZINE, 2011)

The Baltimore Sun headlined on February 23, 1963, "The young college men and women of Morgan decided to see a movie at Northwood or Hang in Jail" (Brown, 2001). Emily can be seen below wearing glasses with the top right corner of the newspaper in her hand in the photo.

As CIG negotiators gave the news of the settlement to the women protesters at City Jail, they greeted the news with screams and tears, hugging each other and jumping up and down, news outlets reported. The next day, on the coldest Washington's Birthday on record to that point in Baltimore, 23 African Americans, some of them the former protesters, quietly bought tickets at the Northwood Theatre and watched "In Search of the Castaways," a Disney flick advertised as "An Avalanche of Adventure" starring Maurice Chevalier and Hayley Mills (Zizori, 2020).

Baltimore Movie Ends Segregation

From News Dispatches

A week-long struggle that packed Baltimore's jail with 413 Negro and white pickets and attracted thousands of spectators struck down a movie-theater's racial bar yesterday.

counts, despite contentions by the group that the protest was orderly.

The demonstrators, most of them from nearby Morgan State College, started their campaign last Friday night.

cepted help in posting bond. Municipal Court Judge Joseph Finnerty rejected pleas for reduced bail. Juanita Jackson Mitchell, attorney for the students said, "These students are not criminals. They are

he, were guilty of settling lower defendants arrest several days having been too. Late yesterday Solm Sodaro at

FIGURE 19 NEWSPAPER ARTICLE ANNOUCING THE DESGREGATION OF NORTHWOOD MOVIES, 1963

PHOTO 44   MORGAN STUDENTS INVOVLED WITH THE FIRST DEMONSTRATIION. EMILY IS CIRCLED IN THE NEWS CLIPPING IN THE TOP ROW. (AFRO-AMERICAN T. B., 1963)

Emily was questioned, "Were there any tensions at that time within the groups of people protesting?" Emily replied,

> Oh no, well, it was overwhelmed with students, we all knew each other. The correctional officers would let us meet in the cafeteria and we would hold talent shows. Now, the AKA's, the Ques, Alphas, and other students would sing and do their songs, they would change up the words to songs like, "Oh freedom, oh freedom." While in Jail, many of the conditions such as overcrowding, lack of a bathroom, and shower access would drive many to anger and turmoil, especially when they did not expect to do more than a few hours inside the cell. The anxieties, fears, annoyance, and fits of anger began to fill within some people and groups.

Achieving desegregation was an all-enduring and jolting task, it was understood that not everyone had the fire inside of them to rise to the occasion like those who took part in the demonstrations. Emily believes that even if people were not outside of the picket lines, but prayed and gave encouragement to the people involved for safety, guidance, and victory. Brown asked Emily in 2003, *"What do you think about the results coming from the movement, and what do you think they were?*

> The results...well. They were good, I mean we got integration. Through integration we in reference to awareness, we just did not understand that we still had to organize and mobilize because we integrated and assimilated, so we would not be eliminated. In the process we did not protect our heritage, and our interest. Now people are just beginning to understand and trying to do - what they must do - to make things right in this country (Brown, 2001)

Overall, Emily had to about civil rights activism in 2019:

You must be willing to stand up for what you believe in and if you want to make changes you are going to have to struggle, it is a lifetime struggle. (and) people may not necessarily agree with you or they may agree with you on some issues, but when it gets down to really moving on those issues, they are not willing to go as far as you would like to go. They are just going to do it. That is the same thing in this town (in reference to Roosevelt). I went to meetings and stood up and spoke out and people came up to me, 'girl, you have a lot of nerve. How do you do that?' I just do what I must do. I understand that if I do not do it, it is not going be done. Sometimes you must be on the cutting edge, you've got to say what's right and stand on principles. And people, even though they may be uncomfortable about it, you have just had to tell it like it is. Whether it is a Black audience or a white audience, or an integrated audience, you must just be able to do what you must do and say what you have to say because our people have been struggling for hundreds of years for justice and equality, and fair play. Just that about all those brothers and sisters who were lynched, cattle pronged. Imagine female getting cattle prongs stuck up her [body] and people ripping people's babies out of their stomachs. I mean… all that kind of stuff happens to our people and then I am going to be afraid to speak?! That is all I have is my independence, my freedom of speech. I just try to do the right thing and say what I have to say, try to make things right, because it is just too much.

"The Delta's showed what sisterhood was."

PHOTO 45 L TO R: EMILY, JOYCE FREEMAN, AND MARCIA SAXON-HAZELTON ON THE STEPS OUTSIDE OF TRUTH HALL ON MORGAN STATE'S CAMPUS, 1963-65 (COURTESY OF EMILY MOORE)

Emily has had the ability to use any situation to learn from or teach towards. Before the demonstrations, Emily and her friends were vetting whether they would be a great match for either Black Greek organization, but it was her time during the Northwood demonstrations that would define Emily's choice. Emily recognized the strength of unity within the Delta women as they went back and forth between jail cells and demonstrations. Emily loved that the women of Delta Sigma Theta was not allowing the conditions to faze them, break their bond, or disrupt their purpose of demonstrating. The events solidified Emily's choice because their actions were of the characteristics that Emily held within herself. Emily had wanted whichever sorority she sought to membership in, to be about hard work, unification, and bonding through life and its struggles. In the Jail, it was the first time Emily was able to see the groups without their glamor and colors, to see them as the people they were and the sisterhood that they kept in the face of adversity.

> *Now let me tell you what happened with the Deltas when we went to jail. There were two older Delta's and two older Akas,' they were seniors. We watched how they all interacted in these circumstances, to see what their sisterhood looked like to us. When the Delta's went to jail, all the Deltas that were inside with us joined and demonstrated within the jail, like everyone else who could not and did not want to bail out. When the AKAs went to jail, we saw that many were bailed out and went home. I saw that and I was like, "Look at that sisterhood!" we became more for the Deltas* (Brown, 2001)

The Alpha Chapter of Delta Sigma Theta Sorority Incorporated was founded at Howard University in Washington, D.C, on January 13, 1913. A society for black collegiate and elite women of their time, the ladies' the Woman's Suffrage Movement March for

Women's right to vote became their first presence with participation in American social activism. After the Northwood Demonstrations, Emily and Marcia would go on to pledge to the Alpha Gamma Chapter of Delta Sigma Theta at Morgan. Emily and Marcia would "Cross the burning sands" on October 25, 1963, as the 28th member of her line, Marcia was number 29 in the line of thirty women. For over 60 years, Emily has networked with youth and other professionals to help promote prosperity and community service for the Black American community and the world. She has been a part of countless fundraisers, events, and ceremonies to help bring honor to achievers and dreamers of the future. With solidified bonds that will last a lifetime, Emily loves being a part of Delta Sigma Theta and stands by Crimson and Cream to the fullest, a dedicated lifetime member. Marcia briefly recalled a pledging moment, though naturally, she could not go into full detail:

> We always ere Rough Rides for each other. When we
> pledged it was rough. They took us over to Howard and
> exchanged lines with the Howard Delta's and our brothers
> of Omega Psi Phi. It was rough, but we made it through!

FIGURE 20 EMILY'S ORIGINAL SORORITY PADDLE FROM 1963. (COURTESY OF AYANNA MOORE)

FIGURE 21 SORORITY BLOCK FOR THE ALPHA GAMMA CHAPTER OF DELTA SIGMA THETA ON MORGAN STATE'S CAMPUS, 2022. (UNKNOWN)

Certificate of Membership

To whom these presents shall come Greetings:

We hereby certify that

Emily Moore

is a duly accredited Initiated Member and is granted all rights, honors and privileges as provided by the Constitution, By-laws and Ritual of Grand Chapter.

In witness whereof we have herewith set our hand and affixed the seal this 25th day of *October* 1963

Alpha Gamma
CHAPTER

PRESIDENT OF GRAND CHAPTER

SECRETARY OF GRAND CHAPTER

CHAPTER PRESIDENT

CHAPTER SECRETARY

FIGURE 22 EMILY'S CERTIFICATE OF MEMBERSHIP TO DELTA SIGMA THETA , 1963. (COURTESY OF EMILY MOORE)

SUMMERS SORROWS: WITHOUT STRUGGLE, THERE WOULD BE NO SENSE OF VICTORY

As mass demonstrations and protests grew, so did the responses of white supremacists who also served as law enforcement. In May 1963 demonstrations at Kelly Ingram Park in Birmingham, Alabama took a merciless turn when firefighters pelted demonstrators of all ages with high-pressure firehoses. As people fled, and resisted being turned back, they were viciously beaten and bitten by police dogs in an attack after the men, women, and children. News coverage of various demonstrations and murders brought worldwide discussion about the United States and the treatment abroad of Black people across the globe to a public forum. CBS and NBC television stations supplied live news feeds of the attempted demonstration. For the Civil Rights movement, television ensured that the events could not be dismissed or erased. Journalists reported the unjustifiable force and anger released against the peaceful civil rights protestors, exposing the injustice and inhumanity that was practiced day and night to preserve Jim Crow segregation laws. Emily thinks that television was one of the most effective tools of Civil Rights besides the leaders and participants themselves. The importance journalism contributed to the civil rights movement is what inspired her to always carry a camera after her time at Morgan.

President Kennedy, in response to the events, confirmed that he was working on a civil rights legislation bill with other Civil Rights leaders. He reminded the American people to focus on the humanities of the nation and the moral cloth they must stand for. On June 12, 1963, Mississippi NAACP field secretary, 37-year-old Medgar Evers was murdered outside his home in Jackson, Mississippi. Evers' skills as field secretary made him critical of the network of organizing meetings and mass demonstrations, including the upcoming March on Washington for Jobs and Freedom, making his murder a strategic plan towards dismantling the organization of Civil Rights efforts. As a military veteran, Evers was buried with full military honors in Arlington National Cemetery, and was awarded the Springarn Medal of the NAACP after his death. In June 1963, President Kennedy responded to the violence:

> He [Black and brown people] cannot enjoy the full and free life which all of us want, then who among us would be content to have the color of his skin changed and stand in his place? Who among us would then be content with the counsel of patience and delay?" (Kennedy, 1963)

The assailant Byron De La Beckwith was tried twice in 1964; both trials resulted in hung juries. Thirty years later he was convicted of the murder of Medgar Evers.

Summer of 1963: The Moore's Move to Roosevelt

After the commercialization and zoning of Bennington Park, the Moore family moved into Roosevelt between May and June 1963. Emily returned from her sophomore year to a new house, in a familiar neighborhood, but she was more elated because of the proximity to the former Roosevelt Lake Park. Emily spent a brief period in New York that summer as she went to New Jersey to stay with Marcia, as she would the summer after in 1964. Emily romanticized Roosevelt and the uniqueness of the town's center, Nassau Road that it once had before the effects of "white flight' and "blockbusting" practices, coupled with the drug epidemic that was rising in Black communities.

> We had a Movie theater, Black owned barbershops; we also had a shoe shop, and a bank before Bethpage. It was a nice little town, even the uniqueness of the town. If we really had been organized then, and not allowed a four-lane highway to be rebuilt for Nassau Road... you could see it." She went on to say, "Well if you see towns like Roslyn, and other areas in the north shore, you can see the difference, the old and new, the culture. Roosevelt was a unique town, and slowly they took it away. Everybody came through Roosevelt. (Brown, 2001)

Roosevelt used to be home to a movie theater, diners, Flora's Fashion retail store, and a skating rink Emily further described the former existence of Roosevelt's scenery. As towns around Roosevelt, specifically in the white majority neighborhoods around Nassau, kept their original town centers, Roosevelt did not. Emily expressed that she should have tried to do more to preserve the essence of Roosevelt and lead the objection against the Town of Hempstead for turning Nassau Road, the town's center of the square-mile town, into a four-lane road in the 1980s. Emily mentioned that Hempstead used to have a bank in the center of the village, and even held about $1,000 in it in 1968, but the bank had to be closed because people kept trying to rob it.

In the present time, one may find Long Island towns like Glen Cove, Sea Cliff, and Westbury kept portions of their original town architecture. Unlike these towns, the geographical radius of Roosevelt only allowed businesses to develop on Nassau Road. When the population dynamics shifted in Hempstead, Roosevelt and Freeport so did the revenue of the towns. Roosevelt went through a series of store shutdowns as whites moved their businesses into white neighborhoods. Roosevelt would become known as the first ghetto of Long Island due to the discriminatory real-estate and bank systems that made it hard for Black citizens to obtain financial loans for business and resources. The Roosevelt School District would become the town's primary source of state tax revenue. In 2002, The Washington Post article entitled *"Separate and Unequal in Roosevelt, Long Island: A New York Town's School Struggle Against the Toll of Segregation"* covered the effects of segregation, red-lining, and "white flight" turned Roosevelt into one of the first suburban ghettos (Powell, 2002). In the article, a long-term resident of Roosevelt reflected on the change of dynamics, *"It was the greatest white flight ever' [...] You would not even see the real estate sign-- people just sold in the middle of the night."*

The changes would be reflected within the adolescent and young adult populations. The specific needs of students in the district were continuously met with changes in budgeting and cuts of resources. Lifetime Roosevelt resident Don E. Crummell, dearly known as "Coach," by the Roosevelt community recalled his time as a young adolescent involved with the Roosevelt School district boycotts for integration that occurred between 1962 and 1964. Newspapers quoted NAACP representatives who admitted that they were not prepared for the demonstrations that the Roosevelt community enacted. Newspapers quoted the NAACP representative admitting that they were not prepared for Roosevelt's demonstrations as they awaited the decision to enact the desegregation of schools on Long Island through the court decision involving the Malverne School District. Malverne is a 15-minute driving distance from Roosevelt. The decision determined if school boards had the option to enact segregation and integration on their terms on Long Island. Nonetheless, the NAACP and four other groups would go on to organize a two-day boycott of Roosevelt schools and an indefinite boycott of local merchants beginning next week. During this time, 1,211 of 3,478 students, and parents of the Roosevelt community stayed out of school in protest, picketing outside the three white elementary schools. While these children were absent from Roosevelt schools, they attended two "Freedom Schools" that were arranged by the NAACP. The demonstrations would cause Roosevelt School district to lose about $3,000 in state aid, around $27,000 in today's market.

NAACP Ends Roosevelt School Boycott

By Richard Kwartler

Roosevelt—More than one-third of the pupils in this school district stayed away from their classrooms for the second consecutive day yesterday as the NAACP concluded its school boycott and announced that no further demonstrations were planned.

Dr. Walter Scott, a boycott leader, said, "We feel that the second day of the boycott was most successful, just as the first day had been." He said that the Roosevelt-Freeport branch of the National Association for the Advancement of Colored People had "no further plans to boycott." The civil rights group, he added, did not expect to hold any other kind of demonstration while awaiting a decision on the Malverne test case by the U.S. Supreme Court. That case, which may be heard next month, centers on the question of whether State Education Commissioner James E. Allen Jr. has the power to order a district to end racial imbalance in schools, which is what the NAACP has asked Allen to do here.

Roosevelt Superintendent of Schools Daniel Terry released figures showing that 1,211 of the district's 3,478 enrolled pupils were absent yesterday.

figures for the other schools were: Harry D. Daniels Elementary, 105 absent of 494; Centennial Avenue Elementary, 40 absent of the predominantly white enrollment of 524; Washington Rose Elementary, 255 absent of 679; junior high school, 239 absent of ***, and senior high school, 135 absent of 600.

About 90 of the Negro children who stayed away attended two "freedom schools" set up by the NAACP, an increase of about 15 over Thursday's attendance at the two schools. The two-day total of absences, 2,446, could cause the district to lose almost $4,900 in state aid.

Negro and white pickets marched yesterday morning outside the Centennial, Washington Rose and Theodore Roosevelt schools. The only incident occurred at Theodore Roosevelt. An unidentified Negro woman, a member of the picket line, yelled at a reporter not to question a Negro boy going into the school. When the newsman began talking to the youth, the woman pushed the boy toward the school door, telling him, "Your mother sent you to school and you don't have to talk to reporters." The boy then entered the building. One of the Nassau County ***

FIGURE 23 NEWSPAPER ARTICLE ABOUT THE ENDING OF THE ROOSEVELT BOYCOTT. (CRUMELL, 1964)

Meanwhile…. Summer in Atlantic City

During the summer of 1963, Emily was able to stay with her best friend and now sorority sister Marcia, who was from to the Atlantic City area of New Jersey. They both worked at both Club Harlem and Von Blaine Steakhouse on the Atlantic City Boardwalk. During this time, the March on Washington for Jobs and Freedom would occur later in the summer, wanting to contribute funds towards the event. [25] On August 28, 1963, more than 200,000 people went to Washington, D.C. for the congregation at the Lincoln Memorial. Participants and spectators from all over the world watched and listened as Reverend Dr. Martin Luther King, Jr. delivered his famous, "I Have a Dream" speech. Emily and Marcia did not attend the event but in retrospect wished she had attended. (Brown, 2001). The summer would end tragically with the Sixteenth Street Baptist Church bombing in Birmingham, Alabama in September 1963. The church was known as a hotspot for civil rights activity, and an unknown person threw a pipe bomb through the

---

[25] Second march organized by A. Philip Randolph, along with other Civil Rights powerhouses such as Rev. Martin L. King, Jr. of the SCLC, Roy Wilkins of the NAACP, John Lewis of the SNCC, and James Farmer of CORE.

basement window of the church after services. Sunday school was held in the basement where Denise McNaire, Cynthia Wesley, Carole Robertson, and Addie Mae Collins were at the time of the explosion, they were killed. Riots erupted later that day, leading to the death of two more Black youths.

To add to national political havoc, in November 1963, President John F. Kennedy was assassinated in Texas.[26] Emily recalled the event:

> I was in Hurt gymnasium, and I heard it from another student that the president was assassinated, that he was dead! I left the gym, and when I came out, I saw the head ROTC guy on campus physically marching towards the flagpole in the Quad in regular clothes. He let the flag down at half-mass.[27] I went with Marcia, who practices the Catholic faith, to the Catholic church and lit a candle for him and said prayers. We made our boyfriends at the time take us to Washington, D.C to see Kennedy in the Capitol Rotunda. There were thousands of people waiting all day to see him.

In May of 1964, President Lyndon B. Johnson, former vice-president to Kennedy delivered a commencement address to the University of Michigan spring class. Johnson told the audience what he thought it would take for the United States to become 'The Great Society.' A portion of the speech on racism and integration stated:

---

[26] "The great society" was the political agenda of Lyndon B Johnson, the biggest set of domestic laws since FDR New Deal programs of 1930s. It provided Medicare, Job Corps and trade schools, low rent housing and head start. (Pg. 32-36)

[27] Edward P Hurt, head of Morgan athletics and Bears football coach.

It rests in abundance and liberty for all. [...] it demands an end to poverty and racial injustice, to which we totally committed in our time, but that is just the beginning." Throughout the remainder of his speech, he advocated for "Americans to come together and learn to settle their indifference, or they would lose a sense of community as a country. The expansion of America will change and if we do not afford the same opportunity for knowledge for every child then there will not be full prosperity." He ended his speech with the question, "So will you join in the battle to give every citizen the full equality which God enjoins, and the law requires, whatever his belief, or race, or the color of his skin? [28] (Johnson L. B., 1964)

President Johnson continued John F. Kennedy's policies for managing the Civil Rights movement by signing the Civil Rights Bill into United States law on June 2, 1964. This was an upset to republicans since Johnson was from Texas. The Civil Rights Bill banned discrimination based on race, color, sex, and religion. It went down as one of the major victories for the progression of Black people in the United States, but it did not stop the oppressions that were quilted into the nation's fabric already.

August 1964: The Mississippi Democratic Party Convention

During an oral interview conducted for a college research paper on the Civil Rights Movement, Danielle Brown asked Emily, "Who would you consider to be the person you looked up to the most during the Civil Rights Movement?" Fannie Lou Hamer was the answer Emily gave, adding "*Oh, I looked up a great deal to her because I understood her plight*" (Brown, 2001). Hamer was a native of Mississippi known for having an education in her community, selflessly putting herself at the forefront of the voter's rights movement in Mississippi. In June 1963, Hamer was arrested for trying to vote. During her time in custody, Hamer and another lady were beaten half to death and sexually harassed by the police who questioned them. Upon hearing the news of the event and that there would be a trial, Emily admired Hamer for holding her ground against law enforcement in the court of law. Hammer was braver than most counterparts due to her testimony, as she was met by death threats.

Emily returned to Atlantic City in the summer of 1964 as she did the summer before, working the same jobs she had the summer before. In the same period, the National Mississippi Democratic National Convention on Voting Rights was taking place in Atlantic City from August 24th - 27th, just before Emily's return to Morgan for her senior year. Hammer was on the ballot box as the nominee for the second district in Mississippi during this election (Mastrovia, 2012). During the convention, Fannie Lou Hamer coined the phrase, "I am sick and tired of being sick and tired," a quote that Emily still uses often. Emily did not attend the actual convention because of work, but she was able to view and hear Fannie Lou Hamer, SNCC's Stokely Carmichael and Civil Rights leader and U.S. Representative Adam Clayton Powell speak while on the Atlantic City Boardwalk. Emily remembered Powell saying that "*being black was more a way of thinking than having to do with skin color. [...] and a Black person can be black as coal, but if you do not have the right-thinking, it does not mean anything.*" The concept Powell spoke about created a change in the generational mentality of what it meant to be black in America for future generations.

After the convention, Emily and her friends decided to quit their jobs to help raise money on behalf of the MSDP along the

Atlantic City Boardwalk. During Emily's time at Morgan tuition was between $4,000-$6,000 a year. Emily had decided that she would take out a loan for her final year, it was the only time she felt she had to (Brown, 2001). In response to everything that was taking place in front of her eyes, Emily said, *"Look, FREEDOM is more important than work."* During her employment in the summers, Emily only worked to provide herself with food and shelter, donating the rest to the different organizations of the Civil Rights movement anyway. Voting Rights was just as important as Civil Rights to Emily and for the rest of their summer, they worked the boardwalk. In recollection, she still felt that she was very wise in making that decision at the time as she was able to meet many civil rights activists that would later become prominent figures within black American history.

PHOTO 46 FANNIE LOU HAMMER ON MICROPHONE, EMORY HARRIS (TO THE LEFT), KWAME TURNE (IN HAT), SAM BLOCK (IN GLASEES) ELEANOR HOLMES NORTON AND ELLA BAKER (IN SUNGLASSES) DURING THE CONVENTION ON THE ATLANTIC CITY BOARDWALK. (VIGEANT, 2022)

Emily mentioned that she drove with Stokely Carmichael and other people to New York when the summer convention was over. Marcia reflected on their time in Atlantic City:

> *Emily and Patty stayed at my grandmother's house with me, it was the year they had the democratic convention in Atlantic City. We had worked at the Von Hanson Blain Steakhouse, to make money to pay for our college. It was on Kentucky Avenue, next to Club Harlem. We had a good job, with good pay. After breakfast, there was a breakfast show which was at six in the morning. We saw many famous people, even Sammy Davis Jr. and Frank Sinatra perform and come for breakfast. We met Fannie Lou Hammer and Stokely Carmichael, we met them all, the speakers of the civil rights movement. Emily rode back with Stokely.*

> *- Marcia Saxon-Hazelton*

The fight against racial injustice, and found success was always met with tragedy. By the end of the summer, five bodies of civil rights activists were found in the woods of Mississippi in June 1964. The Freedom Summer Murders is the story of three men, James Chaney, Andrew Goodman, and Michael Schwerner, two white men and one Black man, who went missing on their way home along the backroads of Mississippi after helping with voter registrations. There was a massive search that ensued for them enacted by the FBI; simultaneously, they found the bodies of civil rights workers Henry Hezekiah Dee and Charles Eddie Moore in the process of the search. The two were killed by the Ku Klux Klan because of rumors that they were planning to arm African Americans in their area around Philadelphia, Mississippi. The three men would be found in a fourteen-foot-deep hole, Eight of sixteen who were accused of involvement and conspiracy included a police Deputy and Sheriff, and a Baptist priest. These murders hastened the passing of the Civil Rights Act of 1964 (History: Famous Cases & Criminals: Mississippi Burning, n.d.). The event of this tragedy is depicted by the movie Mississippi Burning that was released in 1988.

Four Mississippi Boys in a white woman's living room

For Black American families, it was common that, in the summer months, children would be sent between the North and South to bond with their distant relatives and learn an understanding of the differences between their worlds. New York had a liberal sense of politics, but the social tolerance of ideals such as interracial coupling, and Black people roaming certain areas could still bring trouble. Emily recalled that kids and their family members would come to Freeport, Hempstead, and Roosevelt in the summers, even moving to stay with family members. Nonetheless, Emily still was not ready for the visual of four Black men from Mississippi standing in Anne Pollocks, a white woman, family home in Baldwin, a once predominantly white town next to Freeport. It did not matter how liberal New York was, it was not a common sight to see.

Anne Pollock was a woman that Emily became friends with during high school who had transferred from Roosevelt. While Anne studied at Harvard University, Emily would visit and stay over in the dorms as she demonstrated around campus and the area. This summer, Emily could not recall if Anne's parents were around for that moment in time, but Anne spent time in Mississippi helping with voters' rights activism as Emily had done in New Jersey. Pollock's family was of a liberal democratic background. They would invite Emily to events that they hosted and vice versa, but the moment still seemed extreme to Emily and the men as she thought about how to make the gentlemen feel more secure and at ease with their environment. Emily decided to invite Pollock and the gentlemen to her Aunt Marie's house for dinner.

Anne excelled at her mission because Emily claimed that Ebony magazine did an article on her for being a white woman deeply involved with Voter's Rights. Unfortunately, the magazine could not be recovered as a source.

> There was a picture of her [Anne] and some of the other people from Mississippi; that was the summer of 1964. When I returned from Atlantic City, Anne called me and then I went over to her house. I remember coming to her house with a magazine with her face in it. She had about five or six Black boys from Mississippi in her house. You could tell those boys were losing their minds. There they were -- with this white girl, when in Mississippi they could be killed for looking at her (Brown, 2001).

During the time they were in New York, they all went to different churches and fundraised for SNCC (Brown, 2001).

> We would split up, we took one student from Mississippi, a white and Black student. We went around and stood up and we told them that we were collecting an offering. We went to all the churches we could. We must have raised about $400. Enough money for them boys to fuss over! They never seen so much money before it seemed, so they were having second thoughts. I told them: Look, I am taking the money into Forman! Let him do what he wants with the money, and I took the money to New York City to their headquarters.

Senior Year: I am woman

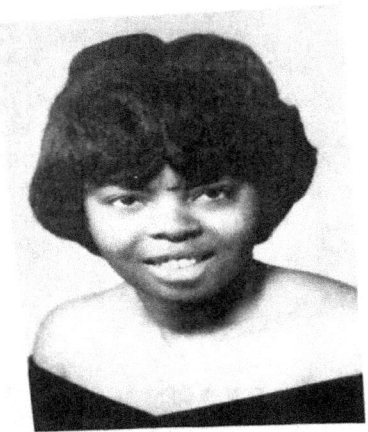

Emily Moore
Physical Education
Delta Sigma Theta Sorority; Physical Education Club; Gamma Sigma Sigma Sorority; Cheering Squad; Student Athletic Representative; Hockey Team; Basketball Team.

PHOTO 47 EMILY'S MORGAN GRADUATION PHOTO, 1963. (MORGAN STATE UNIVERSITY, 1965)

It was the spring semester of Emily's senior year, and graduating seniors were trying to figure out their next journey as they embraced adulthood. Once again, just like high school, Emily did not apply to graduate schools like most prospective graduates but this time it was because she had applied to the Peace Corps as she proposed to do in 1961. She was now in anticipation of her acceptance into the program. Emily's experiences at Morgan made her an effective as a community organizer, debater, and educator.

By the end of her time at Morgan, she came to understand that a movement can truly be effective if there is organization and bonds that evenly tie the people past initial wants, and towards beneficial results. Overall, Emily did not say too much about her campus life, besides how busy it became for her, especially as a Delta Woman. When Emily attended Morgan, the Greek Organizations had their displays, and hangouts at various spots on the main campus, and required time for community service and various social engagements. She recalled how she hung in the "quad" or "The Yard" with her friends and Delta's sisters. By the time Emily was ready to graduate from Morgan, she served on the student board for the School of Physical Education and Health.

As a forward-paced woman, Emily had always looked to change the narrative of her people, understanding there would be sacrifices she would have to make to move forward. Emily refused to move in the path of the gender-stereotyped roles of the 1960s. It was previously recognized that there was no women's tennis team at Morgan before Emily's time as a student. As a first-year student and sophomore, she met approximately ten women who consistently played tennis. As women's tennis grew to be popular among the women athletes on the campus, women wanted to charter a team. For Emily, the journey to gain a women's team was tough at that time. She described Coach Hurt, the chair of Physical Education, as chauvinistic and narrow-minded about the advancement of women's athletics. However, this rejection did not settle for Emily or the other women tennis players who attended Morgan. Naturally in response, Emily drew up a petition. Coach Hurt underestimated Emily's ability to gather people for common causes, it was possible Coach Hurt did not know Emily and her reputation on campus as a multifaceted activist. Emily was able to gain enough signatures to begin charting a women's team on campus to represent Morgan. During her college sports career, she achieved victories and awards for her athleticism.

Later in the school year, Emily tried to get a letter of recommendation from the physical education department for her to join the Peace Corps. In what Emily saw as a rebuttal to the grief she gave the physical education department to establish the Women's tennis team, Emily was denied a letter. She could not understand as a graduating senior and a member of the student board of the physical education department. Emily did not have the energy to go toe-to-toe with the department at the time. Fortunately, Emily's academic courses were mainly science-related, as she was required to take anatomy, biology and other health courses, which enabled her to seek a letter from the Science Department. She received the recommendation with no hesitation, saying *"If one thing doesn't work, you find another thing or way."*

Emily is a woman who is not easily stirred, even as a young woman, and she knew what she wanted out of life very early and was not going to let anything that was not God's Will get in her way. Emily had already made it her life's mission to help the people of the world. For Emily at the age of twenty-one, a partner of any degree would have to be "on the move," or be able to accept that she was a woman on the go, and to support or recommend her decisions rather than deter her from them. As Emily told her story at 80 years old, Emily had not reflected on the romantic side of her life, and concerning her age, and marital status of single, it was not a critical subject to be factored in. Fortunately, she did mention one relationship during her senior year with a man in question whose name remained unnamed, but the story remembered. Instead of the young man displaying support, or even joining the mission, he gave

her an ultimatum about leaving for the Peace Corps.

> *I wanted to travel to Africa; I had hoped I had the chance. He said, 'Emily! If you go to Africa, I will not go! I will break up with you!' I responded, "Well this is goodbye!" I took myself back to New York and prepared for my journey. I was not going to let nobody stop my fight to make the world better.*

Emily graduated from Morgan College in the spring of 1965 with a

bachelor's degree in physical education.

Gamma Sigma Sigma Girls Service Sorority

Gamma Sigma Sigma was founded in 1953, by girls who wished to assemble college and university women in a spirit of service to humanity.

OFFICERS

President ....
First Vice-President ....
Second Vice-President ....
Third Vice-President ....
Secretary ....
Treasurer ....

ROSTER

Olivia Addison, Ruth Banks, Sondra Brown, Constance Daily, Caralyn Dotson, Anna Gaile, Myrna Granger, Janet Green, Chris Jacqueline Miles, Claudette Mitchell, Emily Ine Rodgers, Marcia Saxon, Carletha Sm Smith, Rosemond Smith, Vera Walden, La Delores Watkins, Cheryl Little, Sandra Wells.

FIGURE 24 MORGAN STATE MEMBERS OF GAMMA SIGMA SIGMA GIRLS SERVICE SORORITY. (INPICTURE, EMILY)

Seated, left to right: B. Davis, L. Johns, E. Smalley, N. Monroe, C. Lee, K. Brown, J. Parker, J. Stanley. Standing, left to right: J. Taylor, C. Hunt, E. Robinson, J. Wadkins, E. Moore, L. Jackson, R. Barnes, P. Hendricks, N. Parham.

Health and Physical Education Club

This organization, composed of health, physical education, and recreation majors, seeks to promote the professional interest of the members in this field.

FIGURE 26 HEALTH AND PHYSICAL EDUCATION CLUB, EMILY TOP ROW AND CENTER. (MORGAN STATE UNIVERSITY, 1965)

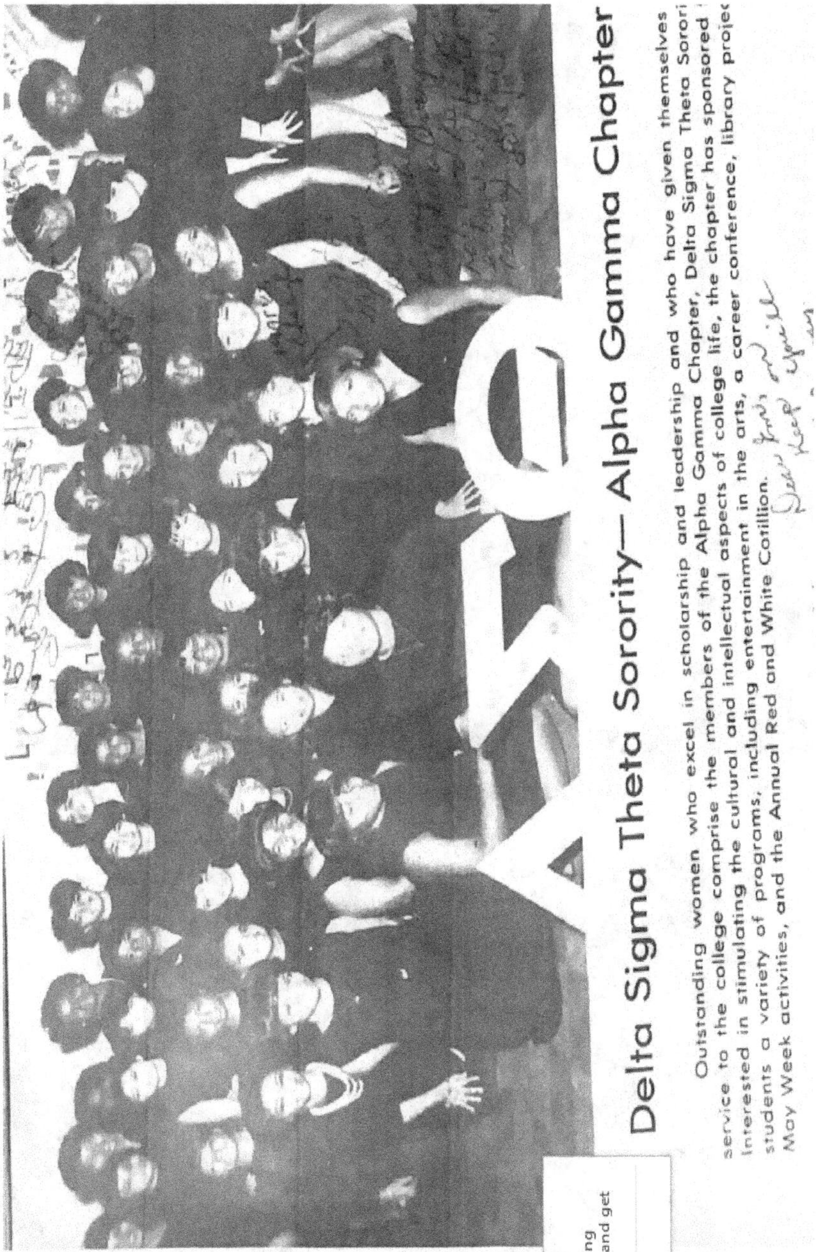
Delta Sigma Theta Sorority— Alpha Gamma Chapter

Outstanding women who excel in scholarship and leadership and who have given themselves service to the college comprise the members of the Alpha Gamma Chapter, Delta Sigma Theta Sorori[ty]. Interested in stimulating the cultural and intellectual aspects of college life, the chapter has sponsored [for] students a variety of programs, including entertainment in the arts, a career conference, library projec[ts], May Week activities, and the Annual Red and White Cotillion.

FIGURE 27 ALPHA GAMMA CHAPTER OF DELTA SIGMA THETA, 1963 EMILY IN THE TOP ROW, MIDDLE. (MORGAN STATE UNIVERSITY, 1965)

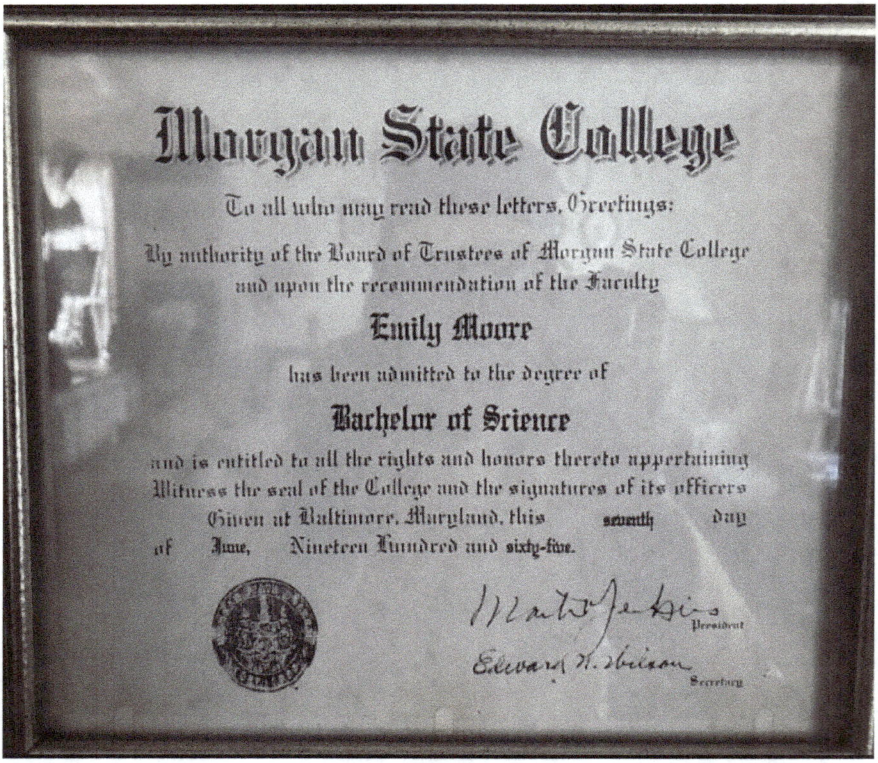
Morgan State College

To all who may read these letters, Greetings:

By authority of the Board of Trustees of Morgan State College and upon the recommendation of the Faculty

Emily Moore

has been admitted to the degree of

Bachelor of Science

and is entitled to all the rights and honors thereto appertaining

Witness the seal of the College and the signatures of its officers

Given at Baltimore, Maryland, this seventh day of June, Nineteen Hundred and sixty-five.

President

Secretary

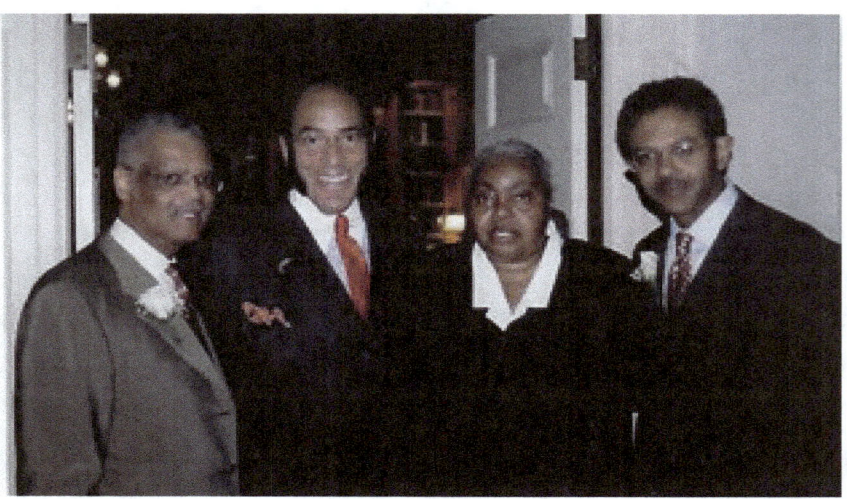

FIGURE 28 EMILY'S BACHELOR OF SCIENCE DEGREE ,1965. (COURTESY OF AYANNA MOORE)

PHOTO 48 L TO R: EARL S. RICHARDSON, EARL G. GRAVES, EMILY MOORE AND UNKNOWN MAN. (COURTESY OF EMILY MOORE)

SERVICE TO THE WORLD AND THE PEOPLE: PEACE CORPS

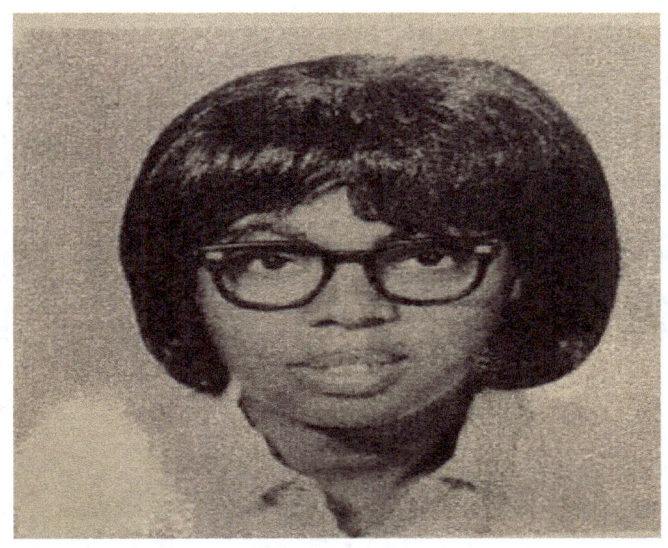

PHOTO 49 EMILY'S PEACECORPS MEMBERSHIP GRADUATION PHOTO. (THE PEACE CORPS , 1967)

It was Emily's freshman year of college when she heard President Kennedy coin the phrase to the republic of the United States of America, *"Ask not what your country can do for you - ask what you can do for your country,"* on the radio, as he was inaugurated as President in 1961 (1961). The war against communism created great tension between the United States and Russia that continues in foreign policy relationships in the present day. It was uncanny, through the tension, the president admired that the Russians had a program where they sent their professionals abroad to help others. In March 1961, Kennedy founded the Peace Corps as an initiative for young and older American citizens to help underdeveloped countries across the world (Papers of John F. Kennedy, 1961). Those who are selected for the program are assigned to an area to serve for a term of two years. The volunteers would serve in one of the following educative, scientific, medical, political, or developmental fields. It was at Kennedy's funeral in 1963, that Emily and Marcia decided they would apply for the Peace Corps when they were going to graduate from Morgan with their degrees.

Emily started the onboarding process with the Peace Corps in August 1965. When she was asked if there were any regions or communities she preferred to serve, to which Emily responded, *"Whichever country needs me the most!"* Emily wanted to serve and teach the children of Africa, people of her descent. Emily decided that her life's purpose was to teach children and young adults of the world what it meant to train themselves to be prepared for the future, what it meant to have civil rights and how to keep them. With dismay, Emily was chosen to teach in the Spanish-speaking country of Valenzuela. It would have been thought to be great news for Emily since Marcia was already serving in Valenzuela. It meant that the two of them could teach side by side. In retrospect, Valenzuela would have been a bountiful experience between the two women knowing they had each other's back indefinitely. Disappointed in the choice, *"Send me where I am needed,"* Emily reiterated to the staff that oversaw her profile. Emily knew of no Black volunteers who chose to go to Africa and felt like it was the best atmosphere to supply a service to black people of the world. Emily was selected to serve in Africa and was set to begin training in September 1965. Before Emily could be sent to training, she had to go to Philadelphia, Pennsylvania for three days to complete physical and mental health evaluations. She recalled hugging her mom and dad goodbye before she left, as she did not return to America until 1968.

After passing the evaluations, Emily's first active training assignment was to teach high school science at an all-girls high school in St. Thomas. Emily was qualified to teach science because of the various science classes that were needed for physical education majors such as biology and anatomy. Once again, Emily expressed what she had wanted out of the internship, that she would be more comfortable and effective teaching physical or health education. When questioned 'why so persistent?' by the staff and she replied:

> My forte is physical education and health; Training young people so they can become who they want to be; to get them mentally and physically to remain persistent when times are tough! That is the key. That is my method.

Emily was assigned to teach in Liberia or Angola when she completed her training as a science teacher, not a physical educator. Emily was told if she were truly dissatisfied that she would have to leave Africa and go where physical educators were needed. The staff did not think it was in the best interest to remove Emily so late in the training process, now that she was familiar with the other members and volunteers of the Corps. Fortunately for Emily, there was a black American woman who was a principal at one of the high schools who reached out and offered to take Emily as a physical education and health teacher in Benin City, Nigeria.

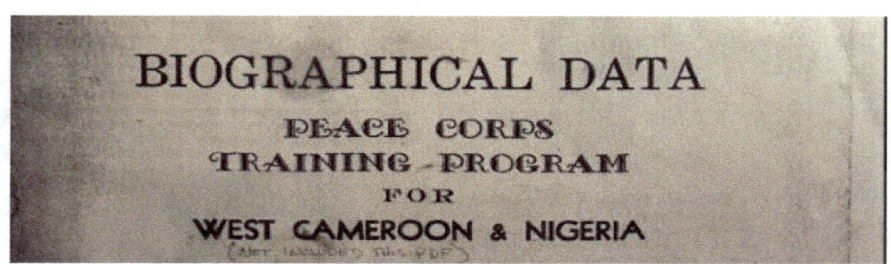

FIGURE 29 BOOKLET EMILY RECEIVED DURING TRAINING. (COURTESY OF PEACECORPS)

Emily took a flight to the Caribbean countries of St. Croix and St. Thomas to begin language, physical and survival training courses because the countries have the most similar climates to Nigeria and the other countries of Africa, making it ideal for simulation. Emily was the only woman of color in the group of volunteers who were training to go to the continent of Africa. Emily was now in her early twenties. A proud and educated woman who faced opposition during the Civil Rights movement. She did not let others' opinions about her skin ruin her journey or outlook on life. Fortunately for Emily, she had not encountered any racial instances.

PHOTO 50 EMILY AND GROUP OF VOLUNTEERS SHE MET AND SERVED WITH IN ST. CROIX AND ST. THOMAS. (COURTESY OF EMILY MOORE)

There was another woman and one brother who worked at the St. Croix training post, but I spent most of my time in St. Thomas," "During training, we lived in tents; the guys who went to serve in Cameroon pitched them; they did their training in St. Croix. I lived in a tent with three other girls, two white girls from South Carolina, and another from New York too. Five white girls and Emily Moore in a tent! We had latrines; we had to go outside to the bathrooms. The showers were set up like tents and when you ran the water it was cold! Everything was preparing us for the situation. We had no lights, no heat, and no air conditioning. We all got up at five in the morning and ran a mile, ran down the hill and back, then ate breakfast. "We trained from sunrise to sunset with classes, presentations, and physical training. He had language classes and psychologists that would meet with us each week to check on how we were adjusting.

Lagos, Nigeria-1966

PHOTO 51 PEACE CORPS STAFF, VOLLUNTEERSAS AND NATIVE NIGERIANS UPON ARRIVAL TO LAGOS. EMILY BOTTOM CENTER IN SUNGLASSES (COURTESY OF EMILY MOORE)

When Emily arrived in Lagos, Nigeria in January 1966,

nothing she trained for with the Peace Corps could prepare her for what she saw upon arrival at Lagos International Airport. On the same day of her arrival, Nigeria had the first day of a military coup that was enacted by the Igbo military, resulting in the airport becoming under seizure! [29] Emily found the situation humorous as she shared that *"The Igbo military took over every entry point, except the American Airlines gates! They did not touch any of the Americans; the United States was the number one military power in the world!"* Emily, other volunteers, and staff were safely escorted to their designated areas where buses were ready to take them to their assigned posts. Emily was the only one who went west into Benin City, Nigeria. Historically, Benin City once served as the center of Nigeria during the Benin Kingdom dynasty from the 1600s to 1897. Benin City was known for its artisanship and ironworks, contributing to elaborate pieces of brass, bronze, copper, ivory, and various woods that told the history of the Benin people. In 1897, Benin City was burned to the ground in response to British explorers who had been denied entry to the city during a time of sacred celebration.

---

[29] Junior army officers overthrew the rule of Nigeria's Civilian Government. The coup would later result in a civil war in 1967.

During Emily's two years in Benin, she continued to keep a steady reputation as a successful physical education teacher and coach at the Anglican Girls Grammar School. Emily has collected various photographs from her time in Africa that capture her teaching young women physical education, but also giving her time to the young women who were now caught between and growing up in territories of a Civil War that was occurring between the Igbo Military and the Hausa/Yoruba Military.

While in Benin City, Emily coached her students to qualify for an event that was like the Junior Olympics during that school year. The opportunity gave her the chance to meet the opposing militia leaders to briefly thank them for the opportunity. One thing she remembered about her students and the event was that every athlete was gifted with a new pair of white sneakers. Her student-athletes wanted to wear the new shoes, like everyone else, but she told them that they could not wear them during their meets because those were not the shoes they trained to run and win in, contributing to the methods and discipline in the training style of Emily Moore.

PHOTO 52 EMILY FACILITATING A PHYSICAL EDUCATION CLASS. (COURTESY OF EMILY MOORE)

Emily performed exceptionally well as an educator and coach. She had become an educational officer for the school and even had the opportunity to be the coach for the Mid-Western Regional track team. During her time in Nigeria, she was also able to converse with the eastern region of Nigeria's military leader Chukwuemeka Odumegwu. While in the Peace Corps, she loved her time in Africa and spent her holidays traveling and exploring the Canary Islands, Ghana, Dohoney, France, Greece, Italy, Morocco, Tanzania, Turkey, and Togo. Emily spoke about her time when she got to experience

Turkey with a group of random women.

> One time, I was on the plane, on my way from Cyprus (Greece) to
> Turkey and I met a group of women who were from Greece on their
> way to Turkey as well. I was going for adventure, but these women
> were heading to Turkey to get an education because it was illegal
> for them to learn in Greece. They invited me to come stay with them
> by their school, and I did. I had a wonderful time. See, back in the
> day, you could do things like that.

After her extensive travels, Emily decided not to return to the

United States immediately after she completed the Peace Corps

program. Instead, Emily had decided that she wanted to continue

touring and learning about the world because she did not know the

next time it would be possible.

> Well, the travel passes that were given to us in the Peace Corps
> allowed us to use a ticket that was reusable to travel anywhere for
> a certain period. I used it until I decided that I had to return home.
> Leaving Africa, I traveled to the Middle East, Turkey, and Rome. I
> decided to learn French, so I went to Paris.

By 1967, the civil and political unrest became too dangerous,

and the volunteers were forced to pack up quickly to evacuate

Nigeria. When Emily was interviewed by the United States Tennis

Association in 2022, she recalled being stuck on a barge for three

days before they could make an evacuation, stating that *"We*

finished the water and food on the first day," and being stuck near

crossfires, *"We heard shots, and we were on a flat barge. Where can you duck and hide? They were running around with M-16's!"*

(Sode, Eastern: 2021 Eastern Hall of Fame: Dr. Emily Moore, 2022).

PHOTO 54 EMILY WITH THE STUDENT VOLLEYBALL TEAM. (COURTESY OF EMILY MOORE)

PHOTO 53 EMILY IN THE CENTER WITH A CLASS OF HIGH SCHOOL GIRLS. (COURTESY OF EMILY MOORE)

PHOTO 55 EMILY ON A MOTOR SCOOTER

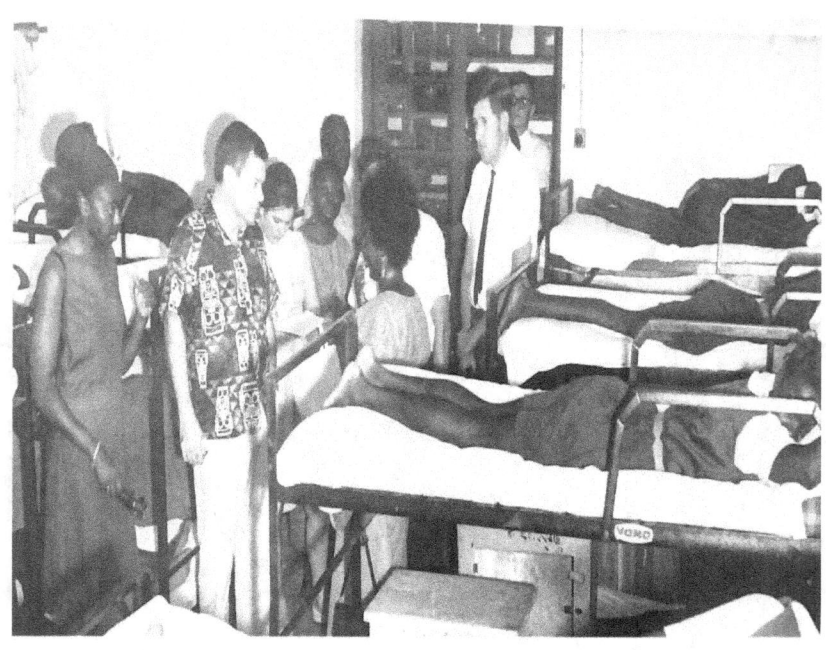

PHOTO 57 EMILY ON A TOUR OF THE SCHOOL GROUNDS. (COURTESY OF EMILY MOORE)

Emily Moore, (P.C. 137721) 24, is from Roosevelt, Long Island, New York. She received her B.S. in Physical Education from Morgan State College. She has a varsity letter in hockey and basketball. Her special skills also include tennis, volleyball, table tennis, folk dancing, badminton and bowling. She has done volunteer work and during the summer worked in the field of Family Services at the Recreation Center. For the past two years she has officiated at Intramural Games.

FIGURE 30 INFORMATION ABOUT EMILY IN THE PEACE CORPS GRADUATION BOOKLET. (COURTESY OF PEACECORPS)

AMERIKKKA ON FIRE: THE RACE RIOTS AND THE RISE OF 'BLACK POWER'

Emily knew that people were *"sick and tired of being sick and tired"* about the prejudice and racially based acts of violence that continued from law enforcement, and the Ku Klux Klan and branches of Neo-Nazi groups throughout the United States. Collectively, Black Americans were done with the lack of effort towards no change, and/or reformative action. The addition of the Civil Rights Act of 1964 and the Voting Rights Act of 1965 to U.S. Law did not bring the peace that Black and brown American Citizens sought. There was no immediate effect on this cause, as White Americans who opposed desegregation continued to be disgruntled by the ruling of integration. In the political world, politicians continued to create economic, social, and political loopholes and hardships that would continue to deter the legal process and progress of Black Americans. Notably, black, and brown people were harassed and falsely accosted by local law enforcement in major black and brown-populated cities such as Chicago, Illinois; Compton, California; Detroit, Michigan and Harlem, New York. Law enforcement across the nation used extremely obsessive and deadly force when dealing with prospective and non-prospective suspects who were of black and brown skin complexions. Back in the United States, the Civil Rights movement transcended into the Black Power Movement as the fight for equality took on the anger of Black Americans. Black people took to the streets with riots and looting of central businesses within their neighborhoods in response to the injustice.

If it was not already hard for Black Americans to gather resources and properties, rioting made it harder for the recovery of families of all backgrounds who had given everything into being business owners. I never approved of rioting and acts of violence because these actions took away from their own community resources, affecting Black ownership. It took away from who we really were as a people and culture, giving reason for the other side to NOT want to give us our liberties. African and Black Americans have never been a violent people, they have been an oppressed people.

In August 1965, The Watts Riots took place as a community response against Los Angeles Police Department enforcement who used excessive force on two Black men after being pulled over for erratic driving in the Watts neighborhood of Los Angeles. Allegedly, the driver of the car failed the sobriety test but pleaded and insisted that they were right around the corner from their residence and should be allowed to park and walk instead of facing arrest. Eventually, family members of the man who lived nearby arrived at the scene. The situation escalated into a physical altercation which included the dragging of a pregnant woman on the ground. The surrounding community saw the force used against the men, but more importantly the pregnant woman. The riots resulted in thirty-four deaths, over a thousand injuries, and arrests. The riots lasted for 6 days and devastated the overall Black community's financial wealth for over 50 years (Civil Rights Digital Library, 1965).

The Chicago riots took place in July 1966 because of an armed robbery where the assailant, a Black man, was seen by citizens being shot at by police as he fled on foot. The perpetrator was caught, but by then a crowd had formed protesting the arrest, and then another mob began to form at the liquor store, eventually turning into a looting situation. Emily was away from the United States when riots began to erupt. Emily's poem *"Long History of Pleading"* references the events of the Watts Riots in the Watts neighborhood of Los Angeles, California in August 1965, and then the Chicago West Side Riots that occurred in July 1966. The Chicago Tribune reported:

> *On July 13, around two hundred youths looted a drug store and threw stones and fired shots at police, wounding seven policemen. Stores were set on fire with rioters pelting responding firemen with stones. During a raid on an apartment building, twenty-one*

members of a "paramilitary group" were arrested. A police captain said he received reports the group was planning on waging guerrilla warfare and had caches of automatic weapons and explosives stashed throughout the city. (The Chicago Tribune, 1966)

The rise of Black Power and the Black Panther Party for Freedom

By 1966, Stokely Carmichael (Kwame Tume) was the president of SNCC. He had come a long way as an activist since Emily had met him in Atlantic City. Tume worked closely with Gloria Richardson, who led the SNCC chapter in Cambridge, Maryland while Emily was attending Morgan, which made Emily very familiar with who he was and had become.[30] Tume's ideologies were strongly influenced by Garveyism and Malcolm X philosophies as he pushed for black inclusion in the future organization of SNCC. Tume retorted that his decision to remove white members was based on the overall view of the mission. Tume viewed that white participants took away from the bigger picture of it being an issue plagued by Black people. Furthermore, the empathy given by the public to

---

[30] Gloria Richardson – once the head of the Cambridge Maryland Nonviolent Action Committee during the Cambridge Movement. She led demonstrations over economic issues, healthcare access and substantial housing. (The Associated Press, 19)

demonstrations was displayed due to the involvement of white people, rather than seeing racism as an offense against humanity. During the Civil Rights Movement, as the president of SNCC, he decided to remove all white members of SNCC for a short period. Kwame Tume would become known for coining the phrase *'Black Power'* in 1966. The phrase produced a new wave of black philosophy towards black social, economic, and political affairs while keeping their life, liberty, and happiness. This created a target on Tume's back as it revolutionized Black Americans against the oppression of law enforcement and white oppressors.

> *Black power also represented Carmichael's break with King's doctrine of nonviolence and its end goal of racial integration. Instead, he associated the term with the doctrine of black separatism, articulated most prominently by Malcolm X. "When you talk of Black power, you talk of building a movement that will smash everything Western civilization has created," Carmichael said in one speech. Unsurprisingly, the turn to Black power proved controversial, evoking fear in many white Americans, even those previously sympathetic to the civil rights movement, and exacerbating fissures within the movement itself between older proponents of nonviolence and younger advocates of separatism. Martin Luther King called Black power "an unfortunate choice of words. (Seidman, 2012)*

The Black Power ideology gave way to the popular rise of The Black Panther Party for Self-Defense/ Black Panther Freedom Party (BPP). In response to excessive force from law enforcement,

BPP was founded in 1966 in Oakland, California, by young activists Huey P. Newton and Bobby Seale. The BPP advocated Black Pride, Black Nationalism, and self-education and self-policing of their neighborhoods to combat the systematic oppression that continued to plague inner-city communities (Smithsonian: National Museum of African American History and Culture, unknown). The Black Panther Freedom Party harbored the militancy and inclusion rhetoric that Marcus Garvey displayed in the 1930s and that Malcolm X brought to the occurring Civil Rights movement. The Black Panther Party also catered to the economically impoverished by creating and funding free lunch and extracurricular programs for children. Those programs would pave the way for state and government-funded programs such as Women, Child and Infant (WIC) and Head Start daycare programs. The BPP invoked all constitutional rights granted to them as "equal" citizens by the law of the land during all their public demonstrations.

> At one time there were children that passed out in class from hunger or had to be sent home for something to eat. But our children shall be fed, and the Black Panther Party will not let the malady of hunger keep our children down any longer. The Free Breakfast for School Children =To Feed our children.
>
> The Black Panther March, 1969

The BPP programs included self-defense and armed defense training, as the BPP openly exercised their Second Amendment rights. This mass organization did not sit well with local, state, and national law enforcement, leading to the increase of gun statutes and penal laws in the states of California, New York and Illinois, states where the BPP had the most influence. The Black Panther Party grew to a have membership of over 100,000 Black Americans by the 1970s. The organization's main chapters were in Oakland, California; Chicago, Illinois; and Philadelphia, Pennsylvania, which supplied multiple resources to the black communities of their areas. The BPP exercised their Second Amendment – the right to bear arms in conjunction with their First Amendment - freedom of speech against law enforcement and political oppression, making them a prolific target of law enforcement entities. The BPP's support of women in leadership roles and ranks within their chapters, made them very successful in harnessing overall unification within the groups, because it was based on work ethic, not race nor gender, another reflection of BPP and its program to be ahead of its time in ideologies.

Friends of SNCC and the death of MLK

It was now the fall of 1967. After completing the Peace Corps, and traveling to various countries, Emily was now living in Paris, France, trying to keep up with what was in the U.S.A. to the best of her abilities. When asked why Paris? Emily responded, *"I really wanted to learn French and thought the best way was to be there. I still had time left on my Visa for the Peace Corps to travel, so I took advantage."* The racial climate of Europe varied from country to country, and terrain but overall, Emily was not met with the same opposition from White European people in the way she had from White Americans. European countries such as Italy and Sicily were known for being highly receptive to Black American soldiers during World War II. In retrospect, these countries were more occupied with the effects of post-Nazism and communism, where everyone was liable to face death for opposition to regimes, rather than racism.

I loved it there in Paris. I was a radical activist more than ever too. I could walk anywhere and not get bothered, but they loved me in Italy! We were guarded but I always tried to be on my own because I had no fear of seeing other things. I met Muslims who got to spoke of how Charles De Gaulle the president of France, at one point did not want Malcolm X to come to Paris during this international trip because he did not want him to get assassinated on their territory

by an anti-Islamic and another white supremacist. They said that
he was bigger than the Muslims, and they were right.

In 1967, Carmichael decided to part ways as president of SNCC to travel abroad and gain further concepts of self and meaning to life. Carmichael would also meet with international civic and human rights leaders to broaden the message of Civil Rights to the rest of the world. Though Carmichael stepped down as leader, he still was a staunch advocate for starting an international chapter of SNCC. Once again, wherever Emily went, something significant would occur. In October 1967, Carmichael came across 25-year-old Emily Moore in a sea of the international student body while in the international cafeteria. In that cafeteria, Carmichael asked Emily to organize and run an SNCC chapter in Paris.

> *I was in this large eating place; it was where all the international students went to get food. I was on the line, and I was asking someone if they knew French, and I heard,' Emily!? What are you doing here?' I turned around and it was Stokely Carmichael! At this time, Stokely was still a part of SNCC, he came to speak in Paris. We, most of the students that were there went to see him speak, and after we met up at different places. He later asked me to organize Friends of SNCC in Paris because of my fundraising history with SNCC and MDMP. I agreed.*

To know Emily personally, then it is agreed that if Emily says that she is going to do something, it is going to get done. As Emily agreed to help be one of the organizers for the Friends of SNCC. she worked relentlessly to help format and organize with other students towards making the chapter prosperous. For about six months, Emily remained in Paris, and she recruited members to organize a small headquarters at a Quaker center in downtown Paris. The organization proved its difficulties for Emily as consistent U.S. correspondence was difficult because of the riots, coupled with the fact that Carmichael's status as president of SNCC and BPP Prime minister stood in the wind due to allegations of trying to overthrow the government in Guinea in 1968. Ture would go on to leave SNCC, but Emily tried to organize, making it even more difficult with the organizational dysfunction at the time in the States. Emily worked herself so much that her health was starting to decline; her friends noticed she was told she had to take a break. Emily was on her way to Switzerland when she heard news that Dr. King died on April 4, 1968.

> [...] I was organizing, doing a whole lot of stuff in Paris. I was exhausted and really getting sick. The weather there is cold and dry, and then wet in the wintertime! I just came back from Africa for two years and it was hot. My body was really taking a beating. I was going away for about a week, maybe a couple of weeks, because they said I had to get AWAY. I was going to Switzerland to meet some friends and just relax. I was literally about to get on the train

when I decided to call my friend just before. She said, "Have you seen the paper? Come, tell Julian. That was Julian Harvey, I stayed with her and family when I was in Paris. They took me down to the train station. Anyway, my friend told me that Dr. King had been killed, they told me to get a paper. That was April of 1968. The group SNCC disbanded in 1968 too.

One day after confirmation of MLK's death, Ture went to Washington, D.C. to speak to the people, but afterward, the Washington D.C. riot occurred, and the government wanted to blame Ture for insinuating it. With MLK deceased, Emily felt that she had to return to America, so she could prepare her community for what was next to come. She told Julian and her family, *"I am going back to the U.S. because that is the belly of the beast,"* but it had a tremendous effect on Emily which ultimately brought her back to the United States. Emily felt the heartache behind his death just like millions across the world, there were Americans who felt that "the dream" was now over. MLK was the voice and formidable force behind the Civil Rights Movement, and for Emily and countless people around the world, it seemed like MLK death diminished the remaining energy and the picture behind the idea of remaining non-violent in the fight for civil rights. Emily returned to Long Island to organize a memorial service for Dr. King and hoped to make it down to the funeral in Atlanta, Georgia, which she did. Emily recalled

seeing predominant figures of the civil rights movement at

the Ebenezer Baptist Church in Atlanta, and the sorrow she felt for

Coretta Scott-King, his wife, and his young children. Ironically, at the

same time, Marcia ran into Emily after the funeral.

> I was walking, and I must not have paid too much attention in the park. I almost fell over someone. When I looked to see who it was to apologize, it was Emily! I said, Emily?! And she responded, Marcia?!," I was living in California by then, so it was great to had catch up with her because I thought she was still overseas in Africa, or somewhere! We went to have dinner after it all.

The Black Panther Party would eventually become the

number one subject of the Federal Bureau of Investigation (FBI) and

the Central Intelligence Agency. Under the case name

COINTELPRO, U.S. law enforcement agencies colluded to enact a

string of legal and illegal operations to disrupt and infiltrate black

political groups under the direction of J. Edgar Hoover, the first

director of the FBI.[31] The organizing of Friends of SNCC was a

short-lived journey as Carmichael would later be foiled by British

Intelligence as infiltrations led to the discrediting of him as a member

of SNCC. The allegations and distrust also led to the removal of him

---

[31] COINTELPRO an operation of infiltration and dismantling of black led political groups. J Edgar Hoover would serve as FBI director from 1935-1972.

from the Black Panther Party for whom he served as the Honorary Prime Minister in the 1970s. Tume would focus his knowledge and influence on Pan-Africanism, revisiting the Back-to-Africa ideologies of Marcus Garvey and Paul Cuffee until he died in 1998.

Poems of the time: Just Like It Is

In 2008, Emily self-published *Just Like It Is*, a book of poetry from when she was in the Peace Corps until the 1970s. The book included subjects on herself, and experiences; followed by the rhetoric influenced by the pain and time that she and the Black culture had experienced as they fought against black oppression. The first poem "Me" expressed her feelings of certainty about the path she was choosing as an activist. Emily was certain that her life path was to help her people become well and move into advancement to obtain a better life socially, mentally, and economically. She would reflect on her understanding that every choice taken must be of importance if she were to truly help the most important plight of her life. In her works, Emily affirmed that she never had the demeanor of 'relaxing and just being in 'togetherness' of the hippie movement that was appearing. She felt that she had a more affirmative stance on racial, and social inequality, anything for that matter, but tried not to talk negatively about anybody for their choices and mistakes. Emily always advocated for people to *"just try and do their best and do what is right,"* in their part of any movement for society and humanity, just as Fannie-Mae had taught her.

Once again, for every victory came defeat within the Civil Rights movement, even after the signing of the Civil Rights Act in July 1964. In February 1965, Malcolm X was assassinated in Harlem, New York during a speech given at the Audubon Ballroom by members of the Nation of Islam. His assassination had always been thought of as an FBI infiltration maneuver, or retaliation due to the turmoil he gained with the Honorable Elijah Muhammad as he rose as a vocal figure to what it meant to Black Americans to take on the "fight" for Civil Rights. As mentioned before, Emily had the chance to meet Malcolm X in 1962, in honor of his passing; Emily drafted a poem since she was not available to travel back to the United States. Emily saw the changes that were occurring between time, energy, and rhetoric of younger generations as they became angrier about each occurring grievance. Emily's reflection on

Malcolm X in 2020:

> Malcolm was feared by white people because he brought everyone to one voice, one mind, one result, through organized actions. The worst vision of the American government is an organized and unified front against the oppressor. Especially from people of white America who have dehumanized, disgraced, and disenfranchised since the beginning of the establishment of American democracy. Black people with every reason have the right to be angry when they truly have nothing to lose.

Malcolm X

> Malcolm X, a very together Black man, who challenged life and liberty in the fight for Black people liberation.
> Malcolm X talked to me like the million others he spoke to on the streets, college campuses, lecture rooms, churches and in his travels around the world.
> Malcolm X, I met at Morgan state college. He was a tall, Black thinking proud man and what he projected was beautiful. Black people being aware of their enemy and preparing for survival.
> Malcolm X realized that Black people were not aware of how essential Blackness, Black Power, White power, and togetherness as Black people was so important.
> Malcolm X's message entered too many narrow-minded people's minds, who were not ready at the time, but today we are fortunate because those words are still alive for all those who need a second chance in order to understand tomorrow.
> Malcolm X's reaction to what is considered a Black Revolution is evolving for all those who are willing to fight for the Black liberation.
> Malcolm X's contribution to humanity which will never die is Malcolm X.

Stokely Carmichael

A cry of Anger
A cry of fear
A cry of distrust
A cry of disgust

He stood the test.
With the great trust
He worked and slaved for all of us.

He carried signs.
Down picket lines
Marching miles
Went to jail.
Didn't get no bail.

He no longer
Feels the same.
Got beat proper.
To no avail
He got a plan.
And he's plenty mad.

He's blaming the people.
Of the world for his senseless pain.

FIGURE 31 FLYER OF THE BOOK RELEASE FOR JUST LIKE IT IS, 2008. (COURESTESY OF AYANNA MOORE)

Africa

So much tradition is this land.
Folklore and tales.
Juju, drumming and dancing all night long.

Thick and rich the earth of man,
Dark as night the people walk the land.
Magnificent things passed on for many years.

So much culture is misunderstood outside of this land.

Benin City, 1967

Long History of Pleading

Black people
Long history of pleading for equality with reason.
Black people displeased,
All reasoning gone out to destroy.
The Mans' doing what's pleasing.

Black people ramping and raging,
Treating down walls,
Burning down stores,
looting and stealing

Black people making a change,
Acting strange,
All seem in vain.
Just like a sweepstakes

Benin City, 1966

Third Quarter: 1968-1975

EMILY MOORE THE EDUCATOR 1968-1972

A New York newspaper article entitled *Separate and Unequal In Roosevelt, Long Island: A New York Town's Schools Struggle Against the Toll of Segregation* reviewed Roosevelt's journey as town. Historically, the formerly white-populated Long Island town became the area where real estate brokers sent low-income and Black families to buy and rent homes. The shift changed the way the homes were occupied and tended to as property owners allowed overoccupancy of homes in areas of Long Island, promoting slum-like conditions. In the article, a longtime Roosevelt resident, Diana Coleman described how when the real estate people found out that the professor at Hofstra was a woman who was black, they told her they would " need to find a place where you would feel more comfortable," and they took her to Roosevelt in the 1970s (Powell, 2002). She continued to describe how the stores and commerce died in Roosevelt as white Americans moved to other neighboring towns such as Garden City, Lynbrook, and Rockville Center.

Emily initially joined the Roosevelt School District in 1968 as a physical education teacher at Ulysses Byas Elementary School. [32] As a proud and politically militant Black woman, Emily was the kind of teacher who spoke to children about African American history, civil rights, and the law. As a resident of Roosevelt, Emily would catch her students at Roosevelt Park as she would practice her tennis skills on the weekdays or after school, making her popular and closer to the community and its younger generation. Through the organization of fundraisers and events for the community and youth, Emily was gaining notoriety and popularity among the citizens of Roosevelt.

Emily committed much of her time to supporting Roosevelt youth and other Black youths of Nassau in between her master's studies at Hofstra. As grand as her achievements and results were, her Civil Rights activities made her a hazard to the Board of Education members who were nervous about the attention and influence Emily would bring to the Roosevelt community and student body. It was not unknown of her arrest in Baltimore, or her

---

[32] Renamed in honor of Ulysses Byas, one of the first black Superintendents on Long Island who served for Roosevelt from 1977 to 1978. He led Roosevelt and Hempstead School districts out of major budget crisis (Columbia university, 2012).

encounters with civil rights leaders both dormant and active of various statuses. Reputation of Emily's connections followed her when it came to local, state, and federal law enforcement branches, as they knew of her involvement a Civil Rights as an SNCC organizer overseas. Unfathomed, Emily remained faithful to her plans of helping the Black culture and the youth of Roosevelt. Emily recalled her father giving her a warning about being a new educator but a highly respected and influential activist, "that black stuff isn't going to get you nothing but trouble girl," Emily still agrees after all these years that her father was right, but that never held her back from activism. Marion Moore, Emily's older sister, made a statement about Emily and her involvement as a Civil Rights activist when they were young women.

> Well, Emily and I are like night and day. I did not know all what Emily had done, I did not know all her activities prior to her moment in Morgan. She hid it from the family for a while, until received a newspaper clipping in the mail from a relative or friend that had her in it in Baltimore. I knew that she became more politically active at Morgan State area more than here, I was never so active. The first thing that I took on was politically were things that happened after. I was also on the Roosevelt School Board; I was on it when Emily had first become a teacher for the Roosevelt School District. Of course, she was already outspoken, but the district had decided that she was too progressive for them when it came to fighting for the Black people. I got up the ladder quickly because I did not stir up anything politically. Most of the jobs I had, I was the only Black person, or only Black women in my profession. I went to college, I started at Nassau, no Black people in accounting, went to Hofstra, the same. Something happened where they decided not to give her

tenure. I had told her, that is why she must be wise about her activities.[33]

---

[33] Nassau Community College, Hempstead, New York
Hofstra University, Hempstead, New York

The shooting of Lawrence "Larry" Blaylock

In November 1971, a sixteen-year-old male named Lawrence "Larry" Baylock of Freeport was killed by Nassau County Police after being shot in the back during in a foot pursuit in Roosevelt. It was Thanksgiving week or weekend when Baylock and another assailant were accused of being seen in possession of a stolen car in Lynbrook. The teenaged assailants made it to Roosevelt where the police would catch up to the teenage assailants on Bennett Avenue, prompting Baylock and an unidentified assailant to flee the car. Nassau County police officer Frank Parisi pursued Baylock on foot. Officer Parisi claimed that Baylock eventually made it seem like he was going to draw a gun at one point during the chase, prompting him to shoot at Baylock in response to his gesture. There was no gun reported, and compile controversy that Baylock had been mentally challenged by the neighborhood residents. An investigation took place, the police officer faced trial with the verdict of not guilty. Community residents of Nassau felt that it was not a fair trial because the jury did not "reflect its peers." The verdict was met with angry rhetoric from locals (Policeman cleared in LI Youth's death, 1971). Emily admits to helping the residents of Roosevelt and Freeport organize various meetings to discuss demonstration plans after the incident, but once again none of them ever spoke of choosing rioting and looting.

Ǝxit 22 Southern

FREEPORT 8-9601

Mona Lisa

24 Nassau Rd.

Roosevelt, L. I., N. Y.

CLOSE COVER BEFORE STRIKING MATCH

FIGURE 32 MONA LISA DINER , ONCE LOCATED ON NSSAU ROAD. THE DINER WAS AFFECTED BY THE RIOTS (COURTESY OF EMILY MOORE)

News coverage from *The Washington Post* covered the protest that took place on December 2, 1971. *Over two hundred protesters arrived at the County Executive Building in Mineola demanding the involved police officer be suspended from his job. The protesters made their way inside the Board of Supervisors hearing room. Allen D. Calhoun, a Freeport resident, and a Black Democratic committee member could be heard telling the Nassau County officials,*

It is dangerous to be black and live in Nassau County...that the feeling in the black community was one of anger and despair... you're going to have to tell us just what kind of future a person has in Nassau County (Silver, 1971).

According to Emily, the youth of the neighboring communities of Hempstead and Freeport took the event and the verdict the hardest. Within the small timeframe of Baylock's death and the verdict on the shooting, the youth came together and began to demonstrate, but it turned into a series of lootings in Roosevelt. Emily told what she remembered from that event.

> *What happened was that night, there was a meeting at the youth center in Mansfield, they got mad and wanted to leave and go to the streets! I got a phone call from the men at the center. I told them to stand at the doors, and do not let the kids out! But they did not have any backbone. They let the kids leave. They had a diner on Nassau Road, they broke that window. Somebody knocked a white lady down, and almost killed her. The colored folks just acted crazy.*

Emily and other residents in the area were accused of instructing and/or influencing the group of youth to riot, but the accusations were false.

> *They blamed us for causing the riot. I had helped organize several meetings with various freeport residents to go down to the court houses. But I did not attend any of the demonstrations because I went to Puerto Rico with Dorothy Height! and was still in Puerto Rico by the time the riots came about. when I came back to New York, I was able to get a lot of kids out of jail because their parents did not want to go to court to bail them out, a lot of the parents had their own troubles as well. The kids were in the streets and schools yelling, 'off the PIGS, PIGS this, PIGS that,' I told them that that was not going to get them the results they were seeking. We decided to*

*give the children a mock trial. We got the kids **together**, we picked who would be the judge, the jury, then we practiced, and then we held the mock trial, we invited everyone, even some Nassau Counties police officers came, we even had little pamphlets. They told us that they had done a fantastic job.*

Long Island Newsday newspaper article:

FIGURE 33 NEWSDAY LONG ISLAND COVERAGE OF MOCK TRIAL DONE BY STUDENTS OF ROOSEVELT. (NEWSDAY LONG ISLAND, 1972)

Roosevelt – twelve days after a Nassau County grand jury refused to indict police officer Frank Parisi in the fatal shooting here of 16-year-old Larry Blaylock, an all-black "people's tribunal" found the Nassau County patrolman "guilty of first-degree murder." The hour-long mock trial in the Roosevelt Youth Center was conducted by two dozen Black teenagers and young adults complete with a judge, 12-man jury, prosecutor and two defense attorneys who argues that the unarmed Freeport youth "signed his own death warrant when he turned as if to shoot" Parisi. There was no stand-in for the white 24-year-old Nassau County Patrolman. The dead youth's mother sat silently in the first row but declined to comment on the verdict. "We are talking to the community, no to the whites. The whites will not listen," said the Rev. Robert C. Chapman, a Roosevelt resident who is executive director of the department of social justice of the National Council of Churches. While the jury deliberated, the Rev. Mr. Chapman told the one hundred spectators that the killing of Blaylock, who was mentally [challenged], represented, "An American kind of Justice that has demanded a life for a car." According to police accounts Baylock was a passenger

November 27, in a stolen auto that police chased for six miles after, police say, the driver tried to run down a Lynbrook village policeman. The auto stopped in Roosevelt, police said, Parisi chased Blaylock on foot and shot him once when he believed Blaylock was wheeling to shoot. The driver of the car has not been apprehended. A Nassau grand jury composed of twenty-two whites and one black has decided not to indict Parsi. The teenagers and adults and children who had come to watch the tribunal sat quietly through the proceedings. But there was applause as the prosecutor, a young man who identified himself only as "Brother David," summed up his case with the commend, "We do not need mad dogs running amok in our community under the name of 'law and order.' We are not dogs. We will not be treated as dogs." The tribunal gave Parisi an undefined "sentence" that it said would be carried out at "the peoples convenience. "It's good for the community, for community spirit," a Black teenager said after the trial. Another youth said, "It is a start. It will not stop here!

Around this time, Emily recalls being brought in for questioning about her civil rights activities, travels abroad, and connectivity to the BPP from the FBI. They also asked her about her connectivity with the youth, and adults of the Black communities, seeking information. Emily told the investigators, "*I am not here to do your job. I am here to make the kids better than I am.*" Emily further explained that she was not involved in the organizing of any riots associated with the Larry Baylock case. After all, why would she promote violence in the black youth? A group of people whose lives she has dedicated her time to, to bring difference and positive change within her community. Fortunately, Emily had an alibi being that around the time of the riots, Emily was invited to the country

Puerto Rico by her friend Prathia Hall Wynn, (1940-2002). [34] Wynn

moved to Roosevelt in the 1960s, and during that time she ran for

the Board of Education for Roosevelt. According to Emily, the

students of Roosevelt were invited to Puerto Rico by Dorothy

Height. Emily was asked to chaperone the students for the week

that they were there. They left before the demonstrations advanced.

Dr. Dorothy Height was a prominent Civil Rights and Women's

Rights activist who primarily worked in the effort towards the

betterment of Black American women and children through

organizing various programs. Here is what Emily said in reflection on

her time with Dr. Height.

> *Dr. Height was a visionary; she brought all the staff and children to Puerto Rico too! I supervised the students for the whole week. The trip was to provide Black students with experiences that many Black children could not afford. We were there for a whole week, at the end of the week the children put on an hour-long presentation, they sang young black and gifted, told some history, and a girl did poetry and read from a book she kept. Some children recited things, and they did great. During the trip, Dr. Height asked me to be a lifetime member of the National Council of Negro Women (NCNW), and I accepted the offer That is my story in 1971! (Emily Moore)*

---

[34] Wynn was a womanist, theologian, ethicist, and civil rights activist who has been credited with being a key inspiration for Martin Luther King Jr.'s 1963 "I Have a Dream Speech." (Samuel Momodu, 2020)

FIGURE 34 LIFETIME MEMBERSHIP CERTIFICATE TO THE NATIONAL COUNCIL OF NEGRO WOMEN. (COURSTESY OF AYANNA MOORE)

Emily recalled another moment she and Dr. Height had together,

> *We went to look at a building to rent to run a program or have an event in. We went to a nice building, but the white man acted like we would not be able to afford a place like that when he told us it would be $5,000 dollars. We left the room laughing because we had exactly $5,000 in our pocketbooks.*

PHOTO 58 L TO RI: WY TEE , DOROTHY HEIGHT, AND EMILY. 2000'S. (COURTESY OF EMILY MOORE)

Emily mentioned that she would always make sure to give Dr. Height a hug when she would run into her during various conferences with NCNW and other organizations. Dr. Dorothy Height passed away in 2010.

FIGURE 35 NEWSDAY COVERAGE ABOUT EMILY'S TERMINATION (ALEXANDER, 1972)

After various battles with the Roosevelt Board of Education, on May 18, 1971, *Long Island Newsday* labeled Emily as a 'Firebrand', as they covered the various reasons for tenure denial, which included her vigorous Civil Rights involvement. For 60 years, Emily had been no stranger to Long Island publications, but as one of the first news coverages about Emily, it seemed as if the paper was trying to label her as a troubled adult who brought instability, and an uncertain influence over youth. In the article, it was said that Emily was known as a "problem child" as an adolescent growing up in Freeport by her peers and other Freeport locals. There was also a nudge at her political activism, which she had been involved in from an early age as if being vocal for racial equality was absurd at any age. For Emily, it did not matter what was said in publications as the position she took in life was more important than any ridicule. Emily felt she was given her mission by God to educate young people. As a vocal person, Emily knew that she would put herself and others in difficult and frustrating positions as she looked to bring differences to Roosevelt School District, beginning with the staff and their mannerisms of teaching the black youth, which did not make her an immediate popular figure among teachers and staff.

Newsday: The Long Island Newspaper

Ousted 'Firebrand' Strikes Sparks
By Micheal Alexander
May 18, 1972

Roosevelt – When Emily Moore was growing up in Freeport, she was called a problem child. As a civil rights advocate marching on a picket line in Glen Burnie, Md., she was thrown in jail. Ans during the controversy that led to her ouster as a teacher by the Roosevelt School Board, she was labeled a firebrand.

"People have branded me all my life," the former physical education teacher said recently. "But I like to think of myself as an educator and a Black woman involved in a people's struggle for human rights."

Today, the 30-year-old activist is busily involving herself in new roles and new identities. Since being denied tenure as a teacher, she was elected as a delegate to the Black Caucus national convention in Gary, Ind., she outpolled all her opponents to win on of ten seats on a local anti-poverty board, and she has launched a campaign for a school board position.

Now that she is working as a counselor at the Roosevelt Youth Center and the Ujamaa Academy in Hempstead, Miss Moore's view of her ouster has mellowed, and she speaks easily about the events leading up to it. "I ran into trouble with the board on many levels," she said in an interview at the youth center. "I thought the programs in school were stifling and the teachers were not working in the best interest of the students or the community, I challenged them on that and for the contradictions that I saw. What it said and did was not just to be badgering but for some understanding, clarification and for some correctness."

Last May, her activities led the Roosevelt school board to charge her with insubordination, absenting herself from school without permission, criticizing her colleagues and habitual lateness. Miss Moore's appeal to the state education commissioner charging that the board had denied her tenure solely because of her political activities was denied.

Her efforts have brought her wide support among Black people in the Freeport and Roosevelt areas. During the hearings on her ouster, young blacks demonstrated on her behalf and many adults signed petitions arguing for her reinstatement. "She had always been a doer." Ralph Wynn, a Roosevelt resident, and chairman of Nassau's delegates to the black convention said. "By no means is she one to sit back without trying to work for a solution. She is certainly one of the most energetic and concerned persons in this community. What she has accomplished since being fired is a mandate from the people...."

Born in East Meadow to what she describes as "hard-working, struggling, poor parents," Miss Moore grew up in Freeport and attended school there.

A former Peace Corps worker, she has travelled throughout Europe and Many African countries. But today, she says she is basically a homebody. She lives with her mother in Roosevelt and spends most of her free time at home reading books on Black history and writing poetry "whenever the urge hits me."

Her love for the community, she says, goes hand in hand with her hope for its youth. "I know what it is like to be known as a problem child and be held back in school because teachers think you can't learn," she said. I know because these same things happened to me. So, I try to instill in them that they can make it. "

She says that, as an example to youth, she has stopped drinking liquor and smoking. "The young people are our future, and we need their best," she said.

But she is not without critics. Some claim that she is seeking a school board spot merely to feed her ego and "win a popularity contest." One resident who declined to give her name said she though Miss Moore was running for the board to get back at the school system for her ouster.

She has an answer: "Education is too dear an issue not to be involved in it. A personal vendetta is not my thing. When I open my mouth, I knew the price of a job. It hurt to be denied the right to teach in a community I practically grew up in. But Roosevelt is a community of the future. It needs help from every resident living here. It is going to take time, but we have to maintain the struggle if the struggle is to ever end." (Alexander, 1972)

Since the 1970s, *Long Island Newsdayr* articles have served as the outlet that publicly marked the beginning of her journey towards educational betterment and quality for the Black people of Long Island. In various instances, Emily has been quoted about the underserving of Black young people in education and supporting the fight against injustices locally and abroad. No matter the words, Emily knew and felt the Black people of her community felt that she was doing her job for the youth, and that could not be taken away from her. Outside of Education, Emily served as a delegate for the Black Caucus of New York and served on the Anti-Poverty Board of Nassau County. As far as Emily was concerned, she was doing the very best that she could for her people by becoming involved politically and financially for her people. As she continued to grow as a champion for her people, she and her peers knew that the power dynamics of Long Island did not favor it. In response to the article Emily said, *"People have been branding me my whole life, but I like to think of myself as an educator, and a black woman involved in the people's struggle for human rights."*

Despite community outreach and petition, the Roosevelt School District officially terminated Emily from her position as a physical education teacher in 1972. Various residents and students during this time could attest that the school board felt that their positions were threatened by Emily's presence and influence due to her strong popularity, militancy and unapologetic activism and demeanor. Emily denied her accusations of being a major influence because she knew the black community of Long Island was already on the rise of being more awakened to suppressing systematic oppression. Emily recalled that MLK visited Rev. Dr. Arthur L. Mackey, Sr. Church on Frederick Avenue, months before he was assassinated. Overall, Emily explained,

> *They [the district] wanted yes ma'am and yes sir type of people, especially when it came to the people of my skin color. I was not*

that type of person; I was never that type of person. I also understood that there was a deeper awakening amongst the younger generations that could go either way, so I became a force for them in chance for a better education and future.

The Community Prevails

The local communities came together for Emily and formed a committee that supported her reinstatement as an educator with the Roosevelt School District. The committee wrote a letter on her behalf and passed it out around Roosevelt. The letter read:

> *Can we afford to lose a teacher with these credentials? Can we afford to allow this extremely qualified Black Woman to be another victim of this system? Remember, if we cannot protect Black women in our own community, then we can forget any ideas we may have of our children ever being successful in this county -- a county that blacks have been a key factor in building.*

Roosevelt graduate, Historian, and Colgate University alumni, the late Sheldon Parrish published a book about Roosevelt's history entitled 'One Square Mile' in 2009. In the book, there is a chapter called *Stars and Stories*, which includes a reflection on the impact Emily had on the Roosevelt student body and community during this time of termination. According to Parrish, residents of the Roosevelt community and student body highly regarded her as an endearing champion of proper education ethics and techniques of the Black

youth of Nassau County, especially Roosevelt. He began this

segment on Emily revealing the time he beat Roosevelt native and

National Basketball Association Hall of Famer Julius "Dr. J" Irving in

a game of tennis at Roosevelt Park. Parrish considered himself one

of Emily's protégés and was excited to see Dr. J heading toward the

tennis courts instead of the basketball courts. It is evident that Irving

was not the best tennis player, as he was a professional hall of fame

basketball player, it is quite clear, but Dr. J must have learned for a

brief time with the Junior Alliance Tennis youth, or through physical

education classes as a Roosevelt student. But it was known, anyone

who touched a tennis racquet in Roosevelt, was taught by Emily

Moore.

> *... I spoke about a middle school experience that caused me to have to walk out of class without permission from the teacher. I was in Mrs. Levenbrown's class in room 206. She was a good teacher and usually quite inept at maintaining her class, but this was a different kind of day. See the murder of Dr. Martin Luther King Jr. had such an effect on mobilizing people until the people who killed him probably wished they hadn't and just harassed him the rest of his life.*
>
> *It was the early seventies now and the major white flight had taken place. Blacks were the majority race in town and for a lot of people that was a new unfamiliar place. There was a woman from the Freeport/Roosevelt area who had gone to Morgan State University and was party to a bunch of counter protest. Then upon graduation, went on to the Peace Corps to help people in underdeveloped counties. She was now on staff at the Roosevelt Junior Senior High School.*

During a time when we were in the process of fighting for the simple things, Emily Moore was an empowering student to fight the good fight because she felt quite frankly, "no struggle, No peace." The school board fired Ms. Moore because the all-white school board believed she was a threat to the students. But like Martin, they should have let her be. So, when that door of classroom 206 burst open that day, it was this kind of anxiety that embraced the thrust. I hope she would not mind no but Shereva Scott said to everyone in the class to get up and get in the line with the group behind her. Poor Mrs. Levenbrown tried to counter with "whoever gets out of their seats will get a phone call home tonight. Now under normal situations that would have been quite enough to deter us but then Shereva recanted, "If you don't come out, we will come in and get you." Something about how she said that made me brush by Mrs. Levenbrown and head for the door. I decided that I would take my chances home. When I got outside the classroom and saw how long the line was, I was even more impressed with my decision…

I heard that some males jumped that big counter in the main office and went up to the principal Mr. Here forth, and that all the white students had been called in the Nurses Office until they could be escorted out. Now this is sort of what shock jock Howard Stern talks about he got out of town before this event. I believe. I guess the intensity had been building because a few weeks earlier I was sitting in the junior high cafeteria and a fella; that I will call Big Brother Harrison was sitting on the cafeteria table and a teacher I shall name Mrs. Parks asked him to get off the table. Well, 'Big Brother, a member of a big family with certain reputation did not like Mrs. Parks tone. He asked, "Who are you talking to? Mr. Parks responded, "You, Boy!!!" …. If you count the dots I just typed, in less time, Big Brother was over to the other side of the table where Mr. Parks stood and punched him in the mouth. I do not know who was more shocked me or Mr. Parks. As people rushed in to observe the situation, I backed out because I didn't want to be in the position of "witness", but the riot changed the whole mind set of the district. More Black teachers were hired do the district came closer to mirroring the look of its students. Black history courses were implemented. The students even won the privilege of a "smoking lounge" for the "seniors." A couple of years later Ms. Moore did get her job back and the relocation of the Council Administration eliminated the space where the smoking lounge was located. But if I may preface the courses on Black History, I would have to release my disappointment nationally to the way our leaders have tried to make our history as important as mainstream societies' history. As a child, I remember the great efforts fought in order to have black history courses taught in public school. There was a need for our people to further out knowledge beyond a quick study of reformers, inventors, and sports figures as well as a need to educate society.

Parrish ends his reflection on what the introduction of Black History to schools meant for the Black community, and how it has changed due to commercialization. In the same statement, he credits Emily for never losing sight for black excellence in Roosevelt.

> The fight was basically won. Then we fought to make the month of February, "Black History month. Well society was smart enough to figure it out that they count mount some bogus celebration during February and do away with the courses. No disrespect to Stevie Wonder, we supplied great efforts towards honoring Dr. Martin Luther King Jr. s' birthday as a national holiday. Now the media and the whole county publicly honors one day. I grew up in a proud "Black" town who has celebrated a lot of "Black" history months but the last few celebrated in this predominately "Black town/school district was short of embarrassing. The most challenging – of all was recently under a Hispanic principle., the majority holiday (Black History Month) was basically ignored or given symbolic reverence. A short time late, during a Hispanic celebration, a stringed quartet traveled the building all day playing nothing but Spanish folk music. This was in 2003 but our past is filled with these kinds of events.
>
> I must tell you though; few people in this town fight a fight with such – determination as Ms. Moore. She has even fought with Rev. Al. Sharpton and others across the state and nation. Budget votes are her specialty. When Coretta Scott king passed, she drove all the way to Atlanta because she felt that it was her responsibility to be there.
>
> Ms. Moore has been a mentor and Tennis coach in the community for 40 years. Her summer program has existed in Roosevelt Park (Rev Mackey), many have gone on to do great things with their lives. I was one of Ms. Moore's first tennis students. (Parrish, 2009)

In 2016, Parrish spoke to the Freeport Leader newspaper about the disparities that Roosevelt had encountered and persevered through, as it seemed that curriculum and teachers that were good for the students at Roosevelt High School were taken

away from them, including Emily Moore.

In 1972, Sheldon Parrish was sitting in his eighth-grade social studies class at then-Roosevelt Senior-Junior High School when he heard a low hum coming from the hallway. As he listened closely, he could make out a crowd rushing to the classroom door, and they were singing a strange song, "I got the feeling, I got the Feeling, I got the feeling there ain't gonna be no Sh- like that."

The door burst open, and a high school girl ordered the students out. Despite threats by the teacher, Mrs. Levenbrown, to call parents, the class stepped into the hallway to find a sea of Black students singing together. Downstairs, some of the high school students confronted the principal in his office, locking the door behind them. (Boyd, 2016)

The riot occurred after local woman Emily Moore was denied a position in the district because of her "troublemaking" activities – participating in the March on Washington for Jobs and Freedom in 1963, at which the Rev. Dr. Martin Luther King Jr. gave his "I have a dream" speech, and lunch counter protest, Parrish said. It was not the beginning of racial conflict in Roosevelt, but rather one of many consequences of tragic history of prejudice and neglect.

Yet, despite such a disadvantage past, the Roosevelt community has persevered, and is growing stronger – and more diverse— every day.

Don E. Crummell: "My Coach before I was Coach."

Don E. Crummell would find himself protesting for the future of Roosevelt once again; Not for class integration, but representation.[35] Crummell was now a junior at Roosevelt High School, and like most students in Roosevelt, he knew who Emily was and what she had done for her students of Roosevelt District. Crummell was a part of the student-led demonstrations that occurred on Emily's behalf. This is Crummell's statement:

> I remember it like it was yesterday, I was a young Black teenager looking to find my way in the Roosevelt school district. The district that at the time was 90% African American with a staff that did not reflect or understand other Black students as a collective. As a young kid, Dr. Moore was a Physical Education teacher who we all flocked to ask the questions of Why? Moreover, how can we fix it? Because of her popularity for whatever reason, the district administration felt threaten. This is where I learned what the term tenure meant. As a young student we just understood that Dr. E. Moore was being denied "tenure" meaning she would lose her job.
>
> The students were not having it and we boycotted classes, demanding that they reinstated her. Being threatened that we would all be suspended if we did not go back to class, we organized. With the guidance of the now Dr. Harry Mathews, we organized a silent March throughout the building for 3 hours, you could hear a pin drop it was so quiet. Many of us at our homes were facing another kind of pressure from our parents asking why we were doing this, some understood but many did not.

---

[35] Crummell, Don E, Lifetime Roosevelt Resident. Roosevelt School district retiree. Served as attendance and master scheduler, and coach for Girls Varsity Basketball and Softball for over 30 years. Lifetime friend of Emily.

Coach Don Crummell on Emily Moore:

The moral of this story is that Dr. Moore has always taught us not to be afraid to stand up to anything if you believe in the cause. I live my life every day for students under this motto. Now we have come full circle, this is the same women who the Roosevelt School district did not want to give tenure, she has had a marvelous teaching career and is a viable member of that same Roosevelt School board.

PHOTO 59 EMILY AND DON, 2010S

Dr. Seretta McKnight: "She had our respect."

Lifetime Roosevelt Resident and former Tennis student Rev. Dr. Seretta McKnight recalled the protest that took place in Roosevelt when Emily had been terminated. This is what she had to say about how the community respected Emily, what she stood for, and how she stood for it.

> *Aretha Franklin gave us 'Respect' and James Brown gave us our anthem 'Say It Loud, I'm Black and I'm proud'... and we did. This struggle did not miss our one square mile hamlet of Roosevelt. We even had our very own Angela Davis (inclusive of the big afro) in the person of Roosevelt resident, Ms. Emily Moore: activist; educator, physical education teacher; Founder; a lover of Black folks and children. Her mantra: "a Luta continuum – the Struggle Continues;" "build a base;" and "tell your stories' still resonates today. Emily hails from a large, loving family. My parents knew her parents well and they knew Emily, her work, and her commitment to make the world better. They were her greatest supporters. I remember my dad standing up for her when the school district went to fire her...our Angela Davis. Yet, she was the one they called to diffuse our student protests and unrest, when the administration could not. Emily had that type of influence with the students because she had our respect.*

The Hot Seat: Roosevelt School Board

After her termination, Emily sought a seat on the Roosevelt District school board. The Long Island Newsday wrote an article that announced her running. Emily did not win the election and was faced with strong opposition. *"All these people, Mr. Charlie, big men, powerful men, tried to stop me from running. Tried to intimidate me! The nerve of those men! But I did not let them stop me!"* said in reflection. Emily felt that the district simply was not ready for a Black woman such as Emily to be the face of anything, a woman ahead of her time. Others felt that Emily was trying to feed her ego, but Emily is far from egotistic, as for Emily, she has always expressed that the ego should not exist when it comes to the education and welfare of children and growing young adults.

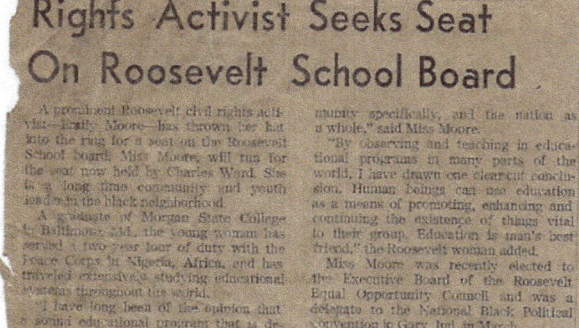

FIGURE 36 UNIDENTIFIED NEWSCLIPPING ABOUT EMILY;S RUN FOR SCHOOL BOARD. (LONG ISLAND NEWSDAY)

The Article reads:

A prominent Roosevelt Civil Rights activist -- Emily Moore -- has thrown her hat into the ring for a seat at the Roosevelt School board. Miss. Moore will run for the seat now held by Charles Ward. She is a long-time community and youth leader in the Black neighborhood.

A graduate of Morgan State College in Baltimore, Md. the young woman has served a two-year tour of duty with the Peace Corps in Nigeria, Africa and has traveled extensively, studying educational systems throughout the world.

"I have long been of the opinion that a sound educational program that is designed to meet the unique needs of today's youth is the only solution to the many problems now facing the Roosevelt Community specifically, and the nation as a whole," said Miss. Moore.

"By observing and teaching in educational programs in many parts of the world, I have drawn on clear cut conclusions. Human beings can use education as a means of promoting, enhancing, and continuing the existence of things vital to their group. Education is man's best friend," the Roosevelt woman added.

Miss. Moore was recently elected to the Executive Board of the Roosevelt Equal Opportunity Council and was a delegate to the National Black Political convention in Gary, Ind. in March. She is currently studying for a master's degree in Counselor Education in Hofstra University Hempstead.

During all of this, Emily earned her Master of Science in education and counseling degree from Hofstra University in 1972.

The following is a *New York Times* newspaper article dated to 1972:

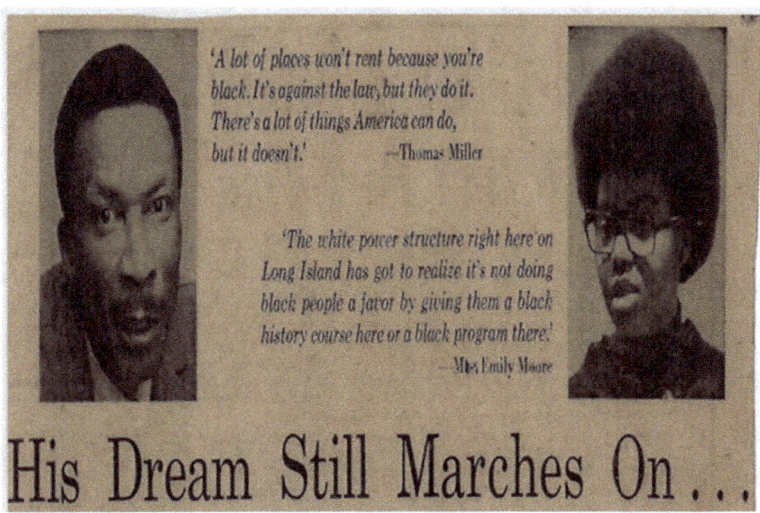

'A lot of places won't rent because you're black. It's against the law, but they do it. There's a lot of things America can do, but it doesn't.' —Thomas Miller

'The white power structure right here on Long Island has got to realize it's not doing black people a favor by giving them a black history course here or a black program there.' —Mrs Emily Moore

His Dream Still Marches On...

FIGURE 37 NEWSDAY CLIPPING ABOUT EMILYS VIEWS ON WHITE POWER STRUCTURES IN LONG ISLAND (COURTESY OF LONG ISLAND NEWSDAY).

Since Mr. Galloway (superintendent) took over, there have been improvements in the schools. For example, reading scores have risen by about ten percent, he said. But, according to Emily Moore, who works with the Target Area Youth Board, and lives in the community, residents still 'do not see that they are getting value for their money—they are paying top dollar and getting second-rate value.

Mrs. Emily Moore shares neither the Rev. Dr. King's prayerful optimism, nor his belief in underlying goodness in white America. She foresees the whirlwind, "As far as I'm concerned, we're not getting anywhere in racist America," she said, "Though things may be better by degrees, she said, she shares a rage with other young blacks over what that regard as oppression of young black leaders. There are targets of resentment, among the police. "They don't treat us like human beings. They don't really understand." The government: "The white power structure here on Long Island has got to realize it's not doing Black people a favor by giving them a Black history course here or a black program there." Mrs. Moore, of Roosevelt, a junior high school teacher, sees the whirlwind intensifying. "The kids no are so wide awake, so aware with reference to themselves. America is in trouble because these kids are going to "do their thing. (unknown, Outlook is Bleak in Roosevelt, 1972)

This is a letter in response to her loss of the School Board Election June 14, 1972

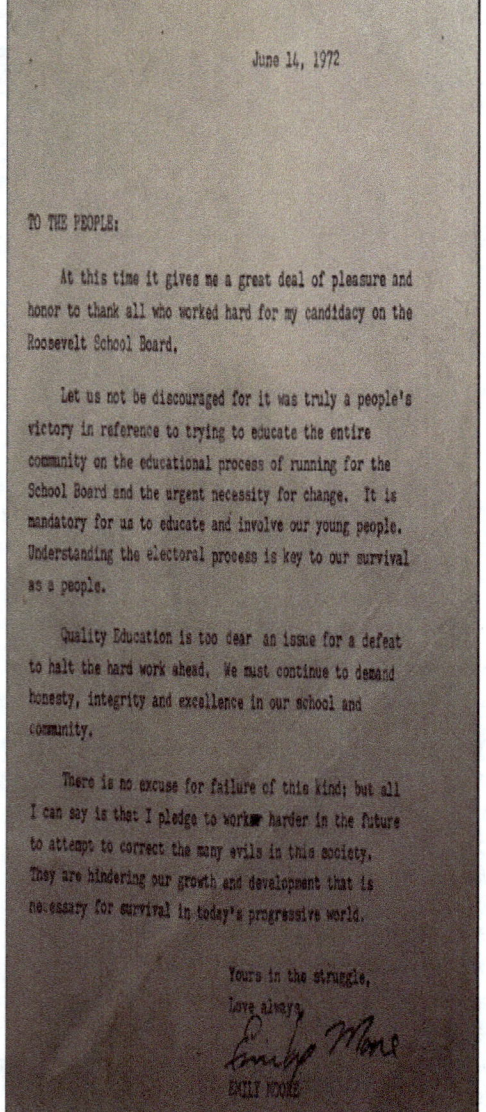

June 14, 1972

TO THE PEOPLE:

At this time it gives me a great deal of pleasure and honor to thank all who worked hard for my candidacy on the Roosevelt School Board.

Let us not be discouraged for it was truly a people's victory in reference to trying to educate the entire community on the educational process of running for the School Board and the urgent necessity for change. It is mandatory for us to educate and involve our young people. Understanding the electoral process is key to our survival as a people.

Quality Education is too dear an issue for a defeat to halt the hard work ahead. We must continue to demand honesty, integrity and excellence in our school and community.

There is no excuse for failure of this kind; but all I can say is that I pledge to work harder in the future to attempt to correct the many evils in this society. They are hindering our growth and development that is necessary for survival in today's progressive world.

Yours in the struggle,
Love always,

Emily Moore

EMILY MOORE

To the people:

At this time, it gives me a great deal of pleasure and honor to thank all who worked hard for my candidacy on the Roosevelt School Board.

Let us not be discouraged for it was truly a people's victory in reference to trying to educate the entire community on the educational process of running for the school board and the urgent necessity for change, it is mandatory for us to educate and involve our young people. Understanding the electoral process is key to our survival as a people.

Quality education is too dear and issue for a defeat to halt the hard work ahead. We must continue to demand honest, integrity, and excellence in our school and community.

There is no excuse for failure of this kind; but all I can say is that I pledge to work harder in the future to attempt to correct the many evils in this society. They are hindering our growth and development that is necessary for survival in today's progressive world."

FIGURE 38 LETTER TO THE COMMUNITY(COURTESY OF EMILY MOORE)

In the 1970s, Emily served as the president of the Roosevelt Economic Opportunity Center, the building sits and remains on the property line between Freeport and Roosevelt on Babylon Turnpike. This afforded Emily broad connections between the youth and adults of neighboring towns through her fundraising, programs, events, civil rights, and general outreach. Emily also was a staunch supporter of the Roosevelt Youth Center as she taught tennis and physical education everywhere she could in Roosevelt. Emily was known for her fundraising organizing skills and success for the children, the community, and her tennis program simultaneously. Emily wrote of the issues that were occurring and the efforts needed to keep the Roosevelt E.O.C running as it was on the brink of controversy for reasons before her arrival. The topics were as follows:

Recruitment Problems

I think it is germane to interject at this point some of the problems trying to recruit organizational and institutional representation. Civic groups, churches, educational institutions all appeared to be hesitant about accepting seats designed for them on the Board because of the unpleasant controversial history of the Roosevelt E.O.C.

No Staff Support

At this time constant board meetings were taking place without the support of paid staff of the Roosevelt E.O.C. As a matter of fact, the Roosevelt E.O.C office was still closed. The Board of Directors held meetings in the solarium of the Cooperative Service Center. A review of this period will show that the attendance of Board Members under the pressure of meeting once weekly began to show and as a direct result attendance decreased according. We did not have the necessary support during this phase in the form of having access to paper, phone, and supplies. We had to provide much of this material from our pockets in order to conduct Board business.

Training Required

Another point that ought to be made is that the elective board members had no prior experience in conducting business affairs as a group under strict rules, procedures, and guidelines. We all had to be instructed as to what the guidelines are under which this agency operates.

Staff Hired

In the mid part of June, the office of the Roosevelt E.O.C reopened, a community organizer, an assistant community organizer, and a field secretary were put on staff in order to generate support in the Roosevelt community for the E. O. C Board of Directors. Activities in support for its meetings had to be publicized for the newly reconstructed and reorganized Board of Directors. I acknowledge fully that this was a most difficult period but a period in which all organizations have to go through in order to grow and develop. In essence this is a brief synopsis of the first stage in the development of the Board of Directors of the Roosevelt E.O.C.

Second Stage of Board Development

The reason why I can separate these periods as Chairman of the Board into two stages is that if we look at the records of attendance, of quorums, of productive activities the record (minutes) indicates that there are indeed two stages that we can denote our progress by the concern and involvement of the Board and even the community during the second stage by their attendance at our regular schedule meetings. Then the staff gave us support in our activity by

Informing the community of our activity, publicizing by flyers, explaining our progress, in person, to civic, churches, and to other interested groups and individuals which helped us immensely during the second stage but the lack of adequate communication with the community during the first stage left us really on our own on getting information out to the community.

Attitudinal Changes

During the present stage which I consider the second stages there has been a definite change in the attitude of the residents in this community towards the E.O.C. For example, the residents approach us now to become members of the board. Residents in an increasingly larger number attended our board meetings. The residents are truly interested in what we the Board of Directors are doing for them in order to serve the needs of the people in this community. Certain activities were planned, activities such as food baskets for Thanksgiving for senior citizens and needy families were gotten together.

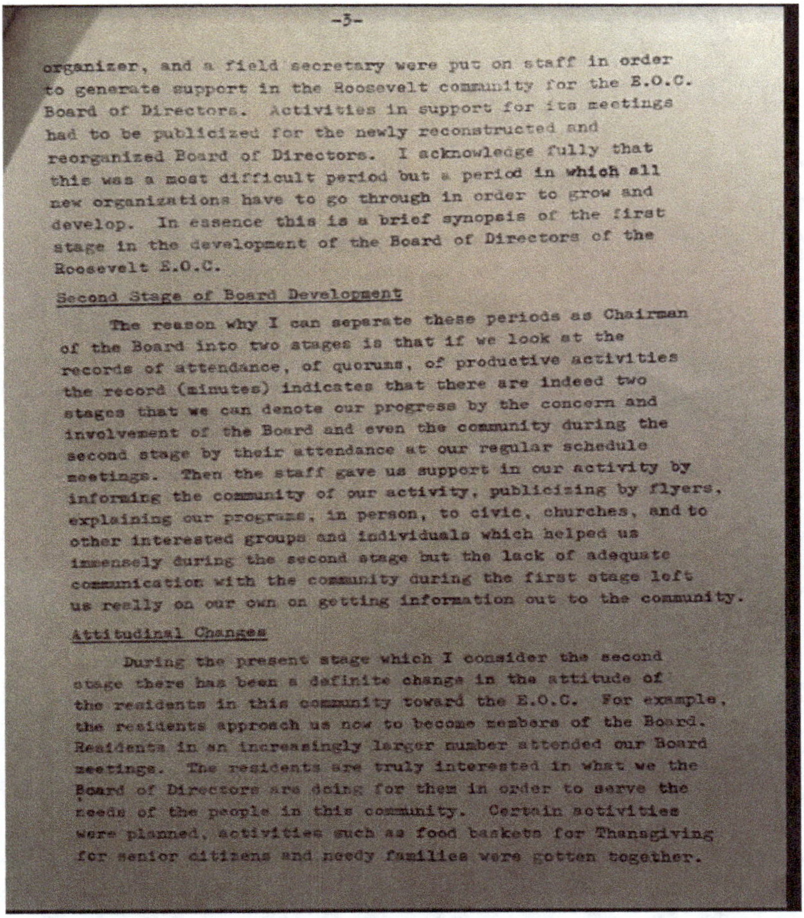

FIGURE 39 DOCUMENTS COMPOSED ABOUT WHAT THE EOC NEEDS IN ORDER TO THRIVE IN COMMUNITY ACTIVISM AND OUTREACH. (COURTESY OF EMILY MOORE)

In the present, Emily displays the same sentiments of the Roosevelt Community when it comes to the organization of community and educative activism that she had over 50 years ago. As a lifetime resident of Nassau County, Emily has been on various committees and has seen failure due to the lack of motion of other members, the organization, and relations to the communities they served. Emily also expressed that the residents on both sides of the table felt that things would be handed to them and the children, *"Expecting an award after every accomplishment, but life does not just work like that. To receive, you must give. Even if it is in the smallest of ways, no good thing is immediate "*

PHOTO 60 YOUTH FROM THE ROOSEVELT YOUTH CENTER, 1970S. (COURTESY OF EMILY MOORE)

UNAPOLOGETICALLY BLACK

In 1971, Emily decided to visit Oakland, California to learn and see the ideologies and practices of the BPP and its movement. While in Oakland, Emily was able to study the BPP and watched them implement their Ten Point Program, the basis of their founding. Emily was finally able to become a witness to the various stories and photos she had seen as BPP delivered thousands of breakfasts, lunches, and dinners to people of all creeds within low-income communities between Oakland and San Francisco. Emily was never ashamed of her interaction with the Black Panther party and Davis because she learned more about creating an organized effort to better her people near and far. Emily viewed the Black Panther Party as the most organized and effective Civil Rights social party within the United States after the series of demonstrations organized by the various Civil Rights organizations.

During various trips, Emily would become acquainted with Angela Davis, a native of Birmingham, Alabama with ties to New York, accused of conspiracy and kidnapping in the state of California since 1970. U.S. President Ronald Reagan, who was the Governor of California at that time, had her fired from her position as a philosophy professor at the University of California-Los Angeles because of her political affiliation as an open Communist Party member (George, 2020). Besides the fight for racial equality on the home front, the United States was still fighting against communism across the world. Davis faced accusations of involvement in the arranged escape of her brother from police custody. Predominantly because she was widely known because of her speeches against mass incarceration. Subsequently, she was also connected to a police murder case because her lover at the time took her gun for the event.

Davis's arrest sparked the Free Angela Movement in the United States in support of her court case, during a time when many of her counterparts were being killed and sent to jail for their involvement with BPP (George, 2020). Emily had not joined the BBP during her time with the members, but she decided that back on Long Island, she would help organize the Free Angela Movement headquarters to raise funds for Davis's legal fees. Emily went to the trial of Angela Davis, placing herself in the courthouse the day she was set free on June 4, 1972. After the trial, Emily speaks of Angela

Davis and her at a BBP member's home, where they ate a spaghetti dinner. Not too long after her time with BPP, Emily was questioned by the FBI again, to no avail. Emily disliked the Federal Bureau of Investigation under the leadership of Edgar Hoover, as investigations infiltrated and slowly violently killed away the leaders of the Black Panther Party and the Civil Rights Movement in the name of conserving white supremacy.

People's Petition Demanding Bail for Angela Davis

To: The Honorable Judges of the Superior Courts for the State of California
Mr. Carle Hoppe, Clerk, Superior Court, Marin County.

We, the undersigned, do hereby petition for the release of Angela Y. Davis on reasonable bail pending trial.

Miss. Davis is presumed to be innocent of all charges, and she has publicly declared her innocence in court. She has no criminal record, she has established roots in the community, and she has many offers of employment. Thus, she meets the legal criteria for bail.

Given these facts, we conclude that Miss. Davis has been deprived of a bail hearing since her capture more than six months ago because she is a Black woman, a member of the communist party, and an outspoken advocate for the rights of prison inmates and political prisoners. These do not constitute permissible grounds for denial of bail. On the contrary, it would be both unconstitutional and illegal to deny her bail for these reasons.

We submit, finally, that it is the grossest kind of denial of equal protection under the law when Miss. Davis is held under punitive conditions of detention while awaiting trial, and Lieutenant William Calley, a felon convicted of the premeditated murder of more than a score of Vietnamese civilians, is released to his own quarters while appealing that conviction. This, we repeat, is gross denial of equal protection under law, and a clear indication that Miss. Davis's prosecution is purely political.

Copies to:

Albert Harris, Deputy Attorney General, State of California
Evelle Younger, Attorney General, State of California
Hon. Ronald Regan, Governor, State of California
Hon. Richard Nixon, President, U.S.A
Hon. U Thant, Secretary General, United Nations

People's Petition Demanding Bail For Angela Davis

To: The Honorable Judges of the Superior Courts
for the State of California
Mr. Carl Hoppe, Clerk, Superior Court, Marin County

We, the undersigned, do hereby petition for the release of Angela Y. Davis on reasonable bail pending trial.

Miss Davis is presumed to be innocent of all charges, and she has publicly declared her innocence in court. She has no criminal record, she has established roots in the community, and she has many offers of employment. Thus, she meets the legal criteria for bail.

Given these facts, we conclude that Miss Davis has been deprived of a bail hearing since her capture more than six months ago because she is a Black woman, a member of the Communist Party, and an outspoken advocate of rights of prison inmates and political prisoners. These do not constitute permissable grounds for denial of bail. On the contrary, it would be both unconstitutional and illegal to deny her bail for these reasons.

We submit, finally, that it is the grossest kind of denial of equal protection under the law when Miss Davis is held under punitive conditions of detention while awaiting trial, and Lieutenant William Calley, a felon convicted of the premeditated murder of more than a score of Vietnamese civilians, is released to his own quarters while appealing that conviction. This, we repeat, is a gross denial of equal protection under law, and a clear indication that Miss Davis' prosecution is purely political.

THEREFORE, we demand the immediate release of Angela Davis on reasonable bail.

June 14, 2972

To the People,

At this time, it gives me a great deal of pleasure and honor to thank all who worked hard for my candidacy on the Roosevelt School Board.

Let us not be discouraged for it was truly a people's victory in reference to trying to educate the entire community on the educational process of running for the School Board and the urgent necessity for change. It is mandatory for us to educate and involve our young people. Understanding the electoral process is key to our survival as a people.

Quality education is too dear, for a defeat to halt the hard work ahead. We must continue to demand honesty, integrity, and excellence in our school and community.

There is no excuse for failure of this kind; but all I can say is that I pledge to work harder in the future to attempt to correct the many evils in this society. There are hindering our growth and development that is necessary for survival in today's progressive world.

Yours in the Struggle

Emily Moore

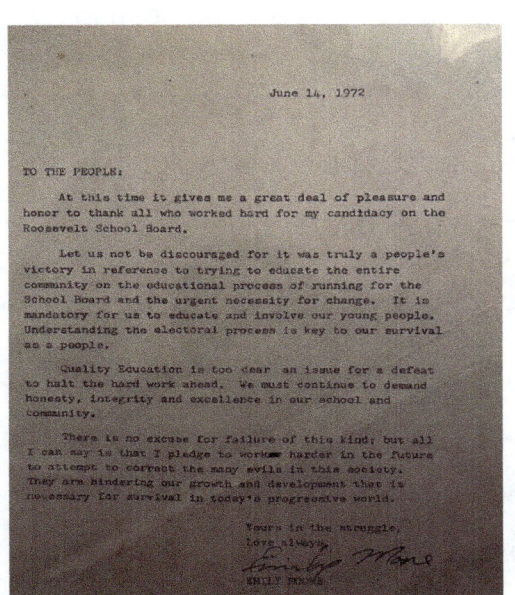

FIGURE 41 LETTER OF APPRECIATION TO THE ROOSEVELT COMMUNITY. (COURTESY OF EMILY MOORE)

To Africa with Queen Mother Audley Moore

PHOTO 61 QUEEN MOTHER AUDLEY MOORE (SCHOOL L. , 2019)

Before Martin and Malcolm, there was Marcus Garvey who was a prominent figure during the 1920-30s, a Jamaican Migrant who became the founder of the Universal Negro Improvement Association (UNIA). In the recognizance of African American black nationalist forebears Paul Cuffee and Martin Delany, Garvey enacted a system backed by the practice of black inclusion, militancy, and economic welfare practices during the Great Depression[36] and Harlem Renaissance Era.[37] He is known as the

---

[36] The Great Depression: Major decline in American economy that occurred between 1929 – 1941 due to stock market crash and banking panics, including international financial troubles and subsequential rise of Federal interest rates (Gary Richardson, Federal Reserve Bank of Richmond, 2013)

[37] The Harlem renaissance: A period of rich artistic and cultural activities amongst African Americans after World War I until the beginning of World War II (1941). Notable artist of the time such as Langston Hughes, Duke Ellington, and Ma Rainey brought consciousness of Black American Culture, embracing their freedom of expression that had been dulled due to legalized racism and segregation. (Harlem Renaissance, n.d.)

founder of Black Nationalism in the United States of America. One of Garvey's most interesting networks was with the state of Mississippi, and the Ku Klux Klan as they too thought mass migration would improve their Black population issues. He was able to reach a mountain of success as the UNIA became the first African American-owned ship fleet, with its main ship named Black Star. Naturally, there was debate among the African American communities about whether they would take on the opportunity since the lands of the United States were all, they knew. Over a million Black people were now generations separated from what African culture, knowledge, and language they ever had.

In 2018, Historian Keisha N. Blain published a Journal Article for the University of New York Press about Queen Mother Audley Moore and her effect on continuing the ideal of UNIA, Black women activists, and Black nationalism as race and politics in the United States of the 20th Century. Blain was able to source a 1973 interview of Moore with *Black Scholar* about the moment she first met Marcus Garvey when she was 19 or 20 years old in New Orleans:

> *"We heard that Garvey was coming to New Orleans, but the police would not allow him to speak Garvey came and they arrested him. The people raised so much sand until they had to let him out the next night"* [Said Audley Moore]

When local police officials tried to block Garvey from speaking during the second night, Moore describes a tense scene in which she and others pulled out guns in defense of Garvey's right to speak. [3] She explained it this way: "I had two guns-one in my bosom and one in my pocketbook... Everybody was told, and everybody knew they had to come armed. We wanted that freedom." Standing with a crown of Black supporters – all with guns in the air—Moore joined the chorus of voices shouting, "Speak, Garvey, Speak!" [4]

Moore's first encounter with Garvey that evening marked the beginning of her political journey into Black nationalist and radical politics. [5] In Moore Words, "Garvey brought something very beautiful to us--- Africa for the Africans. He made us conscious of the fact we belong to a big continent, with all of its gold and diamonds and riches... That we are somebody...That we had a right to be restored to our proper selves. [6] (Blain, 2018)

Audley Moore was a Creole woman native of New Iberia, Louisiana and would migrate to Harlem, New York in her late 20s. Garvey promoted the empowerment of both men and women, allowing women to join UNIA in public and private roles, whereas each division of UNIA made it mandatory that there was one male or female in the position of president or vice president (Blain, To Keep Alive the Teaching of Garvey and the Work of the UNIA" Augley Moore, Black Women's Activism, and Nationalist Politics during the Twentieth Century, 2018). According to Blain's research, it was in Harlem where she became involved with the UNIA, though never holding a formal position, she was frequently at meetings and the first UNIA International Convention (Blain, To Keep Alive the

Teaching of Garvey and the Work of the UNIA" Augley Moore, Black Women's Activism, and Nationalist Politics during the Twentieth Century, 2018). As a major supporter, she brought stocks in support of the Black Star Line, which was a major business venture of Garvey and UNIA. The political exile of Garvey in 1927, and his death in 1940 made it crucial to Queen Mother Moore to continue and educate Black communities about his mission for the betterment of Black people across the globe.

In 1955, Queen Mother Moore created the Reparations Committee of Descendants of United States Slaves, likely the first organization to focus entirely on reparations, followed by the Reparations Committee Inc. (Law, 2020) In 1957, Queen Mother Moore founded the Universal Association of Ethiopian Women, a small Pan-Africanist organization (UAEW) (Blain, 2018). Women who joined the association were once supporters of Marcus Garvey. Queen Mother Moore would also become known for her judicial plight for reparations for the Black descendants of Seneca Village, present-day Central Park of Manhattan, New York. Before 1858, Seneca Village served as New York's Black Wall Street, a metropolis of black wealth and knowledge. As history repeats itself, the white citizens of Manhattan wanted to take over the lands, displeased with all the success that was occurring across from the current Wall, Water and Pearl Streets, areas where slaves were once auctioned off in the past. The residents of Seneca Village were brought out of their properties, which included churches, banks, schoolhouses, and various family homes, for proportionally less profit than its worth. The case was even taken to the Supreme Court, where it was denied. It was a fight she enacted until she died in 1997 at the age of ninety-eight (Pace, 1997).

It is not for certain when Emily and the story of how Queen Mother Moore and Emily met in the 1970s, but Emily recalls learning about her in 1966 when Queen Mother Moore fought the educational system of Brooklyn, New York for underfunding and lack of upkeep of minority-populated school buildings due to improper fund distribution by the Brooklyn educational board. A fight Emily truly appreciated for Black Americans as she began her journey as an educator in 1965 in the Peace Corps. Emily would attend various civil rights conferences and eventually, they created a bond that would bring Emily under the wing of Queen Mother. As a frequent traveler to African countries due to UWEA, Queen Moore would receive her "Queen' title during her visit to Ghana from former Ghanaian President Kwame Nkrumah from the Ashanti ethnic group in 1972.

In June 1974, Emily traveled with Queen Moore and various other women and men of pan-African and diasporic backgrounds to Dar es Salaam, Tanzania to attend the 6th Annual Pan-African Congress Conference (6PAC). The purpose of the annual PAC's was for African countries to come together to assess how to achieve political, financial, and social security in newly independent but exploited territories that were no longer under European apartheid and colonization. This task was extremely difficult as there are over one hundred countries and two hundred languages represented, making Africa susceptible to various dictatorship regimes and political corruption. This conference was its first effort towards combating the damage and trauma that has been done to the African people and their lands by European countries for centuries. Six conferences later, PAC created networks between the African people and the descendants of the Diaspora to help gain international support in their efforts to regain what it means to live with liberty.

Emily attended a PAC before, but PAC6 was spectacular because Queen Mother Moore had invited Emily to join her as a delegate for the conference, as Queen Mother Moore was to be an honorary guest speaker. It was the first conference where it was only people of African descent were invited to be in attendance for the discussion of Africa's future. What was the most important for Emily was that at the conference is that a clear majority of the delegates were women of African descent and the diaspora. (Kentake, 2016). The number of women that attended this conference was a milestone. The women joined together to create an alliance across the globe to combat the oppression of racism and damages that have influenced every part of the world.

Not all African diaspora descendants had the same struggles that Black Americans and current Africans who faced colonization, execution, and apartheid on their native lands, forced to see their lands gutted of resources with their blood for over three hundred years. The purpose of the 6PAC and its gathering of participants was to figure out a way to collectively harness Africa's new independent power and deconstruct neocolonialist regimes to unite the diaspora under a common Pan-African agenda (Farmer, 2016).

Emily and hundreds of participants discussed over four days and presented a plethora of ideals that could be organized for the greater good, but Emily felt their efforts were dulled by male patriarchy.

PHOTO 62 EMILY TO THE LEFT AT THE PAC6 CONFERENCE, SITTING NEXT TO UNKNOWN DELEGATE. (COURTESY OF EMILY MOORE)

It was amazing, I was never surrounded by so many prominent figures and for them to be Black women, educated, there for a cause, it was special. It was unfortunate that the men of the evening could not see past gender and effectively listen to the ideals that the women spoke of in the effort of African people's political liberation. All these women came together with brilliant ideas and resolutions, and at the end of it all, it seemed as if the men did not take in any of it. Like talking to a brick wall.

- Emily Moore

Emily valued her time to be in the presence of one of the most insightful Black women of the 20th century. Emily had the opportunity to stay by Queen Mother Moore as she traveled around the world, but Emily knew that her calling was to teach through education and decided to return to Roosevelt. Emily told Queen Mother, *"Three years, has been more than enough time. I must get back to the children! The children need me."*

After Emily's experience with the Northwood demonstrations, Emily found great importance in photographs and recording the ordeals that she encountered on her journey of life. Specifically, at most events, Emily is known for having a camera around her neck, making her the photographer but not the one being captured in moments of her own. Hence, by the time Emily went to Africa, she became more of the woman behind the camera than in front of it. Emily captured dozens of photos during her time in Africa. In the late 1970s, Emily loaned her audio cassette tapes of the conference and various moments with Queen Moore with Dr. Jenkins. Dr. Jenkins was to transcribe and write his work based upon the information on the tapes. Unfortunately, in a short period, Dr. Jenkins lost track of the tapes during a home move. Unfortunately, not too long after Dr.

Jenkins passed away. Because of this, till this day, Emily does not lend out her resources.

Emily wrote in reflection on her time with Queen Mother Moore.

A FIGHTER FOR RIGHTS OF AFRICAN PEOPLE IN THE
UNITED STATES AND THROUGHOUT THE WORLD
By Emily Moore

Queen Mother Moore attended the All-African Women's Tenth Anniversary Celebration that took place in Dar es Salam, Tanzania during the week of July 24-31, 1972. It was a great historical event and women participated from all over the world.

Queen Mother Moore, actively in the liberation struggle in the United States for over fifty-four years, celebrated her seventy-fourth birthday at the All-African Women's conference to which she was invited by the Secretary General of the conference Madame Jean Martin Cisse of Guinea.

There were over three hundred African women and foreign observers present. It was an international occasion for not only were women from the continent of African and various liberation movements, but also [black]women from Asia, South America, and North America.

The theme was the Role of Women in the Liberation of Africa. The Women expressed their rights as equal human beings in a progressively changing society and the world. They spoke on the crucial issues and situations affecting the women of the world.

The welcome address was given by the chairman, Ms. Sophia Kawawa of the UWT, the women's organization of Tanzania. The Secretary General of the Conference Jean Martin Cisse' also served as the Ambassador to the United States from Guinea, she delivered a key message. The first day ended in the evening with a reception at the Stat House, where Queen Mother Moore had an opportunity to meet with the President of Tanzania Julis Nyerere

Every day was just as exciting as the first and with a full schedule on the affairs of the African women role in the Liberation St5ruggle. Some important messages were brought before the conference floor by some of the Delegates and observers who attended the conference.

On the third day of the conference Queen Mother Moore addressed and assured the AWO that African American people fully understand the tremendous struggles and sacrifices the African people were making to rid their motherland of the scourges of colonial and neo-colonist. The cold fact that Queen Mother Moore added were that everywhere oppressed people were fighting against a common enemy: colonialism, racism, and imperialism. She went on to say many of us have worked long and hard in the spirit of Marcus Garvey to answer the cry of our forefathers, for the redemption of our motherland, Africa. For Garvey said, "Africa is for the Africans, at home and abroad."

It was great feeling to listen to Queen Mother Moore addressing the African Woman's Conference. Imagine, your mother, grandmother and great-grandmother that thought and wondered about the place of their ancestors, a place that many wanted to return unable to because of their oppressive conditions. Because of their circumstances, they were unaware of the greatness of Africa and the real struggle of the people that continued to live there. Yes, and long last, Queen mother Audley Moore speaking in Africa to sisters and brothers as if she was rallying on 125th street or a union meeting, wherever she goes, she tells the story of our struggle, and preaches education, organization unification and mobilization for black liberation.

PHOTO 63 EMILY DURING HER TRAVELS OF TANZANIA. (COURTESY OF EMILY MOORE)

In 2019, Shafeah M'Balia wrote an article for the *African American Intellectual History Society* recapping her time in the presence of Mother Moore in the 1970s that was facilitated by Emily. M'Balia was a student at Roosevelt High School who was involved with student-led anti-Vietnam War demonstrations on Long Island. As a reward for their heroics, M'Balia and other student demonstrators were invited to hear Queen Mother Moore speak at what is now the National Black Theater in New York City, presumably on behalf of Emily. M'Balia remembered that Queen Moore speaking to the young people about their civil rights, and her fight for reparations and unity owed to Black Americans. After the event, M'Balia noted that Emily was able to get Mother Moore to speak further at a private home in the Roosevelt Community later. It was thanks to Emily's encouragement and reward to the students that created one of M'Balia's most memorable moments. It also introduced her to Pan-Africanism, which M'Balia applied to her own life.

> I was one of a group from Roosevelt, Long Island, high school students leading anti-Vietnam War and Black community control demonstrations. I was eager to get further connections to the rest of the Black community and tried to go everywhere and anywhere there was a protest or a cultural event taking place. When I came up the long stairs and around the corner of the building, I was struck

by this elderly lady, sitting alone in the front of the room, commanding everyone's attention. Finger pointed in the air, she held everyone's interest as she talked about reparations and Malcolm X. She was dressed in a floor-length beaded dress with an organza shawl draped over one shoulder and a matching turban.

After her presentation, she opened the floor for questions, and as the small crowd was leaning towards the back of the room, she urged people to come closer. My crew, along with everyone else hesitated a bit and then, in our youthful boldness, stepped out ahead of everybody else. I tentatively raised my hand to ask a question. Her piercing eyes sized me up and she said something like, "Speak, child, speak!" We must have impressed her because some months later, our teacher, former SNCC member Emily Moore, said our little crew was able to convince her to come to Roosevelt and speak to a gathering at a home next door to me.

The ending of Emily's time with Queen Mother Moore did not mean that there was an ending to their friendship and partnership. Emily would remain closely acquainted with Queen Mother Moore for over two decades until her death in 1997.

FIGURE 42 EMVELOPE OF MAIL TO QUEEN MOTHER MOORE THAT IS IN POSSESSION OF EMILY MOORE. (COURTESY OF AYANNA MOORE)

FIGURE 43 INVINTATION TO LUNCEHON BY THE NATIONAL SOCIETY OF AFRO-AMERICAN POLICEMAN AT THE FAMOUS WALDORF ASTORIA HOTEL , (COURTESY OF AYANNA MOORE)

The Struggle Has Ended For
Queen Mother
Audley Moore

July 27, 1898   May 2, 1997

Services:
Friday, May 9, 1997 - 10:00 a.m.

Mount Olivet Baptist Church
201 Lenox Avenue
New York, New York

Dr. Charles A. Curtis, Pastor

Archbishop Abuna Nathaniel
Bishop G. R. Apollo
OFFICIATING

FIGURE 44 OBITURARY OF QUEEN MOTHER MOORE, 1997. (COURTESY OF AYANNA MOORE)

Black on Long Island, 1970s

Between her time as a tennis Coach and traveling, Emily went back to college to receive a postgraduate degree at Nova University, and Brooklyn College City University for educational and counseling licensing. Emily served as the health program coordinator for the town of Roosevelt, organizing health fairs and after-school activities for the youth. She would hold a seat on the Roosevelt Community Advisory Council as the community coordinator. Meanwhile, Black children continued to face racial prejudices in the streets and school halls of Long Island. White school districts tried to cater to the teaching of Black American and African histories in their educative curriculum but were reduced to a month during the newly celebrated Black History Month. During Black History Month, as these schools decorated their halls with primary figures like MLK, Malcolm X and Stokely Carmichael, physical altercations occurred at Bellport High School as white and Black students came into confrontations over their ideals of representation or lack thereof. The white students felt that it was inclusive of and felt excluded, ironically the same sentiments delivered to Black children daily for centuries. When Emily returned to the Roosevelt school district, she made it her mission to prepare students for how to respond in the face of racial tension and oppression they may experience in their journey. Her focus was the fundamentals of physical education, teaching tennis to those who wanted to learn, advocating that physical fitness of the body and mind was what it took to become the next generation of successful professionals for the world. Emily wanted to show black youth that there was a world that loved Black people outside of Nassau County, for what they looked like and who they were. Emily knew that the community of Black youth needed a chance to see and experience more than they were used to; to dream and want for something bigger than themselves and their community.

From the classroom to the tennis courts, Emily understood that she had to prepare her students for the adversity that would be ahead of them. As a witness, Emily knew when those who felt they could use racism and privilege to commit unfavorable actions when the outcomes could be detrimental for the young scholars. She knew she had to help the children of her community face adversity, but how could they know how to if they were never exposed to predominantly white settings? It was not easy for Emily to even get into white tennis programs to play against the students of her program. As far as Emily was concerned about bringing her students to predominantly white areas to play matches, these were her words:

> *My students were taught to carry themselves in a respectful manner, to respect them and they are not just representing themselves, but their families, their friend, their town, and this program! We did not work hard every day, sweat every day, to run away! To count ourselves out because we are somewhere people say we do not belong! I could not let myself, or my students worry about the prejudice and racism of their opposition, and their challengers because wherever we went, we set an example. We understood the injustices because I taught them to do better and be better for themselves. My mission was to educate and expose children to self-respect.*

The caption of this 1970's *Newsday Long Island* article reads:

> *Posters of Stokely Carmichael and Malcolm X are displayed in Bellport High School, along with a portrait of the Rev. Martin Luther King Jr. Anger of white students at the inclusion of the posters with the Rev. Dr. King's picture put up for observance of his birthday anniversary was believed to have led to the scuffles that caused the schools closing yesterday.*

PORTRAITURE. Posters of Stokely Carmichael and Malcolm X are displayed in Bellport High School, along with a portrait of the Rev. Martin Luther King Jr. Anger of white students at the inclusion of the posters with the Rev. Dr. King's picture put up for observance of his birthday anniversary was believed to have led to the scuffles that caused the school's closing yesterday. (Story on Page 5.)

Newsday Photo by Rex Lyons

FIGURE 45 NEWSPAPER CLIPPING OF ART AND PHOTOS MENTIONED THAT SET UNREST IN LONG ISLAND SCHOOLS DURING BLACK HISTORY MONTH. (COURTESY OF LONG ISLAND NEWSDAY)

Fourth Quarter: 1975-1999

THE ALLIANCE JUNIOR TENNIS DEVELOPMENT PROGRAM

PHOTO 64 UNIDENTIFIED ALLIANCE TENNIS STUDENTS AT ROOSEVELT PARK. (COURTESY OF EMILY MOORE)

In 1975, Emily founded the Alliance Junior Tennis Development Program (AJTDP) with the original name Alliance Tennis. The motto of AJTDP is *"to continue to be the vehicle through which we teach discipline, self-control and academic excellence to our young people,"* and has remained the same for the past fifty years. The Junior Tennis Alliance teaches the techniques of tennis, and the etiquette of sportsmanship, but the program also offers leadership training, empowerment workshops, field trips, tournament participation, tennis clinic opportunities, and cognitive development activities that include chess and checkers. Emily gained new acquaintances through coaching the youth around town, and as a physical educator, but still faced the fact that it could be difficult to recruit Black youth on a larger scale into her tennis program. Culturally, tennis was viewed as a "white sport" and was not played as a recreational sport in urban communities. Local recreational facilities also did not supply playing courts, which was common in urban communities, where the closest sport to tennis was 'Handball.'

For teenagers, AJTDP and the introduction of tennis to the community of Black youth of Roosevelt and Freeport could not have happened at a better time. Gaining a small circle of tennis players, with success her participants would grow rapidly in size. Soon enough, many community parents brought their children to learn tennis, making her broadly recognized in the Nassau County area for her efforts. In contrast to what could have been a challenge to gathering tennis students, it became simple for Emily because of her no-nonsense approach to anything she pursued. Her reputation as an educator and activist had already instilled a trust within the Black communities of Nassau County which enabled parents to trust

Emily's and ADJTP to help mold their children into productive student-athletes. ADJTP would supply support and guidance to youth and adults from various walks of life. Providing each student with a unified approach and experience to young black youth that did not alienate them because of their social and economic status, but rather appreciated for their talent and personal drive. For each student, Emily put her heart into ADJTP, with many of the funds for children's participation coming out of her pocket. As a fundraiser, she was *"possibly one of the best fundraisers in Nassau County,"* according to former student Gary Battle.

Former CORE director Lincoln Lynch (with his hands on the boy's shoulders) came to the Alliance Junior Tennis Training and Development Camp in Roosevelt Park to support the young tennis players who were on a trip to Long Island in the 1970s. Among these tennis players are many who went on to earn college degrees, including two physicians and two lawyers. (Courtesy of Emily Moore.)

FIGURE 46 CAPTION OF PHOTO: CORE DIRECTOR LINCOLN LYNCH (WITH HIS HANDS-ON BOYS SHOULDERS) CAME TO THE ALLICANCE JUNIOR TENNIS TRAINING AND DEVELOPMENT CAMP IN ROOSEVELT PARK TO SUPPORT. TWO STUDENTS BECAME PHYICIANS AND TWO STUDENTS BECAME LAWYERS. EMILY IS FURTHEST BACK TO THE LEFT. (COURTESY OF EMILY MOORE)

"One Teaches All": the times of Gary Battle

In 2023, Mr. Gary Battle was interviewed about his training, mentorship, and lifelong friendship with Emily. Battle was one of the first students of ADJTP. Battle joined ADJTP during its early stages. In 1977, eleven-year-old Gary Battle met Emily Moore in front of his Roosevelt childhood home when she approached him and his parents with the opportunity to join ADJTP. Gary described the encounter as simple and to the point.

> One day, I was outside my house in Roosevelt. I might have been throwing a ball or something when Ms. Moore stopped in front of my house and said out her van window, Hey, you want to play tennis? And 30 years later, Ms. Moore and I have had a long journey as coach, mentor, and friend.

Battle specifically remembered one of the first things Emily Moore told him when he started to play for Alliance Tennis.

> Gary, if you master this tennis, you can go far. You can make a lot of money, and in result Ms. Moore put me into positions such as coach, director, and coordinator. She gave me the skills to excel as a leader wherever I went because I knew how to accept criticism, give my best and organize on a greater level than myself. If she did not instill tennis on me, I probably would of went to college, but I would not have been a tennis scholar and champion.

After Battle's first year with ADJTP, he proved himself a skilled player enough to become a Junior Counselor with the ADJTP as Battle would win various tournaments in 1st and 2nd positions. In tenth grade, Battle gained a scholarship to train with the Port Washington Tennis Academy where he would learn from top professional players and coaches on the East Coast. During Battle's 10th grade year at Roosevelt High School, he moved to Folkston, Georgia. As a student in Georgia, Battle would lead as number one in boy's singles for Charleston County, receiving notoriety from sports publications. Battle went to St. Paul's College in Lawrenceville, Virginia on a full-ride tennis scholarship where he would study business administration. During his time in Georgia and Virginia, he would serve as team captain, and number one in singles and doubles matches for each state. Every summer, Battle would return to ADJTP in Roosevelt on Emily's dime to develop and teach tennis skills. Instilled with Emily's *Each one - teach one motto,* Battle would run respective tennis clinics in Georgia, Virginia, and New York, eventually becoming known as the Pyramid Tennis program in association with Avia Myers and the Pyramid Tennis Association. Mr. Gary Battle currently works for the Hempstead School Board as an administrative member and has done so for the last twenty-eight years. For Battle, Emily Moore had been a driving force in his life since becoming her tennis coach and lifetime friend.

Battle graciously brought into perspective what Emily Moore had done for her all of students as a director, coach, mentor and added family member during the late seventies until the early nineties. Emily has been dedicated to making sure that all her students learn the fundamentals of tennis along with leadership and sportsmanship for over 40 years. Battle described the enthusiasm the students had in the summer mornings as a teen and young man while Emily gathered her students from the various local towns when she ran the Indoor Tennis Program out of Freeport Recreation Center.

> We would be up early; camp was around 5-7 am before summer school and other camps the children attended. She did not charge any of the parents to pick up the children, or the camp for that matter, I think. One thing was for sure, the kids were excited to go, they were never late for the van, matter of fact, they would be standing outside ready when we got there!

Little did Battle know, the reason for Emily's early practices was because the white tennis instructors at Freeport Recreational did not want the black children playing tennis with the white kids at 8 a.m. Emily didn't let it take away from the opportunity that they could still practice, and adjusted accordingly for the children, even though she was one of the people who was a staunch advocator for the building of the Recreational Center in the first place. Wherever Emily had students, she looked to make sure that they all experienced and gained benefits according to their progress and work ethic as she had children of all backgrounds in her program.

PHOTO 65 ARTHUR ASHE AND GARY BATTLE. 1980'S. (COURTESY OF EMILY MOORE)

For members of the Roosevelt community, Emily was considered to have been selfless when it came to helping her students. One of the notable issues with Tennis as a sport for low-income minority communities is the cost of equipment, uniforms, tournaments, and travel accommodations. Even in the present day, the costs behind the sport of tennis have made it considered a sport played by rich people in Black culture. Even with groundbreakers like Althea Gibson, and Arthur Ashe were known globally for their accomplishments as Black American tennis professionals, it was not visible for Black communities. To adhere to the needs of her students, Emily converted her garage into a mini store that would supply uniforms, tennis rackets, tennis balls, other sports paraphernalia, books, and snacks at a discount or free through donations from various sponsors and supporters.

Battle remembered attending tennis professional Vitas Gerulaitus's Tennis Clinic twice a week, on Emily's funding.[38] Gerulaitus would personally come to teach and practice with the students amongst the dozens of professionals there, including Arthur Ashe. Gerulaitus was interested in Battle's skills and sponsored Battle to attend and represent on behalf of the Gerulaitus Camp at Harry Hoffman's International Tennis Camp in Florida. During the 1980s when Battle was attending Norfolk College, he recalled Emily and him arranging for her tennis students to stay on

---

[38] Vitas Gerulaitus - Born Vytautas Gerulaitus, Native of Howard Beach, Brooklyn, New York, He was an American professional tennis player. Won double titles at Wimbledon tournament, two Australian Opens, and Two Italian opens.

the college campus in Georgia while they attended a tournament. Battle said, *"Ms. Moore did that so the young students could experience what it was like to be in the atmosphere of college students. She always made sure we had the best experience that she could provide for us to learn and feel like we belonged."* Emily's opportunities allowed them to imagine themselves in the future outside of their normal surroundings.

Battle told of how he and various students like Spencer Belcher, Kevin, and Daniel Burgess Jr., took part in various tournaments with the United States Tennis Association due to the superb skills they refined through additional tennis clinics, and donations from other tennis professionals. As a young player, Battle gained vast notoriety as he grew as a player, becoming a professional tennis player as an adult. Specifically Battle remembered that every summer, the students of ADJTP would drive to the Atlantic Tennis Association tournaments in New Haven, Connecticut for one day, but specifically this summer almost the whole team returned with a trophy or medal for their wins. Battle could not recall a time when a player did not come back from a tournament, or match without an award. Notably, Battle wanted people to remember that when it came to Fundraising, Emily always

had a plan and the will to support all the students.

> Most of the people Ms. Moore serviced were underprivileged
> children and young adults. When we went to California, Ms. Moore
> did not charge them. She would fundraise and gain donations. If
> you knew Ms. Moore, you knew that fundraisers were her thing! She
> used to do it big! But it got difficult overtime with the lack of
> community support. Anyway, Tom Gulado, the Nassau County
> Executive presented ADJTP with a grant for the students so they
> could travel to the tournament. It was just enough.

One of the last remarks Battle wanted to leave on the behalf of

Emily Moore was this:

> Ms. Moore made it all happen because of dedication. Every
> profession there is in this world, there was once a student who
> encountered Ms. Moore. Doctors, engineers, professionals such as
> Rene Blunt, Kim Saunders, Zina Garrison, even Venus and Serena
> Williams, for a short period of time, met and learned with Ms. Moore,
> and she [Emily] didn't go to them. They all came to Roosevelt Park!

The letter below invites the community and supporters to attend their Fundraising tennis Party in June of 1985.

May 31, 1985

Dear Friend,

The Alliance Junior Tennis Development Program was established to provide a viable Tennis program for young people from seven to twenty-one years of age. On Long Island, tennis opportunities for minority youth are limited.

The Junior Tennis Program is special because it affords young people the opportunity to participate in a positive experience designed to develop tennis skills, provide on-the-job training, and enhances academic achievement.

In the months of July and August we run a tennis camp which is held at the Roosevelt Park. During the fall and winter months, we have an afterschool program, held in the gymnasium at the Washington Rose Elementary school, and a Saturday and Sunday morning program at Freeport Indoor Tennis Center, Freeport, New York. Good Programs of any kind cost money, therefore, we feel fortunate to know people like you who can help make this need a reality.

Please join us, we are having a Fund-Raising Tennis Party Saturday, June 15, 1985, at 8 p.m-12 a.m. at the Freeport Indoor Tennis Club, 103 Mills Road, Freeport, New York 11520.

The proceeds from this event will help to continue efforts to expose our youth to many tennis challenges and experiences.

Let us hear from you soon and please accept our thanks for your support.

ALLIANCE JUNIOR DEVELOPMENT, INC

15▮▮▮▮▮▮▮▮

ROOSEVELT, NEW YORK 11575

May 31, 1985

Dear Friend,

The Alliance Junior Tennis Development Program was established to provide a viable Tennis Program for young people from seven to twenty-one years of age. On Long Island tennis opprtunities for minority youth are limited.

The Junior Tennis Program is special because it affords young people the opportunity to participate in a positive experience designed to develop tennis skills, provides on-the-job training and enhances academic achievement.

In the months of July and August we run a Tennis Camp which is held at the Roosevelt Park. During the Fall and Winter months we have an afterschool program held in the gymnasium at the Washington Rose Elementary School, and a Saturday and Sunday morning program at Freeport Indoor Tennis Center, Freeport, New York. Good programs of any kind cost money, therefore, we feel fortunate to know people like you who can help make this need a reality.

Please join us, we are having a Fund Raising Tennis Party Saturday, June 15, 1985, at 8 p.m. - 12 p.m. at the Freeport Indoor Tennis Club, 103 Mills Road, Freeport, New York 11520.

The proceeds from this event will help to continue efforts to expose our youth to many tennis challenges and experiences.

Let us hear from you soon and please accept our thanks for your support.

Sincerely yours,

Emily Moore
Executive Director
Alliance Junior Development, Inc.

FIGURE 47 LETTER ANNOUNCING FUNDRAISER FOR JUNE OF 1985 (COURTESY OF EMILY MOORE)

The *Community Journal* wrote about Ms. Moore and ADJTP:

More than a teacher, more than a coach, Ms. Emily Moore has invested her lifetime in action-oriented ventures, not the least significant of which is her present passion for developing young tennis players into first class athletic scholarship winners heading for competitions all over the world and colleges across the country.

Founder and Executive Director of the Alliance Junior Tennis Development Program, Ms. Moore has had the pleasure of watching over one thousand students of her program go on to successful lives, most of which have included distinguished academic careers funded by full tennis scholarships. Jermain Thomas of Roosevelt is one such protégé. He is entering his junior year at Morgan State University with his tennis game intact and paying the freight. Hempstead's Tamara Johnson, a recent Morgan alumna is beginning her 1st year of medical school in North Carolina, following years of tutelage in Ms. Moore's program.

Throughout this summer, some 50 to 100 youngsters at a time participate in the Alliance Summer Camp Program at Roosevelt

Park where they learn the fundamentals of tennis, court conduct, equipment handling, strategy, and match play under the direction of Ms. Moore and a staff of professional instructors. Many of these students are carry-overs from an early bird program which meets from 6:00 am to 8:00 am during the school year at Freeport Indoor Tennis. This dedication pays off for some of Alliance's student athletes who travel extensively throughout the year to France, Belgium, Pakistan, India, Nigeria, and Australia among others, to represent team and country in international competition.

Ms. Moore herself is quite the world traveler. Following her graduation from Freeport High School in 1961 and receipt of her bachelor's degree from Morgan State, Moore joined the Peace Corps. "I survived three military coups and a civil war during those two years in Nigeria," she reveals. While teaching physical education and health science during that period, she found the time to coach track and to act as the Mid-Western coordinator for the world Olympic committee.

A keen sense of adventure took Moore to Israel, Lebanon, Turkey, Greece, and Italy in subsequent years. She then settled in France in the late 1960's where she became a political activist and organizer. The death of Dr. Martin Luther King, Jr. brought Moore on the journey home to the U.S where, after attending the funeral, she ventured back to Long Island where she accepted a teaching position in Roosevelt. An apparent affinity for working with young people led to several counseling and program coordinator assignments first with the Nassau County Youth Board, and then with Brooklyn College.

It was during her association with the Long Island Alliance for Minority Group Leaders that Ms. Moore was inspired to adopt the name "Alliance" for her tennis program. What is now the Alliance Junior Tennis Development Program, Inc. has grown in size and scope since its inception in 1975. While this non-profit venture seeks out new sources of grants, it continues to sustain itself through fundraisers and instruction fees.

Always the adventurer, Ms. Moore launched an entrepreneurial enterprise last month with the Grand Opening of Moore's Tennis Shop. Here, in addition to selling racquets, balls, and T-shirts, she is able to give some students the opportunity to string racquets, and otherwise become more familiar with the equipment that, if perfectly matched with their skills, will help them achieve their own goals in sport and in life one day.

The awards and honors have been plentiful over the years. Still Ms. Moore, shuffling though her photo albums and memorabilia filled with Arthur Ashe and Althea Gibson, kudos to her, focuses on the accomplishments of the youngsters who have studied with her and gone on to do great and important things beyond tennis. She beams as she mentions Paula O'Connor, who started with her at age 11, and went on to Yale followed by Stanford Medical School.

Tennis is her life, but Ms. Emily Moore knows that it may simply be a door opener for many young people who will eventually travel a different path. They have learned that their relationships, their alliances – with successful mentors and determined peers will lead them somewhere, someday.

More than a teacher, more than a coach, Ms. Emily Moore has invested her lifetime in action-oriented ventures, not the least significant of which is her present passion for developing young tennis players into first class athletic scholarship winners heading for competitions all over the world and colleges across the country.

Founder and Executive Director of the Alliance Junior Tennis Development Program, Ms. Moore has had the pleasure of watching over 1000 students of her program go on to successful lives, most of which have included distinguished academic careers funded by full tennis scholarships. Jermaine Thomas of Roosevelt is one such protege. He is entering his junior year at Morgan State University with his tennis game in tact, and paying the freight. Hempstead's

Tamara Johnson, a recent Morgan alumna, is beginning her 1st year of medical school in North Carolina, following years of tutelage in Ms. Moore's program.

Throughout this summer, some 50 to 100 youngsters at a time participate in the Alliance Summer Camp Program at Roosevelt Park where they learn the fundamentals of tennis, court conduct, equipment handling, strategy and match play under the direction of Ms. Moore and a staff of professional instructors. Many of these students are carry-overs from an early bird program which meets from 6:00 a.m. to 8:00 a.m. during the school year at Freeport Indoor Tennis. This dedication pays off for some of Alliance's student athletes who travel extensively throughout the year to France, Belgium, Pakistan, India, Nigeria and Australia among others, to represent team and country in international competition.

Ms. Moore is herself quite the world traveler. Following her graduation from Freeport High School in 1961 and receipt of her bachelor's degree from Morgan State, Moore joined the Peace Corp. "I survived three military coups and a civil war during those two years in Nigeria," she reveals. While teaching physical education and health science during that period, she found the time to coach track and to act as the Mid-Western coordinator for the world Olympic committee.

A keen sense of adventure took Moore to Israel, Lebanon, Turkey, Greece, and Italy in subsequent years. She then settled in France in the late 1960's where she became a political activist and organizer. The death of Dr.

(continued on page 18)

PHOTO 67 EMILY AND ALTHEA GIBSON. (COURTESY OF EMILY MOORE)

Robert McFadden: "The Junior Tennis Alliance was like a second family"

This is a personal statement said on the behalf of Emily Moore by Robert McFadden, a former student of Junior Alliance Tennis.

I was in sixth grade at Washington Rose when I heard the announcement in class for signing up for Tennis with Ms. Moore after school. My friends and I decided to see what It were about. Initially it was just us all in the gym, bouncing balls against the wall, learning about some technique and rules. Me and five guys decided we were going to see this through. I got decent before I had to stop playing because of my stepmother. Honestly, when that happened, I became sad, depressed because when it was gone, I noticed what it did for me. I guess.

Ms. Moore decided that enough was enough, and she took it into her own hands.

It took her to show up at my house, and with my brother to convince my stepmother to allow me to go back to tennis. She allowed me, but being away for so long, I did not have the confidence to go back into the game headfirst.

Ms. Moore called me one day and convinced me to play tennis down at the park with some friends, so she told me to bring my racquet. Instead, she took me to a tennis tournament, and told me that she signed me up, and that I was playing. I went and played, made it to the quarter finals. It was that same match that the tennis coach from Norfolk State University approached me. It was not even the school year yet, but he offered me a full ride to Norfolk to play tennis. I accepted it, I sent in my papers as soon as I went back to school, I went and graduated from Norfolk with a degree in accounting.

Growing up in Roosevelt was not easy, but tennis kept me focused as the people I played with became my family. It was refreshing to be around a bunch of people of your age range with the same focus, intentions, and goals. Ms. Moore was like a second and first mother to me and many children that went through her program.

When we were first starting, she told us all, 'Tennis will take you places you could never imagine if you keep to it." And she was right, I was able to go to college for free, play in the tennis satellite which is pretty big. I even travelled to six different countries playing tennis. I was number 998 ranked in the tennis world in my prime before I stopped playing, back then I did not know what that meant in magnitude, but as I think on it now, to be that number out of over one million players and rising in this world, amazing.

Ms. Moore had a way of forcing to you rise to occasions you think you are not prepared for until you complete it. I had the honor to present the speakers address for Arthur Ashe' retirement ceremony. I had no idea that I was going to be reading anything, but she handed it to me and said here, you are going to go up and read tonight. I think I did pretty well but that was the kind of person she was. (McFadden, 2023)

```
                              Robert C. Mc Fadden
                                 21
                              Roosevelt, N.Y         5
                                 Home

BIRTHDAY: November 10, 1971

HEIGHT   : 6'3"

WEIGHT   : 165

RACQUET  : Wimbledon Eclipse

GRIP     : 4 3/8

PLAYER   : All court, mostly serve and volley

SHIRT    : X-tra Large

SHORT    : 34 WAIST

SHOE     : 11 - 11 1/2
```

FIGURE 49 PLAYER INFO OF ROBERT MCFADDEN. (COURTESY OF EMILY MOORE)

Arthur Ashe, the champion, and lifetime advocate

PHOTO 68 ARTHUR ASHE AND EMILY. (COURTESY OF EMILY MOORE)

Emily was able to meet many fruitful and influential activists, as well as notable sports players during her journey as a civil rights activist and tennis coach, but she had a standing partnership with tennis Legend Arthur Ashe. Ashe was the first Black man to be on the United States Davis Cup team in 1963 and still is the only black man to ever win the singles at Wimbledon (1975), the U.S. Open (1963), and the Australian Open (1970). The tennis world of minority players and coaches was relatively small in the United States. Emily and Ashe both had a profound love for educating the youth about tennis and the world they lived in. The pair would often come together, along with Althea Gibson, to coach and mentor young Black children on how to play tennis. In 1972, Ashe founded the Harlem Junior Tennis program in Harlem, New York. Emily worked closely together as a coach and mentor to the participants, along with her students. When Emily founded the Alliance Junior Development Tennis Program in 1975, Ashe was a strong supporter of her camp and afterschool program.

In June of 1992, Emily put together a grand fundraiser gala on the behalf of Alliance Junior Tennis Development Program at the Marriott in Uniondale, New York named "An Evening with Arthur Ashe." Ashe served as the keynote speaker. Emily was known as a popular woman, as celebrities that shown up for Emily at the tennis courts of Roosevelt, and other professional settings. For this fundraiser, legendary R&B soul singers Ashford and Simpson performed their greatest hits for those who attended.

PHOTO 69 FROM L TO R: ASHFORD AND SIMPSON, MAN UNKNOWN, ARTHUR ASHE, AND EMILY AT THE FUNDRAISING BANQUET AT THE MARRIOT. (COURTESY OF EMILY MOORE)

ALLIANCE JUNIOR DEVELOPMENT, INC.
TENNIS PROGRAM

Presents

" *An Evening with Arthur Ashe* "

Tuesday, June 16, 1992
7:00 pm

L.I Marriott Hotel
Uniondale, N.Y.

FIGURE 50 PAMPHLET OF " AN EVENING WITH ARTHUR ASHE" (COURTESY OF EMILY MOORE)

Dr. Seretta McKnight was there when Arthur Ashe announced he wanted to celebrate Emily by presenting her with the Junior Tennis Development award for the year 1988 at the Marriott Marquis in New York City. Dr. McKnight recalled,

> *Another great tennis moment was years later when Arthur Ashe and the Black Tennis and Sports Foundation contracted me to produce 'An Evening of Sports Chic' at the newly opened Marriott Marquis in Manhattan. In our initial planning meeting when identifying honorees, Arthur Ashe, the Chairman of the BT&S Board directed that the Junior Tennis Development Award would go to Emily Moore. I sat up straight and said, Miss Emily Moore from Roosevelt? To which, he replied: "Yes. Seretta, do you know her?" I just lit up the room with my smile as I answered in the affirmative adding that she was my teacher, and I was a member of AJDTP first class of tennis players. What a moment that was!*

Emily and Arthur Ashe would go on to develop and keep a long-standing partnership until he passed away in March 1993. It so happened that a group of Emily students were able to meet him the same day he had the heart attack that would later lead to his passing. Emily was also presented the Arthur Ashe Tennis Award in 1995, two years after his death. Emily remained loyal to her views of who Arthur Ashe was as a person and what he represented and did not mind vocally stating her opinion about it. In 2000, a statue was revealed in honor of Arthur Ashe during the U.S. Open at the Arthur Ashe Stadium, of a touching gesture it was to give him that recognition, Emily disapproved of the design of the statue. The statue was in the position of him serving a tennis ball, while there was no tennis racket either. Emily chimed during the public viewing that was not what he was about. *The Queen's Chronicle* covered Emily's disapproval of the statue during the moment but noted how the artist and others were pretty much annoyed by her remarks on the statue. If the audience and reporter truly knew the dynamics of which Emily was to Ashe, they would have probably reconsidered and understood what she was saying was possibly right. Emily felt that the statue should have been more orientated toward his love for educating the children and tennis.

> *"He believed knowledge is power and he believed in dressing appropriately for all occasions. He believed in helping children. But there are no children up there, and there are no books. He is naked! This is the year 2000, so where are the high-tech images up there?"* (Toomey, 2000)

Arthur Ashe at New York City's Katonah Park with up and coming tennis players including students of the Alliance Junior Tennis Program. Later that day, he suffered the heart attack which would prove to be the beginning of the end, as he contracted AIDS from tainted blood given in a transfusion during surgery.

FIGURE 51 AJDTP STUDENTS WITH ARTHUR ASHE (COURTESY OF EMILY MOORE)

PHOTO 70 AJDTP STUDENTS AND STAFF, EMILY FAR TOP RIGHT (COURTESY OF EMILY MOORE)

FIGURE 52 ARTHUR ASHE AND EMILY MOORE (COURTESY OF EMILY MOORE)

In 2001, Emily wrote to the Adjutant General, Major General John Fenimore, to save the Harlem Tennis Center. Reverend Al Sharpton, Governor of New York at the time George Pataki, Congressman C. Rangel, and Comptroller C. McCall all received the letter.

Dear General Fenimore,

I am the Executive Director of the Alliance Jr. Tennis Program. For the past twenty years, our program has frequently used the facilities of the Harlem Tennis Center. The Children from Long Island come into the Harlem Tennis Center for clinics, tournaments, and various other activities. These groups are composed largely of youngsters from low to middle income families. The Harlem Tennis Center made it possible for many young people to obtain scholarships to college. The Center, under the leadership of Mr. Claude Cargill, reduces the rate for my type of community – oriented programs. I recently learned that there are plans to replace the Harlem Tennis Center with a sports complex operated by the Police Activity League. I implore you to reconsider this action. This center is irreplaceable. I am in full support with the actions of the Friends of the Harlem tennis Center to keep this important community resource alive. Over the years, I have seen what a treasured community resources this center has become. People like our senior citizens, who can no longer play tennis here, come in often to play chess or just enjoy the environment. Many youngsters are being led into the Harlem Tennis Center for instructions. The Harlem Junior Tennis Program, Pyramid Tennis program and so many others throughout New York State utilizing the courts of this great center. I strongly feel that it is very important that we Save the Harlem Tennis Center. It is a valuable community asset and should be preserved at all costs.

January 6, 2001

Major General John Fenimore
Adjutant General
330 Old Niskayuna Road
Latham, NY 12110-2224

Dear General Fenimore:

I am the Executive Director of the Alliance Jr. Tennis Program. For the past twenty years our program has frequently used the facilities of the Harlem Tennis Center. The children from Long Island come into the Harlem Tennis Center for clinics, tournaments, and various other activities. These groups are composed largely of youngsters from low to middle income families. The Harlem Tennis Center made it possible for many young people to obtain scholarships to college. The Center, under the leadership of Mr. Claude Cargill, reduces the rate for my type of community – oriented programs.

I recently learned that there are plans to replace the Harlem Tennis Center with a sports complex operated by the Police Athletic League. I implore you to reconsider this action. This Center is irreplaceable. I am in full support with the actions of the Friends of the Harlem Tennis Center to keep this important community resource alive.

Over the years I have seen what a treasured community resource this Center has become. People, like our senior citizen, who can no longer play tennis here, come in often to play chess or just to enjoy the environment. Many youngsters are being led into the Harlem Tennis Center for instructions. The Harlem Junior Tennis Program, Pyramid Tennis Program and so many others through out New York State utilizing the courts of this great center.

I strongly feel that it is very important that we Save the Harlem Tennis Center. It is a valuable community asset and should be preserved at all cost.

Sincerely,

Emily Moore
Executive Director

c: Reverend Al Sharpton
      Govenor G. Pataki
      Congressman C. Rangel
      Comptroller C. McCall

FIGURE 53 LETTER OF PETITION AGAINST THE CLOSING OF HARLEM TENNIS CENTER. (COURTESY OF EMILY MOORE)

To

Emily Moore

Just to say Thanks

Summer Tennis Team

1979

FIGURE 54 AWARD OF THANKS FROM AJDTP SUMMER TENNIS

PHOTO 71 MEMEBERS OF AJDTP WITH THEIR TROPHYS, 1980S

ROUGH RIDERS TO VELT VILLIANZ: A ROUGH RIDER FOR LIFE

In the 1970s Black families faced a rapid decline in family and community dynamics across the United States. Various reasons besides systematic oppression included requirements of the family welfare programs that made it hard for men to be present in the household as it required a lack of male presence and support. The introduction of "Sherm," PCP, and Crack-cocaine into minority neighborhoods, along with the strategic placement of guns around communities by the CIA, thus created a drug and gang-related warfare that continues to plague minority communities in the United States. It also turned the penial system into an industrial complex, as test scores of minority children were being used to create statics of future criminality. The overcrowding of housing projects and homes created chaos with the increase in drug usage and criminal activities to support habits. Just as things seemed to take a turn for the better in communities, the introduction of Crack cocaine and the disease of AIDS/HIV became an epidemic that plagued minority youth for generations to come. In collaboration with the internal crisis of the urban community, educational programs such as vocational schools, and after-school programs were defunded from minority school districts due to the success that they provided to Black young men and women for the future. Overall, local, state, and federal authorities created a hostile environment for youth as they craved wealth, respect, and power rather than knowledge and personification of intellect, creating a culture labeled as "thugs and gangsters."

Neighborhoods across the United States, including Roosevelt, and Hempstead would be the first and lasting communities that continue to deal with the effects of those changing times. Roosevelt became known as the first suburban community to be labeled as a "ghetto," as it continued to lose its economic and educational value, and continued to grow into a center of criminal mischief and focus of Nassau County law enforcement which would last well into the early 2000s, during this time Roosevelt would become known as 'The Velt" and its youth and graduates "Velt Villians".

After taking a five-year hiatus from the classroom, Emily returned to the Roosevelt School District as a physical education teacher at Ulysses Byas in 1981. There was a shift in the emotional and social importance of the youth in the 1980s, as the youth had incurred changes in family dynamics. Generally, students simply lacked guidance and the overall funding for the town of Roosevelt. As an unincorporated town, it proved to be troublesome for state in-school and after-school funding. In the world outside of school, the brewing drug and gang culture affected the town and the dynamics of students that would come through the Roosevelt School District. Although Emily had been out of the classroom since 1971, she saw the change in student dynamics and attitude as the social welfare, afterschool and vocational programs were taken away throughout urban communities of the United States. Teachers who worked in the Roosevelt and Hempstead school districts felt the burdens of the changes between curriculum vs. budgeting, teacher vs. administration, and students vs. society. The Black youth of the 1980 and 1990s, were no longer looking forward to achievements by doing the "right way" to obtain the "American Dream," as for Black youth, it became a dream deferred.

Veteran educators of the district from the 1970s and 80s would become the defying factors that helped catapult students with the community towards the opportunities of higher education and experiences well into the 2000s. As programs and teachers disappeared from the Roosevelt School District there were educators such as Coaches Morris Brandon, Joseph Vito, and Don E. Crummell, along with the Junior Alliance Tennis Program on the external front becoming beacons between sports and high education for the "problem child." Year after year, Emily and other teachers fought against the changes, and the results that occurred due to unstable chairing of the school board, along with failed school budgets, and retractions enacted due to failed state testing requirements. Emily's After School and Summer Tennis program provided a productive resource and escape from the havoc and distraction of the streets for the Roosevelt Youth.

As an educator and coach, Emily was a stickler for grades, and never allowed any of her students to fall below their performance, ADJTP often gave mentorship and tutoring on certain days for her students. Emily has always been ready to go above and beyond in the name of the Children in Roosevelt, the world and greater opportunities. For educators in underfunded districts, there was only so much that a handful of teachers could do within a district that had been subjected to adversity, blatantly rearranged, and geared towards the failure of minority students, best known as the School to Prison pipeline.

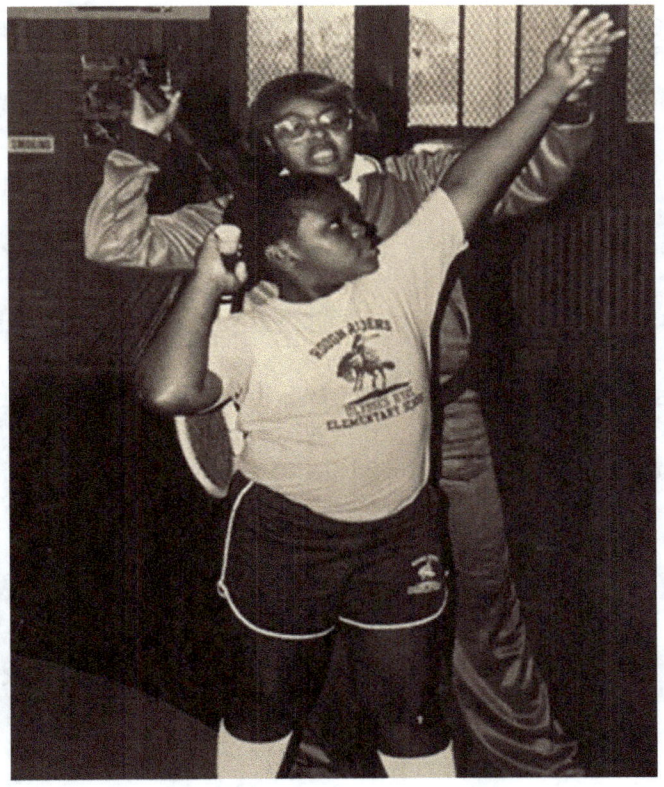

PHOTO 72 EMILY WITH UNIDENTIFIED STUDENT AT ULYSSES BYAS, DATE UNKNOWN. (COURTESY OF LILLIAN WATSON)

What I find most rewarding about my profession is how I have educated and trained more than five generations of students in the last 50 years in the Roosevelt school district and my travels around the world. I am proud of the fact that many students have graduated from schools of higher education, many received scholarships."

Emily often told her students, even if they were misbehaving, *"You come here for a good education, and you're going to get one from me."* Emily has always been known as an advocate for all children, but especially for the children of Roosevelt. Emily has allowed every child that comes to her a chance to learn Tennis, the meaning of physical education, and its relation to success. She allowed all students to prove to themselves that through hard work, determination, concentration and practice, anything they want they can get it because they worked for it. She inspired and has helped guide thousands of children over the last forty years as a physical education teacher, a tennis coach, and a mentor.

Emily took a young boy named Moses as a student when he was five years old. Moses was highly intelligent but like with many young children, the lack of challenge in the classroom brought him trouble from his teachers. As Moses progressed into who he wanted to be, he

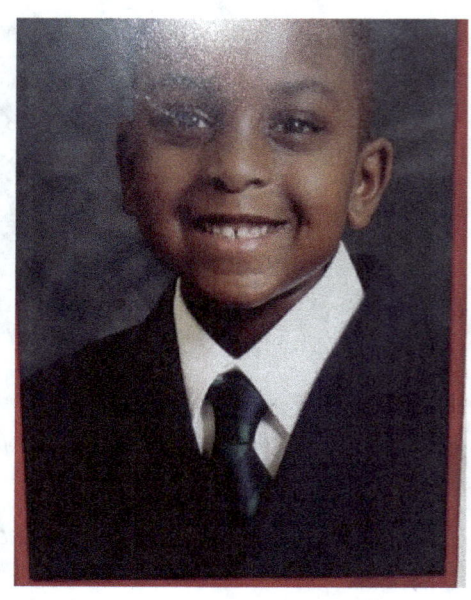

PHOTO 73 MOSES. (COURTESY OF EMILY MOORE)

decided that he wanted to attend the prestigious WestPoint Military

Academy. Emily was able to get a letter of recommendation from an unmentioned congressperson on behalf of Moses.

Moses was accepted to and graduated from the West Point Military Academy. Emily believes that the time, effort, patience, and continuance that she has put into the children, community and the world speak for itself.

Ultimately, she wanted it to be known that the Junior Tennis Alliance was never about her and her capabilities but of the children, pushing their limits to gain success by doing something that would make them the champion of their people in their lives. Emily has dedicated her life to being the champion of education for the people. She has received dozens of accolades for her involvement as a tennis coach and mentor, but to her, nothing compares to the success stories that have come out of her former tennis and Roosevelt students over the past 60 years.

> One of my mottos on education and helping the community is if you are going to use it, use it, but if not give it to somebody else. The younger generations now must create training sessions so our kids can really learn how to read and write, our kids do not know how to author essays, how to be prepared for interviews! Get a group of children and tell them that they need to be trained how to be leaders of this world, to be scholars, athletes, or just simply intelligent. Life is what you make it, not what you want. You must strive for excellence in all that you do, and you learn by doing and you do not learn by just reading something. You must understand it, it is a process, learning and training is a process and that is what I give to

my kids. I start off every school year asking if the children know how to spell the world education, and we go on from there!

After years of battling against the racial disparity in the staffing and hiring process of the Roosevelt school district and its Board, there was finally a public notice published Roosevelt's compliance with the Civil Rights act of 1964 and The Age Discrimination Act of 1975 in 1984.

In compliance with the provisions of Title IX of the Education Amendments of 1972, Title VI of the Civil Rights Act of 1964, and The Age Discrimination act of 1975, the Roosevelt Public Schools prints the following statement which was approved by the Board of Education in August 1984.

It is the policy of the Roosevelt Board of Education not to discriminate on the basis of age, sex, race, color, creed, handicaps, or national origin in its educational programs and employment practices.

The district person responsible for the coordination of activities relating to the above is Dr. Susan D. Savitt – District office 240 Denton place, Roosevelt, New York 11575 (516) 378-8220. Her office will provide information including procedures and forms to any student or employee who feels his/her rights may have been violated.

FIGURE 55   PUBLIC NOTICE OF TITLE VI OF THE CIVIL RIGHTS ACT. (UNKNOWN)

PHOTO 74 EMILY AT ROOSEVELT PARK, YEAR UNKNOWN.
(COURTESY OF EMILY MOORE)

In the 1980s, Emily received the following awards:

1985 – Martin Luther king Jr. annual community service honors and awards –
outstanding citizen contribution to improvement of Education and community

1985- Teachers Award from Roosevelt School District

1987 – Harlem Junior Tennis - Presented in appreciation for
your thoughtful and selfless dedication as a board member
and friend to the kids and their tennis program.

From the Harlem Tennis Junior Tennis Program

6/4/87

Emily Moore

In appreciation for your thoughtful and selfless dedication as a board member and friend to the kids and their tennis program

FIGURE 56 HARLEM JUNIOR TENNIS (COURTESY OF AYANNA MOORE)

Presented to

Emily Moore

The Alliance Jr. Tennis Development Program

In Appreciation for your Dedication, Hard Work, Long Hours, and the Support that you have given us.

Love

The 1980 Summer Camp

FIGURE 57 AWARD FROM AJTDP. (COURTESY OF AYANNA MOORE)

The New York state education system failed minority school districts in the 1990s.

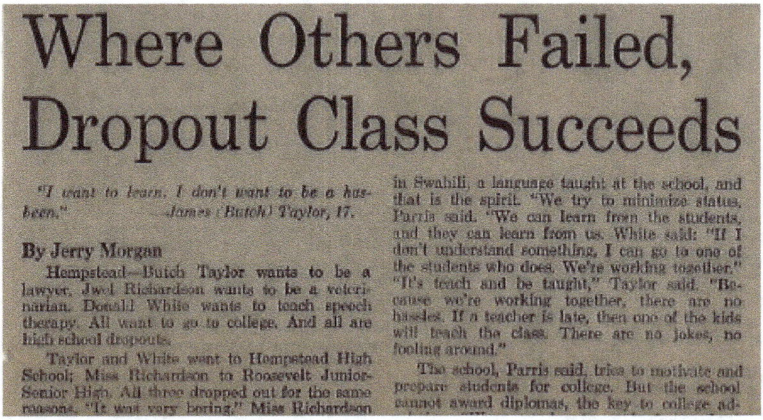

Where Others Failed, Dropout Class Succeeds

"I want to learn. I don't want to be a has-been." — James (Butch) Taylor, 17.

By Jerry Morgan

Hempstead—Butch Taylor wants to be a lawyer, Jwel Richardson wants to be a veterinarian. Donald White wants to teach speech therapy. All want to go to college. And all are high school dropouts.

Taylor and White went to Hempstead High School; Miss Richardson to Roosevelt Junior-Senior High. All three dropped out for the same reasons. "It was very boring," Miss Richardson

in Swahili, a language taught at the school, and that is the spirit. "We try to minimize status, Parris said. "We can learn from the students, and they can learn from us. White said: "If I don't understand something, I can go to one of the students who does. We're working together." "It's teach and be taught," Taylor said. "Because we're working together, there are no hassles. If a teacher is late, then one of the kids will teach the class. There are no jokes, no fooling around."

The school, Parris said, tries to motivate and prepare students for college. But the school cannot award diplomas, the key to college ad-

FIGURE 58 NEWSPAPER ARTICLE ABOUT THE UJAMAA ACADEMY (MORGAN, 199*)

In the 1990s, Journalist Jerry Morgan wrote the article *Where Others Failed Dropout Class Succeeds,* interviewing high school students who all wanted to do grand things with their lives, but dropped out of Hempstead, Roosevelt, Westbury, and Inwood High schools because of the student school courses and environment, *"was very boring."* The school classroom and administration environment pushed out and discouraged students. These students felt unchallenged as if their educational progressions were not of value. One student explained, "I *did not want to learn anything I [She] felt was useless. I [She] could not relate to what I [She] was learning."* Another student said, *"I couldn't cope with the situation in high school. It was just a big game."* The article went on to explain that luckily these students were able to get into a program called Ujamaa Academy that was under the Hofstra University African Studies Institute. Emily worked with the academy as a counselor and viewed that the program worked for the students because of its interactive setting. It allowed the student to learn from the teacher and vice versa, which made students appreciate their learning environment as it did not come with preconceptions and performance expectations of the youth they were teaching. Overall, it made Ujamaa Academy more popular than public school settings.

In the article, one of the coordinators of the Ujamaa Academy explained to the journalist that the kids are not dropouts by choice due to social oppression raised against their differential circumstances and views. One student said that their guidance counselor did not believe in him because he could not complete a certain task and questioned, "How can I be judged by one task when I am also great at others?" In a separate Article, A Roosevelt student in the 1990s was interviewed by *Newsday Long Island* about Roosevelt's decline in its education rank and graduation turnovers. The young woman had expressed that those students, including the young lady, began to skip school to be employed because she did not feel challenged academically. She felt that the younger population would find their selves involved with mischief because the school did not stimulate their minds and often the young women would add to the percentage of teenage pregnancy within Urban communities.

As an educator, Emily worked tirelessly to supply the students of Roosevelt and Nassau County the opportunities and activities to help keep them focused and centered in the right direction of educational achievements. On September 3, 1998, Long Island Newsday issued Emily's words were the Quote of the day. Emily said, *"Change has never been made by people hoping and wishing. Change has come from people standing up and taking a stand."* She then told the newspaper that she had planned to attend the Million Youth March in Washington, D.C. (Long Island Newsday, 1998) One of Emily's favorite things about working with children getting them to learn how to believe in themselves, achieve, and become responsible citizens, ultimately showing students that they don't need a lot materially to make greater change and results. She believed in promoting consistent advancement and encouraged it to others every day in and outside of school.

When interviewed by Elite American Educators in 2014, Emily Moore had this to say about her teaching style and success.

> [My students] They've all graduated from colleges, from Howard to Morgan State to Harvard to MIT," she says. "I told them you could go and be anything you want to be. I have a group of kids who are doctors and lawyers. I am proud that I have trained young people to become leaders and teachers of the world. I let them know from the beginning that we compete in a world with seven continents. It is about 'How can I help contribute to society?' Not going through life and saying, 'what is in it for me? The team spirit carried over to my individual endeavors setting an uncompromising standard of excellence. In every game, you meet on the field with an expectation of fair play. When I learned that in the game of life not everyone was treated fairly, I set out to demand fairness by speaking out against inequality and injustice whenever I saw it around me (Elite American Educators, 2014).

Emily wrote an essay in the 1990s about educational structure being the key to success for children and teens of the 1990s. Emily has always been a firm believer, and example setter of "it starts with the training of the mind and body in the classroom and playing field," not only as a physical education teacher but also as any kind of educator who cares to better their students and youth of tomorrow. The essay:

> Today schools must concentrate not only on teaching reading, writing, and arithmetic but also on providing a proper atmosphere in which to achieve success. Being a physical education teacher, I am acutely aware of the need for children to start at an early age to take care of their bodies as well as their minds.
>
> Physical Education may be the key in instilling positive health and fitness habits that children will have for the rest of their lives. In the

age of the single-working parents and latchkey children, healthy meals are not always a priority. This factor in addition to the more sedentary recreational activities of children including television, and video games has contributed significantly to the problem. Moreover, the health threats including the epidemic and increased drug abuse among young people should be attacked head-on by the educational system. By addressing these issues in physical education classes, another dimension will be added to the usual classroom, an even stronger message will be conveyed to the children.

Rather than allow the current societal trends to dictate what occurs in the educational environment, schools need to anticipate the trends and respond instead of merely reacting to them. The purpose of education is preparation. This includes preparing the mind as well as the body of each child for the future. This requires taking into account the real threats to the well-being of our children, accepting their existence, and addressing them in the controlled atmosphere of structural educational institutions.

Thus, in preparing students for the future, it is of great importance to begin today. This idea was discussed by Harold G. Shane in his article, "Educational foresight for the 1990's." Shane emphasized the need of developing "educational foresight" the ability to understand the variety and the nature of the rapidly changing technological and social aspects of our times and beyond. He also discussed the impact of outside forces on the educational system including the national economy, the Medicare crisis, and increase in violence in our society. To believe that an educational institution can exist without responding to the changes of our world is faced with today is naïve at best. At worst it is in essence the endangerment of our young people. It is the responsibility of our schools to take affirmative steps to prepare students for the difficulties posed by our ever-changing world. (Shane, 1990)

From my perspective as a physical education teacher, I see my role in the preparation of our youth as especially important. Fostering positive self-images among our youth must take place in the field, in the gym, and in the classroom. Together we must create an environment of hope and positivity that our students can carry out of the school and into the world.

As Booth Gardner states in his speech "Educational Change," he states that educators must focus more energy on early childhood and elementary schools, sending out clean messages that the students are capable of learning, even though they may think the odds are stacked against them. We must not engage in limiting our expectations of these children. (Gardner, 1990)

It is apparent that for this educational effort to be effective, all levels of the educational system must be involved. This includes the English teacher, as well as the physical education teacher. There is no room for passing the responsibility for someone else. We must all work together to ensure the future of our own entire society beginning with our youth."

In the late 1980s and early 1990s, popular figures such as comedian entertainer Eddie Murphy, Public Enemy rappers Chuck D and Flavor Flav, and screenwriter Steven White all grew up in Roosevelt and attended Roosevelt District Schools. The Alumni of Roosevelt would contribute their talents and time to the events that Emily would want to make happen. In 1992, Emily was able to "bring Hollywood to Strong Island," giving the children of Roosevelt to see where their hard work, practice, and determination could get them if they believed in themselves as Emily did them. In the 1990s, Emily received Ulysses Byas's Perfect Attendance Award for five consecutive years. Emily made sure she always came to work because each day away, could mean a step back to the youth.

Other 1990's awards include:

> 1993 – *Building for Tomorrow*: For two decades of commitment and untiring service to our youth, programs, and activities.
>
> 1995 – *Arthur Ashe multicultural enhancement award* presented by United States Tennis Association – Eastern Section Long Island Region
> 1995 – *Outstanding Youth Advocate award* presented by the Long Island Youth foundation – Dedicated to culturally educating youth minds,
> 1995 – *Arthur Ashe Coaches Award*
>
> *A Breakfast of Champions – Board of Directors –*
>
> *Roosevelt Unit Police Activity League*

Alliance Junior Development Tennis Program • Roosevelt Board of Education
Arthur Ashe • Public Enemy • Shari Headley • John Salley
and
Spike Lee
cordially invite you to attend a gala benefit reception as
'Hollywood Comes to Strong Island' for the on-location filming at Roosevelt
Park of
Steve White's

Love, Anyone?

. . . the choice is yours

Monday, July 20, 1992 — 7:00 PM - 10:00 PM
Roosevelt Jr-Sr High School
1 Wagner Avenue, Roosevelt, New York

Steve White

Comedian extraordinaire, actor, writer and filmmaker, Steve
hite is the quintessential renaissance man for the 90's. The native
ng Islander, reared in Roosevelt has staked his claim, in the
fervescent world of entertainment!

Steve's film credits include: Eddie Murphy's "Coming to
merica" and "Harlem Nights;" Spike Lee's "Do The Right Thing,"
Mo' Better Blues," and "Jungle Fever;" Renny Harlin's "Ford
irlane;" and Danny Devito's, "Other People's Money."

A graduate of Roosevelt Jr.-Sr. High School, Nassau Community College and Adelphi
niversity, Steve has appeared on: HBO Def Comedy Jam; MTV ½ hour Comedy hour; Comic
rip Live; and Showtime at the Apollo, to name a few.

Now, Steve has returned home, fresh from serving as Director trainee under Spike Lee on
e soon to be released "Malcolm X." Steve has returned home and brought Hollywood with

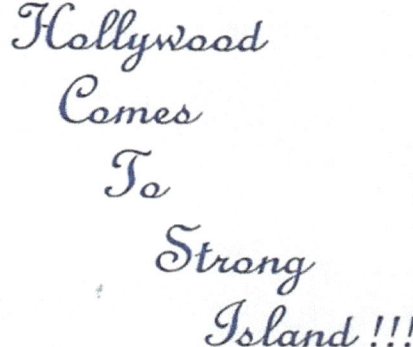

Hollywood Comes To Strong Island !!!

FIGURE 59 PLAYBILL FOR STEVE WHITE'S LOVE ANYONE?...THE CHOICE IS YOUR'S AT ROOSEVELT HIGH
SCHOOL. STEVE WHITE AND FILM DIRECTOR/ ACTOR SPIKE LEE (COURTESY OF EMILY MOORE)

PHOTO 75 STEVEN WHITE AND OMOTAYO ADEDEJI. (COURTESY OF EMILY MOORE)

Presented to Emily Moore Five Year Perfect Attendance Award Martin Luther King Jr. Annual Honors and Awards Program Roosevelt Union Free School District Roosevelt, New York January 21, 1991

FIGURE 60 PERFECT ATTENDANCE AWARD (COURTESY OF AYANNA MOORE)

U.B.S (Ulysses Byas School)

Ms. E. Moore

Best Attendance Award – Faculty 1991

FIGURE 61 BEST ATTENDANCE AWARD (COURTESY OF AYANNA MOORE)

Overtime: 2000 – 2023

Rev. Dr. Seretta McKnight: A student turned lifetime friend.

Emily has had too many students to count and too many stories to just reflect on at her age, but she did mention one of her dear good lifetime friends and former students Rev. Dr. Seretta McKnight. Seretta was one of Emily's first students in 1975, only in the 7th or 8th grade when she started to practice and play tennis for Emily. Moore remembers her father Irving, to be a character, and owner of an oil company that serviced the "Black Belt" of Long Island: Lakeview, Westbury, Uniondale, Hempstead, Freeport, and Roosevelt for almost 40 years. Emily spoke of how Seretta's father would always contribute to the fundraising that was going on within the Freeport-Roosevelt communities, "even if he had it or not."

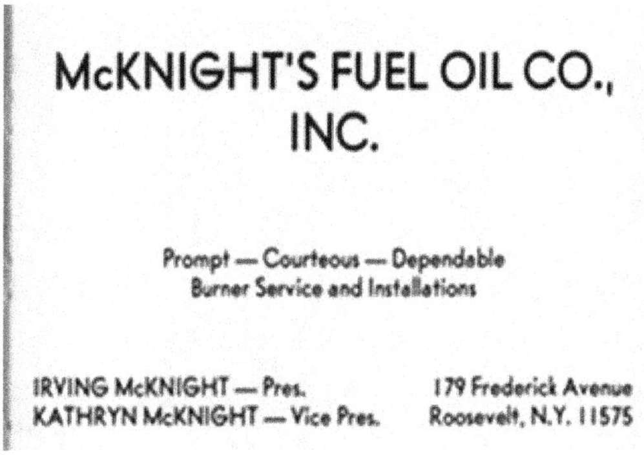

McKNIGHT'S FUEL OIL CO., INC.

Prompt — Courteous — Dependable
Burner Service and Installations

IRVING McKNIGHT — Pres.   179 Frederick Avenue
KATHRYN McKNIGHT — Vice Pres.   Roosevelt, N.Y. 11575

FIGURE 62 BUSINESS CARD OF MCKNIGHT OIL. COURTESY OF EMILY MOORE

Dr. Moore was my seventh-grade physical educator teacher. She introduced me to the game of tennis and travelled us to different tournaments. As a member of the original class of AJDTP (Alliance Junior Development Tennis Program) my parents allowed Miss Moore to take me and get tested at the Port Washington Tennis Academy over on the North Shore. We know what the climate was then. I remember Miss Moore not appreciating their assessment of me. They claimed I needed six months of private lessons, because my style was unorthodox and then she could bring me back for another tryout. Yeah right. That was not going to happen!

Emily proudly mentioned McKnight's achievements saying that she received her doctorate and serves as a minister in Nassau County. In 1991, she became one of the founders of the National Action Network for Justice with Reverend Al. Sharpton Jr. Dr. McKnight is also the founder of the Sisters in the Struggle empowerment group, an internationally known empowerment group within Black communities throughout the United States and the Caribbean Sea. She has also produced her radio station and Television correspondences that educate and uplift the Black community. Emily remembers the day the Sisters of the Struggle was brought together; she was organizing with the group almost twenty years after teaching McKnight.

I organized with them for the Women's March in Philadelphia in 1996, I told her [Seretta], 'I am ordering the bus, and all better get on it! Other than that, I am just ordering one bus.' From that trip came the group Sisters in the Struggle. From that organization came the Breakfast of Champions, a brother group. I have many magazines and pamphlets from both of their activities.

Dr. McKnight spoke on the behalf of Emily as a mentor and friend.

Perhaps the greatest illustration of her ability to reach and continually teach was when she booked the bus for the Million Women's March in DC. Being battle weary from the failed state takeover, I said, you book the bus, and I will get on it. That transformative trip led to the creation of Sisters in The Struggle! That was 25 years ago. Currently, SITS have an Emily Moore Award for Community Activism/Service. Emily Moore has through her activism, and AJDTP produced: doctors, lawyers, educators, activists, architects, preachers, homemakers, civil servants, and all-around successful contributor to society & she is still doing it!

There was also a time Air Force 2 landed out East (Long Island). I called "Em" at the U.S. Open and told her I had arranged for the AJT children to meet Vice President Gore on the tarmac, which was a moment for sure! Full circle, the icing on the cake was Miss Moore selecting me to present her at her induction into the United States Tennis Association Hall of Fame in 2021.

Ain't God grand!

A Strong Supporter Reverend Al Sharpton and the National Action Network

PHOTO 76 L TO R: REV. AL SHARPTON, EMILY, AND DR. SERETTA MCKNIGHT. COURTESY OF EMILY MOORE

In Emily's current years, when she is not involved in the obligations of her career, Emily enjoys watching the sport of Tennis, and the *National Action Network* under the leadership of Reverend Al. Sharpton. Across the world, Reverend Alfred (Al) Sharpton Jr., has been known for his work as a civil and social justice rights activist for over the last fifty years. In the late 1970s, Sharpton served as a youth director in his neighborhood in Harlem, New York, and would further his efforts by becoming a founder of the National Youth Movement to raise money for poor youth and the fight against drugs. Sharpton would then serve as youth director for the presidential campaign of Shirley Chisolm, a congressperson a Brooklyn, New York native, who became the first Black woman to run for presidential office. In 1991, Sharpton along with various others including Dr. Seretta McKnight, founded the *National Action Network (NAN) with the mantra, "No Justice, No Peace."* NAN takes MLK's non-violence stance by aiding and standing for criminal justice, justice reform, police accountability, crisis intake and victim assistance, voting rights, youth leadership, corporate responsibility and pension diversity, all things catered to help those who are underrepresented in the justice system. With all the accolades afforded to Sharpton, Emily views Sharpton as a great man but remembers seeing him as an 11-year-old boy at Bishop Frank O. White's church in Freeport in the 1970s.

An avid supporter, Emily has faithfully attended various symposiums, demonstrations, and marches in support of Sharpton and NAN. Sharpton went on be the voice of the Central Park Five, a group of Black American teenagers falsely accused, accosted, tried, and sentenced for a raping of a white woman in Manhattan. This case increased the racial heat and fear against teenage Black men in New York, which was unfortunate for the Black communities across America because it seems when it comes to Black people, "If one does it, they all do it." It held such rage that "Adding fuel to the fire, weeks after the attack, in May 1989, real estate developer (and future U.S. president) Donald Trump took out full-page ads in *The New York Times*, the *New York Daily News*, the *New York Post* and *New York Newsday* with the headline, "Bring Back the Death Penalty. Bring Back Our Police" (History.com Editors, 2020). The men were freed in 2002 after the true perpetrator confessed, and the State of New York came to a settlement with the group of men in 2014. A documentary on the event *The Central Park Five* was released in 2012, and Netflix released a film on the events in 2019 called *When They See Us*.

Even when Sharpton's name was muddied by the media, due to law issues that pertained to tax evasion accusations in the 1990's, Emily stayed a loyal supporter of Sharpton as he was acquitted of the charges. Dr. Seretta McKnight could once again attest to Emily's support for Rev. Sharpton because they did it together during the Democratic National Convention that took place in Chicago, Illinois in 1996.

> As activists we travelled with the Rev. Al Sharpton, before he was popular because his mission for freedom, justice and equality was righteous then as it is now. A memory that comes to mind is when we were at the Democratic National Convention in Chicago, 1996. As a delegate, we would be at the park protesting with Rev. during the day and inside the convention in the evenings.

The Chicago Tribune wrote that "Rev. Al Sharpton led nearly 300 people from Garfield Park to the United Center, a far cry from the more than 2,000 expected at a rally and march dubbed "Cash the Check." Also stated that when Rev. Sharpton was asked about the march, he replied, "the march was designed to commemorate the 33rd anniversary of Martin Luther King's "I Have A Dream" speech," a strong attachment to Sharpton's and Emily's long battle towards the Civil Rights objective (Lisa Black, James Hill, Laurie Cohen, Jerry Thomas, 1996) e. In 1999, Emily received the Women of Excellence Award for the outstanding example of Womanhood from the National Action Network for her contributions to the community, society, and Civil Rights. To go even further in support of Rev. Sharpton, Emily served as an organizer and fundraiser for Rev. Al Sharpton in 2004 as he bid for Presidential Office. Emily said that even though she and Rev Al Sharpton have interacted, organized, and worked together various times over the decades, she appreciated that while she was going through her health battles, Rev Sharpton would give her a call every so often to check on her welfare.

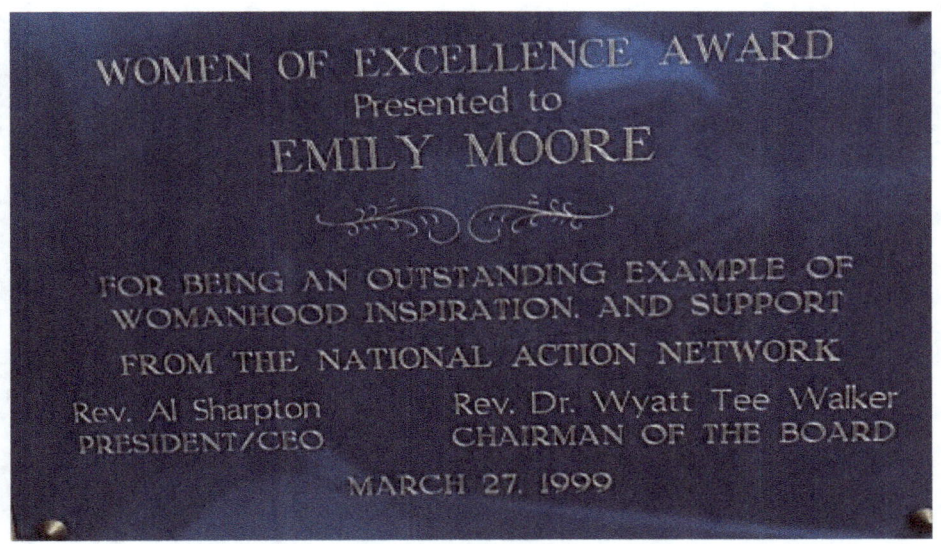

FIGURE 63 WOMEN OF EXCELLENCE AWARD PRESENTED BY REV. AL SHARPTON

This is what Reverend Al. Sharpton said about Emily.

I first Met Dr. Moore in the late 1980s when we were fighting for justice for Yusuf Hawkins who was attacked by a white mob and shot to death in Bensonhurst, Brooklyn, N.Y. She made every rally and stood alongside us even though tension in New York were at a heightened and dangerous level. Through the years, her support has been unwavering, including when I ran for senate and the Presidency. I could not believe that someone of her athletic notoriety would be as active in the movement for social justice, but that is precisely what she has done. I collaborated with her and Dr. McKnight when I ran for office; they were like both sides of the dynamic duo Nassau County, fighting for Black empowerment and getting folks elected to office – they recharged each other's batteries. In 1999, my organization, National Action Network, honored Dr. Moore with the Outstanding Woman of the Year Award for her commitment to the fight for equality, civil rights, and justice. This was in the first decade in which Nation Action Network was founded, which shows just how far back our relationship spans, and how long she has been a warrior for progress. She has been an avid supporter of education, tennis development, physical fitness, and equality across the board. In the three and a half decades of my relationship with Dr. Moore, she has been the ultimate activist, without seeking attention or fanfare for her selfless work. (Sharpton, 2023)

Junior Alliance Tennis student memories:

As Emily has educated hundreds of children, teenagers and adults, it is best to say it is almost impossible to include all the names and achievements of her students. Proud to state, that many of her students have gone to attend colleges such as Morgan State University, Howard University, Norfolk State University, Stanford University, Harvard University, Yale University, New York University, Florida A&M University, Princeton University, MIT, North Carolina A&T and various other colleges and Universities. Here are just a few of the former players and scholars who have been remembered or given words of gratitude for Emily's dedication.

Paula O'Conner

PHOTO 77 PAULA O'CONNER IN THE GLASSES WITH ARTHUR ASHE

According to Emily, Paula O'Conner was highly ranked in the American Tennis Association as a junior. The last thing that Emily knew was that she had completed undergraduate work at Yale University on an academic scholarship and that she had plans to take a year to relax and play tennis, and that she would enroll in medical school, that she may currently be a doctor in San Francisco. After graduating from Yale, she attended Stanford for her further education. In 2021, Paula O'Connor currently serves as Senior Vice President of Clinical Development, at Protagonist Therapeutics Inc.

Daniel Burgess, Sr.

PHOTO 78 DANIEL BURGRESS, SR. MAN, FROM AMERICAN TENNIS ASSOCIAITON, AND EMILY MOORE. COURTESY OF EMILY MOORE

Panamanian-born tennis legend Daniel Burgess, Sr in the 1980s after he settled in Freeport after his professional career. Emily spoke of how she developed a long-standing friendship and partnership. Burgess Sr would go on to open his tennis program in Freeport at the Freeport Recreational Center, he sent his sons to learn tennis under the coaching of Emily Moore with the Junior Tennis Alliance program. Both of his sons would become promising and successful players in the youth tennis world in the 1990s. Daniel Burgess, Sr passed away in 2021. His son Kevin took over the teachings of his Tennis Academy, still running in Freeport at the Bishop Frank O. White Park during the summer.

Daniel Burgess, Jr.

FIGURE 64 DANIEL BURGESS JR.

Daniel Burgess Jr. ...Won the 1998 New England Tennis Association – Open Championship Boys 10 years old Singles Tournament, 1998 New England Tennis Association Championship Boys 10 years old Doubles, 1997 New England Tennis Association

Championship Boys 10 years old Singles. He won second place in the 1998 Pyramid Junior Tennis Championship, and New York Tennis Association Championship. In 1997 at age 8, Daniel finished third in the Boys 10 and under at the American Tennis Association National Tournament held in Florida. His coaches are the best – Daniel Burgess, Sr., and Emily Moore.

Kevin Burgess

I have been playing tennis since I could walk at about two years old. I am now thirty-two and can still recall some of my fondest memories with Ms. Moore. They either involved her calling every individual to focus, and preserver through hard work; or the treks taken to the Harlem Armory, and Alabama for the ATA Nationals (Atlantic Tennis Association). During the treks, Ms. Moore always brought us to places where Black and brown people were trying to build, compete and educate at all levels. The culture of tennis that Ms. Moore curated and promoted boosted excellence while inviting beginners. The predominantly white tennis clubs can be uncomfortable with the racial barriers, but Ms. Moore and my father Daniel Burgess, Sr. made a way. Between 5-6:30 a.m., we would get up at dawn to use the Freeport recreational facilities before indoor tennis opened. This was where Black instructors would work with Black students. My brothers Daniel, Jr. and Shawn Conyers played with Ms. Moore as well. These memories remind me that there is always a way, and if there is not: there is an opportunity! Trail Blazers raised me! My father served as the director of tennis at Freeport Indoor Tennis at the Freeport Recreation center.

Kelvin Belcher

Emily recalled that Belcher transferred to Morehouse College in Atlanta, Georgia, attending during his senior year of college on a tennis scholarship. She remembered his credentials, as he was number two on the varsity team and he completed his last tennis season with a 20- 0 record. Belcher went to play for the USATA satellite circuit and has done radio announcements in Atlanta since that time. Emily smiled and said "Every time he sees me, he calls me coach, all the guys traveled with me, except Kevin because he lived in the city. He claimed me from day one, and he watched what I was doing, what I taught."

Renee Blount

Emily mentioned that she had once trained professional tennis player Renee Blount, a Washington, D.C. native. Though she was a great player obviously, that did not matter with Emily Moore as she told her *"You're not going to be late, not with me. you must get up and work and train. I have one hundred children waiting for me,*

so I will see you before work and after school.

"I took the kids to the U.S. Open!"

Emily had taken students to the U.S. Open for at least 20 years. She recalled how she met with the likes of Tennis Champion and legends Serena and Venus Williams, various times during the events. Emily specifically remembers their father, Richard Williams, coming to the group of youth during their protest the lack of minority inclusion in the Davis Cup Tennis Tournament. Longtime Roosevelt Resident Beverly Cunningham recalled the first time she was able to travel with Emily to the U.S. Open as an adult chaperone.

> *Dr. Moore was my physical education teacher when I was in Junior High School more than 45 years ago. She was energetic, conscious, and driven to nothing less than greatness and excellence for her students and humanity. Dr. Moore was my eldest niece's physical education teacher, whom she still loves and holds in high esteem. My other four nieces and nephews learned tennis in Dr. Moore's Junior Alliance tennis summer camp program, along with countless other youngsters in New York. At the end of one summer, Dr. Moore decided to obtain a bus and insisted that her students attend the U.S Open qualifying finals annually at the U.S Tennis center in Flushing, Queens, New York. As an adult chaperone, I hold this experience dear to my heart, and will cherish it for life.*

Emily has always advocated exposing her students to experiences, visions and ideas outside of the communities they came from. In 2021, Emily told reporters for the United States Tennis Association,

> I am a historian," Moore says. "Whatever state we are going to, [the kids] are going to have to know something about it. So, we would have an educational day to visit the sites after the tournaments were over. We visited colleges like Morehouse in Atlanta, Norfolk in Virginia. And a lot of them went on to those schools. So, through tennis, they were exposed [to these things]. (Sode, 2021 Eastern Hall of Fame: Dr. Emily Moore, 2022)

On Tuesday August 24 the Tennis Camp will attend the U. S. OPEN, at The National Tennis Center, in Flushing New York.

We will leave from Roosevelt Park at 9 AM. We have leased a coach bus and the cost is $10.00 per person. Please pack a lunch for your child. We will return to Roosevelt Park at 3 PM.

We would like for all of the children to attend. It will be an incredible experience for him/her. Please fill out the permission slip below and enclose $10 (a separate slip for each child please).
ALL CHILDREN MUST WEAR CAMP SHIRT.

FIGURE 65 U.S. OPEN TRIP INFORMATION. (COURTESY OF EMILY MOORE)

PHOTO 79 STUDENTS AND INSTRUCTORS OF JTADP (TOP LEFT. -MIDDLE: SPENCER BELCHER, FAR RIGHT DENISE BROWN (COURTESY OF EMILY MOORE)

In 2007, players of the Junior Tennis Alliance qualified for the American Tennis Association National Tournament. Emily fundraised various drives and events to provide funds for student participation and camp trips.

FIGURE 66 BOOKLET OF THE 90TH ANNIVERSAY OF ATA NATIONALS

Emily Moore, President
New York Tennis Association
137 Mirin Avenue ⌘ Roosevelt, NY 11575

A Message From The
New York Tennis Association President

Greetings to all Participants and Supporters of the 2007 ATA National Championships.

As President of the New York Tennis Association and host of the 90th Anniversary of the American Tennis Association's National Championship, I "Welcome you to New York".

We gather at a time in American history when we still face challenges, but the cream (our top juniors) will always rise to the top. The ATA National Championships has always provided positive experiences for our youth and adults in this great sport of tennis.

We are proud of you. You have trained hard for the ATA National Championships and this experience coupled with the discipline obtained through focused training leads to success. There will be standing room only around many tennis courts, but don't let the big city or the many people deter you from your destiny which is greatness.

The committee has planned several phenomenal off-court activates for your enjoyment. I must thank the many sponsors and community volunteers. The opportunities provided to enhance your New York visit would not have been possible without them.

Here's to a safe and happy tennis adventure filled with pleasant learning experiences in the Big Apple, New York.

Sincerely,

Emily Moore, President
New York Tennis Association

"Dare to Struggle, Dare to Win...
No Struggle, No Victory"

ata Nationals 2007 New York

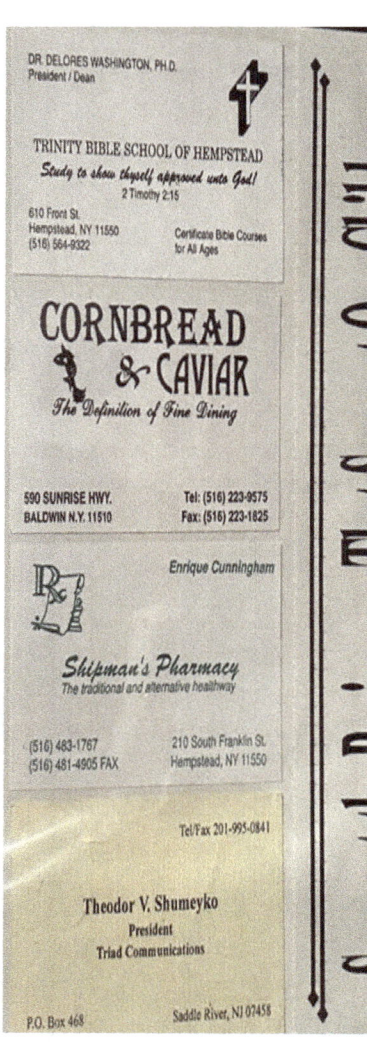

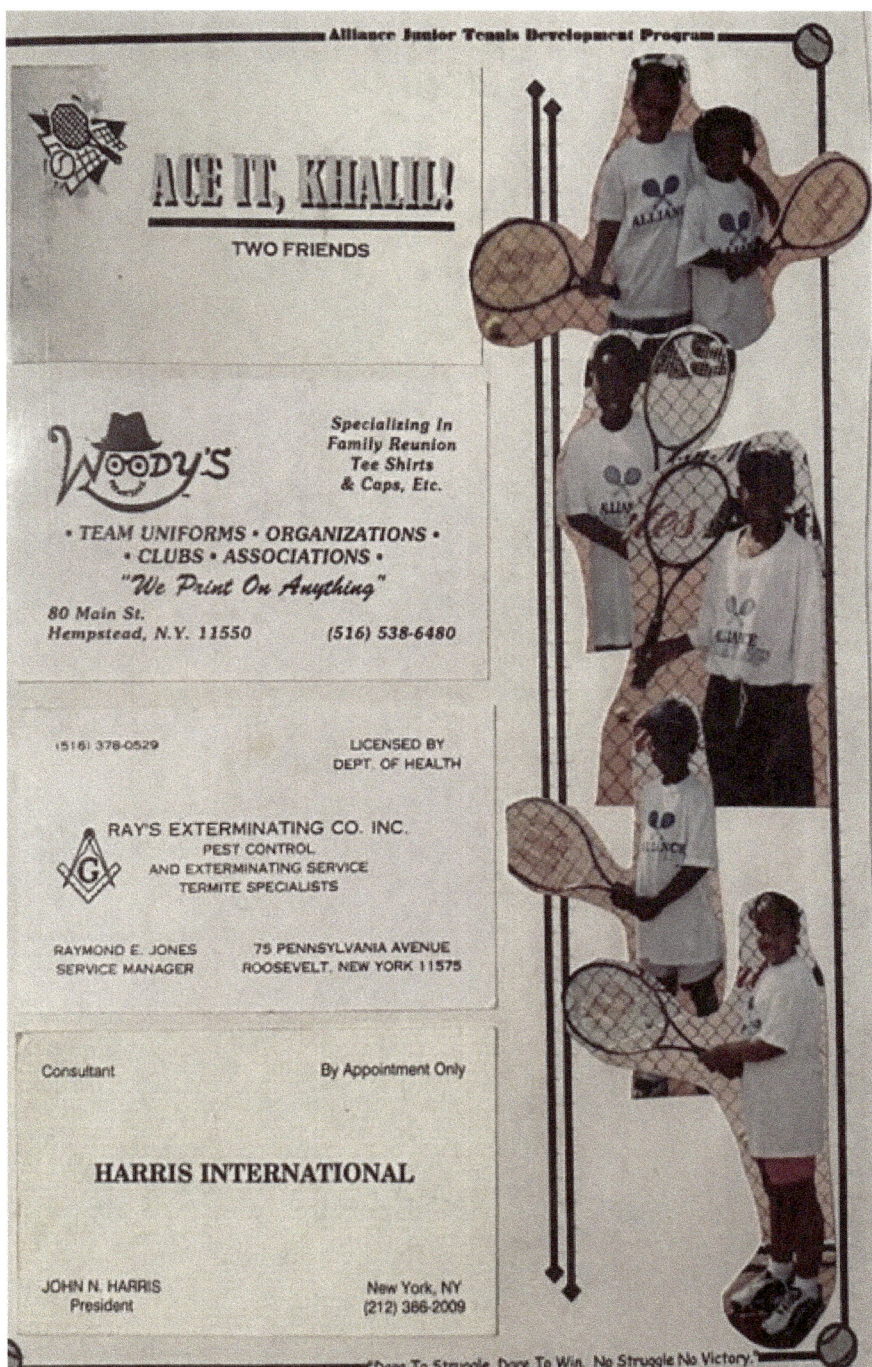

Sister Emily Moore

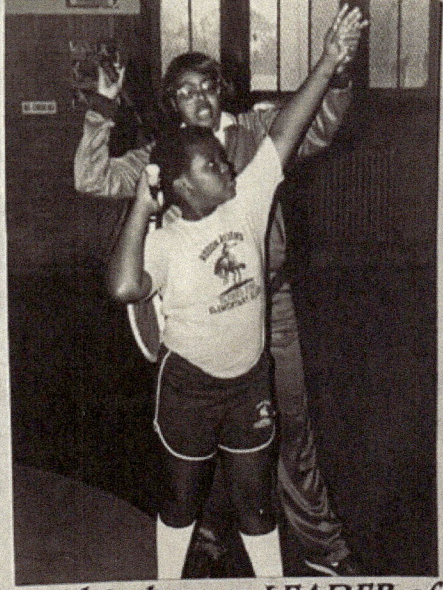

We are Blessed to have a LEADER of your magnitude serve 'our' community.

You make the difference in so many of our young peoples lives.

Your contribution to the transformation of the universe are greatly appreciated.

Your Sister In The Struggle,

Lillian Coggin-Watson

GOOD LUCK TO
ADISA MANDELA HORTON
AT THE AMERICAN TENNIS ASSOCIATION'S JUNIOR NATIONAL CHAMPIONSHIPS, FORT LAUDERDALE, FLORIDA, Aug. 1 to Aug. 9, 1998

AWARDS

1997 ATA NYS INDOOR CHAMPION BOYS 12

1997 ATA NEW ENGLAND FINALIST BOYS 12

1997 ATA NEW ENGLAND DOUBLES CO-CHAMPION BOYS 12

1998 ATA NYS INDOOR FINALIST BOYS 14

1998 ATA NYS OUTDOOR CHAMPION BOYS 14

Nia: Purpose
"To be a great champion. You must believe you are the best. If not, pretend you are."   Muhammad Ali

Student of the Alliance Junior Tennis Program since 1990

"Dare To Struggle, Dare To Win. No Struggle No Victory."

THANK YOU MS. EMILY MOORE, EXECUTIVE DIRECTOR, AJTP

Best of Luck to the

Alliance Junior Tennis Players

Attending The

ATA National Tennis Tournament

KIWANIS CLUB
OF ROOSEVELT

P.O. Box 70
Roosevelt, New York 11575
516 379 6550

Meetings:
1st & 3rd Wednesday
of each month

"Dare To Struggle, Dare To Win. No Struggle No Victory."

Continued Success to All Honorees
and the Alliance Junior Tennis Program

We salute you on this auspicious occasion!!

*S*ISTERS

*I*N

*T*HE

*S*TRUGGLE!!

Seretta C. McKnight
President

316 Nassau Road, Suite 282
Roosevelt, NY 11575
(516) 223-5288 ~
   378-3991(fax)

A Luta Continua ~ The Struggle Continues

Pastor Reginald Tuggle

&

The Memorial Presbyterian Family

Congratulates

Emily Moore

And

The American Tennis Association

Ninety Years Of Excellence

To God Be The Glory,
Great Things He Has Done!

MEMORIAL PRESBYTERIAN CHURCH

189 Babylon Turnpike
Roosevelt, New York 11575

(516) 623-9561

Emily expressed that the passing of this student Shayla Rose saddened her.

Alliance Junior Tennis Development Program

Our heartfelt thanks to **Miss Moore** and **Alliance Junior Tennis** for helping our daughter **Shayla** and countless other children, discover and develop a **"CAN DO"** attitude.

Love and Respect,
Stacy & Trevor Rose

Shayla,
Congratulations on your **Graduation** from Freeport High School, and your brilliant commencement speech as **Class President.** You've earned your wings, **NOW USE THEM!!!**

LOVE,
Mommy & Daddy

ROOSEVELT TEACHERS' ASSOCIATION

recognizes and supports the efforts of the

Alliance Junior Tennis Development Program.

It is our hope that the children of the
Roosevelt Community
continue to receive exposure and guidance
that will sustain positive aspirations
and
nurture responsible citizenship.

*   *   *

We wish you all a successful competition
at the
American Tennis Association National Championship
in Fort Lauderdale, Florida.

"Dare To Struggle, Dare To Win. No Struggle No Victory."

Congratulations
&
Continued Success

Alliance Junior Tennis Program
&
All Recognition Awardees

McKnight Fuel Oil Company
Complete Burner Service & Installation

'Celebrating over 30 years of Service to the Community!'

(516) 378-1510 ~ (516) 378-4272

Irving C. McKnight
President

Kathryn McKnight
Vice President

Seretta C. McKnight
General Manager

"Our Fuel Oil Makes Warm Friends"

'Dare To Struggle, Dare To Win. No Struggle No Victory.'

PHOTO 80 JATDP STUDENTS AND STAFF WITH REVEREND DONNIE MCCLURKIN (SECOND ROW, FORTH FROM LEFT). (COURTESY OF EMILY MOORE)

PHOTO 81 STUDENTS OF ROOSEVELT HIGH SCHOOL GIRLS TENNIS TEAM, 2009. SOME BUT NOT ALL: TOLITHA HENRY, CHIKU, NAILAH CHERRY, DENISE BROWN, VINNIEQUA KENNEDY, SHERELL KENNEDY (COURTESY OF EMILY MOORE)

'MOORE' OR LESS

Humanitarian efforts in Haiti

In 2004, the County of Haiti experienced a category five hurricane called Ivan. It devastated the Haitian community and its lands, killing approximately 1,700 people. During this time, Emily joined Dr. Ron Daniels, President/Founder of the Institute of the Black World 21stCentury, as an Ambassador of Hope and Community Builder for the Haitian Support Project along with hundreds of other ambassadors and volunteers in efforts to supply disaster relief to the Haitian community and the building of a schoolhouse.

> *I have always loved and respected the Haitian community because they were the first to show resilience against slavery and prevail. Even throughout the times, Haiti has been hit with natural disasters, political downfalls, and the exile treatment from other countries due to their fight for their independence.. They fight for themselves and each other all the time against great oppressions.*

In 2009, Dr. Ron Daniels commissioned Emily as a Nation Builder for Haiti.

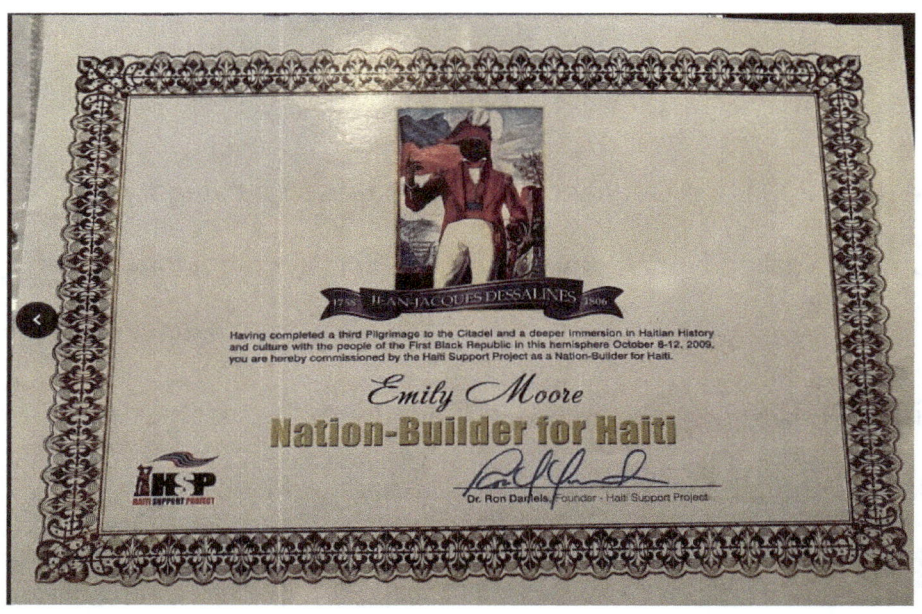

FIGURE 68 RECOGNIZATION FOR BUILDING EFFORTS IN HAITI AND MEMBERSHIP TO TOUSAINT L'OUVERTURE V.I.P CIRCLE. (COURTESY OF AYANNA MOORE)

Having completed a third pilgrimage to the Citadel and a deeper immersion in Haitian History and culture with the people of the First Black Republic in this hemisphere October 8-12, 2009. The Haiti Support Project as a Nation-Builder for Haiti hereby commissions you.

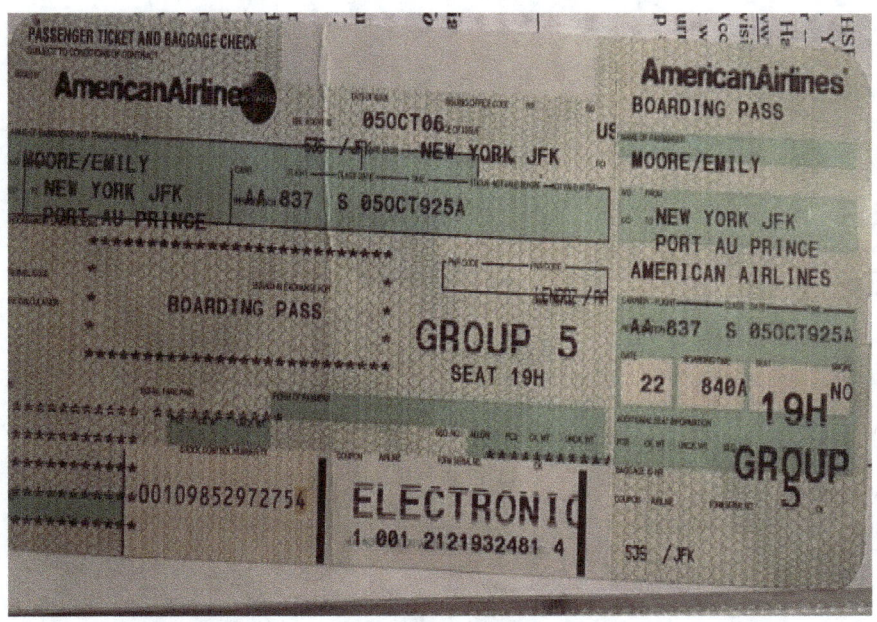

FIGURE 69 PLANE TICKET TO HAITI (COURTESY OF EMILY MOORE)

New England Tennis Association

In July of 2006, Emily was chosen to be enshrined in the New England Tennis Association All of Fame as a Contributor.

FIGURE 70 ENSHRINEMENT ELECTION FOR NEW ENGLAND TENNIS ASSOCIATION HALL OF FAME. (COURTESY OF AYANNA MOORE)

People-to-People

In 2010, Dr. Moore traveled with People-to-People Citizen Ambassador Programs with delegation leader Alpha Alexander, Ph.D., Sports, and Physical Education Delegation to the Republic of South Africa. The mission of the delegates was to visit various institutions of educational settings, governmental representatives, cultural institutions, and the Department of Sport and Recreation. Emily also traveled across South Africa for the first time.

FIGURE 71 PEOPLE TO PEOPLE PARTICIPATION. (COURTESY OF AYANNA MOORE)

Emily was the **Grand Marshall** for the Annual Roosevelt Memorial Day Parade in 2010.

PHOTO 82 EMILY AS GRAND MARSHALL. (COURTESY OF EMIY MOORE)

In appreciation of the efforts and support to the founding and contribution to Hempstead, and Long Island's only African American History Museum in 2011.

Certificate of Recognition
Presented by the African American Museum
to
Emily Moore

Behalf of the African American Museum, Friends, and Board Members we would like to acknowledge your selection as women who has made a positive impact in the lives of those who know you and the community at large. We urge you to continue your great work and inspire future generations of women in their chosen endeavors.

David Byer – Tyre
Director, and Curator
of African American Museum
March 19, 2011

FIGURE 72 CERTIFICATE OF RECOGNITION (COURTESY OF AYANNA MOORE)

On February 26, 2011, Emily was presented a Certificate of Recognition from the Freeport-Roosevelt Branch of the NAACP for being someone "who has given unselfishly of her educational acumen for the betterment of students, in the Roosevelt School District."

FIGURE 73 NAACP CERTIFICATE OF RECOGNITION (COURTESY OF AYANNA MOORE)

Incorporated Village of Freeport, New York

Mayor's Citation in Honor of

Emily Moore

The Church of Transfiguration

On behalf of the Mayor and the Board of Trustees, this is presented to Emily Moore as she is recognized as "The Freedom Rider." She is an exceptional woman who has achieved prominence and distinction in her lifetime. She is being honored today for her contributions to improve our surroundings. He Actions have inspired others to dream more, learn more and become more! Congratulations!

In testimony Whereof, I have Hereunto Affixed my Signature.

This Twenty-Ninth Day of October 2011

Andrew Harwich, Mayor

FIGURE 74 MAYOR'S CITATION (COURTESY OF AYANNA MOORE)

In November 2011, Emily attended a convocation ceremony held by Morgan State University in honor of the students who took part in the Civil Rights movement. The guest speaker was the late Congressman John Lewis. Morgan State revealed its civil rights exhibit that reflected the participation of Civil Rights student activists. Emily is pictured in the exhibit along with the other young women she was arrested with during the Northwood Demonstrations.

MORGAN STATE UNIVERSITY

GROWING THE FUTURE • LEADING THE WORLD

Dear Ms. Moore:

On February 1, 1960, four students from the Agricultural and Technical College of North Carolina — now North Carolina A&T State University — walked into a Woolworth's store in Greensboro and sat down at the lunch counter, refusing to leave until they were served. They were arrested and launched a national sit-in movement for civil rights. Or so the story is often told. The truth is the sit-in movement in the United States began right here in Maryland, years earlier.

In the early 1950s, students of Morgan State College — now Morgan State University — began demanding service at the lunch counter of the Read's Drug Store at Loch Raven Boulevard and Cold Spring Lane. The sit-in movement began there and soon spread to stores downtown and many other locations in and around Baltimore. Morgan students' activism continued into the early sixties, culminating in the integration of the theatre in Northwood Shopping Plaza. Records show that you were among those brave students who stood up for your rights.

On Thursday, November 10, 2011, at 1:00 p.m., Morgan State University will host a celebration of those students who participated in the protests and helped launch a national phenomenon that shaped the Civil Rights Movement of the 1960s. I am pleased to invite you to be a part of this historic event, the highlight of which will be the unveiling of a special civil rights exhibit, curated by University of Maryland law professor Larry Gibson, that will set the record straight and commemorate Baltimore's and Morgan's role in this national movement.

Earlier that day, we would like for you also to be our special guest at the annual Founders Day Convocation, to be held at 11:00 a.m., in the Gilliam Concert Hall of the Carl J. Murphy Fine Arts Center. The keynote speaker will be Congressman John Lewis.

I hope your schedule will allow you to participate in these historic events. Please RSVP, by October 21, 2011, by calling 443-885-3535, or shonae.spence@morgan.edu.

Kind regards,

David Wilson
President

Dear Ms. Moore,

On February 1, 1960, four students from the Agricultural and Technical College of North Carolina—Now North Carolina A&T State University --- walked into a Woolworth's store in Greensboro and sat down at the lunch counter, refusing to leave until they were served. They were arrested and launched a national sit-in movement for civil rights. Or so the story is often told. The truth is the sit-in movement in the United States began right here in Maryland, years earlier.

In the early 1950s, students of Morgan State College – now Morgan State University – began demanding service at the lunch counter of the Read's Drug Store at Loch Raven Boulevard and Cold Spring Land. The sit-in movement began there and soon spread to stores downtown and many other locations in and around Baltimore. Morgan Students' activism continued into the early sixties, culminating in the integration of the Northwood Shopping Plaza. Records show that you were among those brave students who stood up for your rights.

On Thursday, November 10, 2011, at 1:00 p.m., Morgan State University will host a celebration of those students who participated in the protest and helped launch a national phenomenon that shaped the Civil Rights Movement of the 1960s/ I am pleased to invite you to be apart of this historic event, the highlight of which will be the unveiling of a special civil rights exhibit, curated by the University of Maryland law professor Larry Gibson, that will set the record straight and commemorate Baltimore's and Morgan's role in this national movement.

Earlier that day, we would like for you also to be our special guest at the annual Founders Day Convocation, to be held at 11: 00a.m, in the Gilliam Concert Hall of the Carl J. Murphy Fine Arts Center. The keynote speaker will be Congressman John Lewis.

I hope your schedule will allow for you to participate in these historic events...

Kindly,

David Wilson
Presidnet.

Office of the Executive
Citation

Whereas the County of Nassau is proud to recognize those outstanding individuals, institutes, and programs which render significant contributions for the enhancement of our region and the betterment of our residents, and

WHERAS, Emily Moore, is such an individual; and

WHEREAS you, Emily Moore, have worked diligently on behalf of causes and ideals which upheld the principles of human decency, and through the years, you have demonstrated a selfless commitment to the County of Nassau and its residents that warrants attention and gratitude; and

WHEREAS the County of Nassau is proud to extend this commendation

to you, Emily Moore, as you are honored by the H.E.V.N. Coalition's dedication to the community,

NOW, THEREFORE, I, Edwards P. Mangano, Nassau County Executive, on this 21st day of April 2012, do hereby present this citation to

Emily Moore

FIGURE 76 CITATION FROM NASSAU COUNTY EXCUTIVE

Worldwide Who's Who

WORLDWIDE
WHO'S WHO

ACHIEVEMENT | HONOR | RECOGNITION

WORLDWIDE WHO'S WHO

RECOGNIZES

Emily Moore

AS A

VIP MEMBER

THE ABOVE NAMED INDIVIDUAL HAS

QUALIFIED FOR INCLUSION IN

THE 2012-2013 EDITION OF

THE WORLDWIDE WHO'S WHO REGISTRY OF

EXECUTIVES, PROFESSIONALS AND ENTREPRENEURS

IN WITNESS WHEREOF THIS AWARD IS ISSUED AND SIGNED BY

DONALD TRUMP JR.
EXECUTIVE DIRECTOR OF GLOBAL BRANDING AND NETWORKING
WORLDWIDE WHO'S WHO

January 24, 2012
DATE OF ADMISSION

FIGURE 77 WHO'S WHO WORLDWIDE.(COURTESY OF AYANNA MOORE)

Worldwide Who's Who

Officially proclaims.

Emily Moore

As the 2012

PROFESSIONAL OF THE YEAR

Representing the

Education

Industry

FIGURE 78 WHO'S WHO WORLDWIDE. (COURTESY OF AYANNA MOORE)

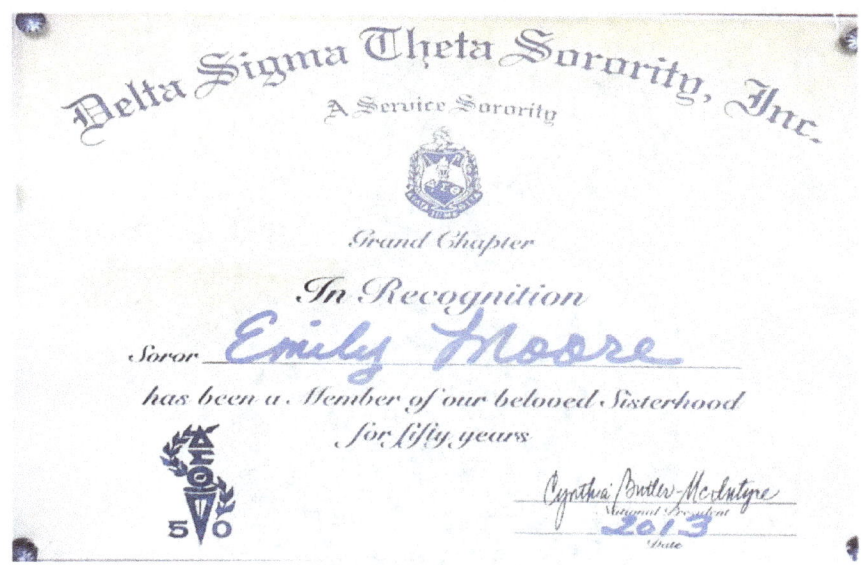

FIGURE 79 50 YEAR MEMBERSHIP RECOGNITION BY DELTA SIGMA THEAT SORORITY INC. (COURTESY OF EMILY MOORE)

PHOTO 83 MEMEBERS OF THE ALPHA GAMMA CHAPTER OF DELTA SIGMA THETA AT MORGAN STATE. EMILY SECOND ROW FROM TOP, SECOND FROM RIGHT. (COURTESY OF EMILY MOORE)

Dr. Martin Luther King, Jr. award

FIGURE 80 MLK COMMUNITY AWARD.(COURTESY OF AYANNA MOORE)

In January of 2014 on what would have been his 85th birthday, Emily received the Dr. Martin Luther King, Jr. Award for her Community activism by the Dr. Martin Luther King, Jr. Birthday Celebration Committee of Nassau County, Inc. The award was presented by Julius O. Pearse, the first Black police officer in the village of Freeport and president of the African American Genealogical Society.

John L. Kearse
Trail Blazer Award

presented to

EMILY MOORE

Civil Rights Historian

Youth Empowerment Institute, INC

2014

FIGURE 82 ELITE AMERICAN EDUCATORS AWARD. (COURTESY OF AYANNA MOORE)

Certificate of Recognition
Has been awarded to

Emily Moore

Educator, Founder & Executive Director,
Alliance Junior Development Program, Inc.

For Inclusion into

Elite American Educators

10/09/2014

Since her time at Morgan State, Emily has received awards and recognition for her involvement in the Civil Rights movement. On December 18, 2015, Emily and dozens of Morgan Alumni were presented with an Honorary degree, Doctor of Law, and *Honoris Causa* for being "the Unsung Morgan College student civil rights pioneers of the forties, fifties, and sixties," by Morgan State University president Dr. David Wilson, honoring their characteristics of being "intrepid, politically astute and civic-minded," in the fight towards integration and equality.

Emily was awarded recognition from Roosevelt for receiving her honorary degree from Morgan State in 2015, her presenter former student and now retired Roosevelt School District athletic coach and timekeeper, Don "Coach" Crummell, told of how Emily could often be heard asking this essential question to teachers: *How are we preparing our children to be global citizens?* He continued to say, "*Ms. Moore has a strong passion for doing what is right and making sure that our children are trained and prepared to face this world that we have set before them.*"

PHOTO 84 DON CRUMMELL AND EMILY MOORE, 2019. (COURTESY OF EMILY MOORE)

The Roosevelt Public Library Trustees
Honors
Dr. Emily Moore

Founder and Executive Director Of

Alliance Junior Tennis
Development Program, Inc.
Dr. Moore Has Shown Dedication, Leadership, And Excellence in All
Aspects of Education in The Roosevelt Community and Beyond, She
Is being Recognized for Her Many Years of Contributions to The
Field

March 23, 2019

Elite Women Worldwide

FIGURE 84 ELITE WOMEN WORLDWIDE CERTIFICATE OF RECOGNITION (COURTESY OF AYANNA MOORE)

In 2016, Emily received a *Certificate of Recognition* from Elite Women Worldwide for her services as an educator, and the role she plays as founder and executive director for the Alliance Junior Development Program.

FIGURE 85 TOP FEMALE EXECUTIVES AWARD. (COURTESY OF AYANNA MOORE)

Top

Female Executives

Emily Moore

Educator, Founder & Executive Director

Alliance Junior Development Program, Inc.

HAS QUALIFIED FOR INCLUSION IN

WORLDWIDE PUBLISHING'S

PRESTIGIOUS ROSTER OF

TOP FEMALE EXECUTIVES

IN HONOR OF

OUTSTANDING PROFESSIONAL

EXCELLENCE & DEDICATION

A court in her Honor

FIGURE 86 SIGN INDICATING THE DEDICATION OF ROOSEVELT PARK'S TENNIS COURT TO EMILY MOORE. (COURTESY OF AYANNA MOORE)

Emily is a woman who is not easily swayed, never changing her views or rhetoric in the name of challenging adversity because of her love of building the mental and physical strength of youth so they can survive in the World. Thousands of former students, parents and adults can attest to the timeless and selfless energy Emily has put into the Roosevelt Community for the past 40 years. In June of 2016, the tennis court at Arthur Al Mackey Sr. Park, formerly Roosevelt Park, was named in honor of Emily Moore, the same park where she has run the Junior Alliance Tennis Development program for the last

50 years.

EMILY MOORE VS THE ROOSEVELT BOARD OF EDUCATION

With over 40 years in the field of education, Emily has been known for helping children and adults in the community. In all her years, Emily is known to be very vocal, not a physical type of person unless it was on the Tennis Courts. In 2017, Emily was falsely accused of abusing a child during school hours. The allegation was that Emily hit and pushed a student, by a teacher. In this situation, Emily refused a Union representative, simply insisting that the person who started the allegation, should file the complaint because Emily was sure of her innocence. Supposedly, there were at least six students who claimed to have seen this event, and specific school security footage that would prove the allegation. In February 2018, Emily was summoned to psychiatric assessments over the allegations by Dr. Solomon. Dr. Seretta McKnight, Gary Battle, and Mrs. Watson attended the assessments with Emily, and Dr. McKnight would later in her written account note how impersonal and dismembered the psychiatrist that was assigned to Emily behaved before the session.

The sessions were mandated by Roosevelt School District,

but it did not seem that it was for the best interest of Emily, but an attempt to oust her once again. McKnight admitted that the interview became intense as the doctor asked if Emily remembered hitting the child, while Emily replied, *"I educate children, I don't hit children."* Very sternly. It appeared that Dr. Solomon seemed to be stern on antagonizing and set on confusing Emily instead of getting clear-cut answers. As she would try to answer, he would cut her off abruptly. Through McKnight's observations, Dr. Moore answered all the questions to the best of her abilities throughout the inconsiderate disruptions displayed by Dr. Solomon Through the ordeal Emily went through various assigned tasks that included number counting and reciting information. To conclude the session, Dr. McKnight and Dr. Solomon reviewed the video that was connected to the allegations, but in conclusion, the video did not support the allegations against Emily Moore.

When asked how she felt about the sessions, Emily replied,

> **Dr. Moore**: *"I feel bad about it; my life is a struggle. People have always had their opinions and they still do.*
>
> **Dr. Solomon**: *"This is a mystery here. As an educator, if you have six children saying the same thing, do you believe, they believe this? "*
>
> **Dr. Moore**: *"You have information I do not have. It would depend on the intent. I cannot speculate as to what if there is any*

malcontent from students. They are given different messages. Adults can exert influence."

Ms. Moore extensively explained her life's work to Dr. Solomon. How over the years she has encountered adults in education who colluded and use children? After this session, Emily informed Dr. Solomon that she would conduct an independent evaluation conducted for her records since the district had not provided her with any information about the allegation and that the letter sent to her allowed her to have her doctor of choice to evaluate her. Dr. McKnight noted Dr. Solomon's frustration in his pursuit of trying to get Ms. Moore to affirm the allegations, even after he had admitted that the video did not supply proof of Dr. Moore putting her hands on a child. Dr. Moore was asked to provide a urine sample by Dr. Solomon, and she replied that she would be negative, but she does have a physical examination coming soon. Upon testing, Dr. Moore was proven negative for any mind- and mood-altering drugs. Dr. McKnight thought it was odd that the doctor shared Emily's test results with her and Mr. Gary Battle before Emily herself. After the testing, Dr. McKnight took it upon herself to ask how the doctor was selected to even interview Emily in the first place. The doctor was unprepared to answer this question and said he did not know. Ultimately referring them to speak to the school district.

Dr. McKnight's conclusion of the whole event,

Dr. Moore is a living legend who has traveled extensively throughout the world and chooses to live, work, and serve the Roosevelt Community. For over 40 years she has faithfully fought for and raised generations of children. As founder and Executive Director of the Alliance Junior Tennis Development program, Dr. Moore has sent numerous children to college on tennis scholarships, coached world-class players, and continues to be recognized by the United States Tennis Association for her boy of work. As an educator in the Roosevelt School District, Dr. Moore Continues to shape and inform the lives of her students. She is more than a physical education teacher. If you attend her class, you will see children learning how to respect themselves, and each other and be leaders. Dr. Moore is an encourager. As she says in her own words, "I educate children. I do not hit children." Therefore, especially after sitting in on this observation, I can unequivocally say that Dr. Moore is of sound mind.

However, I do question the motive, intent, and practice(s), of those who advanced this baseless allegation. Here, are my concerns, which are raised because of this process:

1) Allegations made against Dr. Moore were supposed to be clearly sustained by a videotape. The videotape I saw, in Dr. Solomon's office, clearly showed that Dr. Moore was carrying bags and having the children line up orderly in the hallway. It did not show her hitting a child. Therefore, this should have been squashed at the building level. An investigation needs to be opened to determine the fitness of the building principal who allowed such an injustice to proceed. Why didn't the building principle bring all parties together to address the allegations? It appears that there may be some collusion somewhere in this.

2) Why would the building principal not call Dr. Moore in and she with her the allegations, video, concerns, and write-up? Isn't that what a competent administrator does?

3) Where would the building principle come from? I ask because it is apparent that this principle is inexperienced and lacks sound judgment – which makes me extremely concerned for the safety and well-being of the children and staff in the building.

4) Why wasn't Dr. Moore provided with the same information the doctor had?

5) What is the culpability of the Central Office Administration in this process?

6) Who is advising the Board of education, that they would be so arbitrary, capricious, and gullible in this instance, as to take such an unjustified action: put a living legend through a 913 evaluation?

On its face, this appears to be an attempt to push Dr. Moore out, wrapped up in age discrimination whit a cherry of collusion on top! Or perhaps this is a case of sexual harassment, wrapped in age discrimination. In any event, it is wrong and *unjust. Many that have occupied positions on Roosevelt's Board of Education today have careers and professions due to servant leaders like Dr. Emily Moore.*

Emily's reflection on the event:

It was unfortunate, they tried to oust me once again. I dedicated my whole life to these children, to this school district, and community, and as soon as they heard the rumor, they just shut down on me as if I were nobody. It was a bit of ageism as well, but here I am! One year from my pension! Would I jeopardize my career and my safety by putting my hands on a student? I did not battle cancer and still work to be treated so poorly by the school and board. But do you know what, the people are not Roosevelt Community-based people, they would have been skeptical about the ordeal. But I am innocent and have been proven so. I went back to work.

FIGURE 87 THE PUBLIC ADVOCATE FOR THE CITTY OF NEW YORK CERTIFICATE. (COURTESY OF AYANNA MOORE)

The Public Advocate

For the City of New York

This Certificate is Awarded to:

Dr. Emily Moore

Office of the Public Advocate

In recognition of your commitment to building and strengthening safer communities across our city

November 22, 2019

Black Tennis Hall of Fame

The American Tennis Association was founded in 1916 to create a circuit for black tennis players. In 2004, the ATA began a Black Tennis Hall of Fame to honor its players and contributors to Tennis. In 2019, Emily was inducted by the Black Tennis Hall of fame as a "Regional Legend".

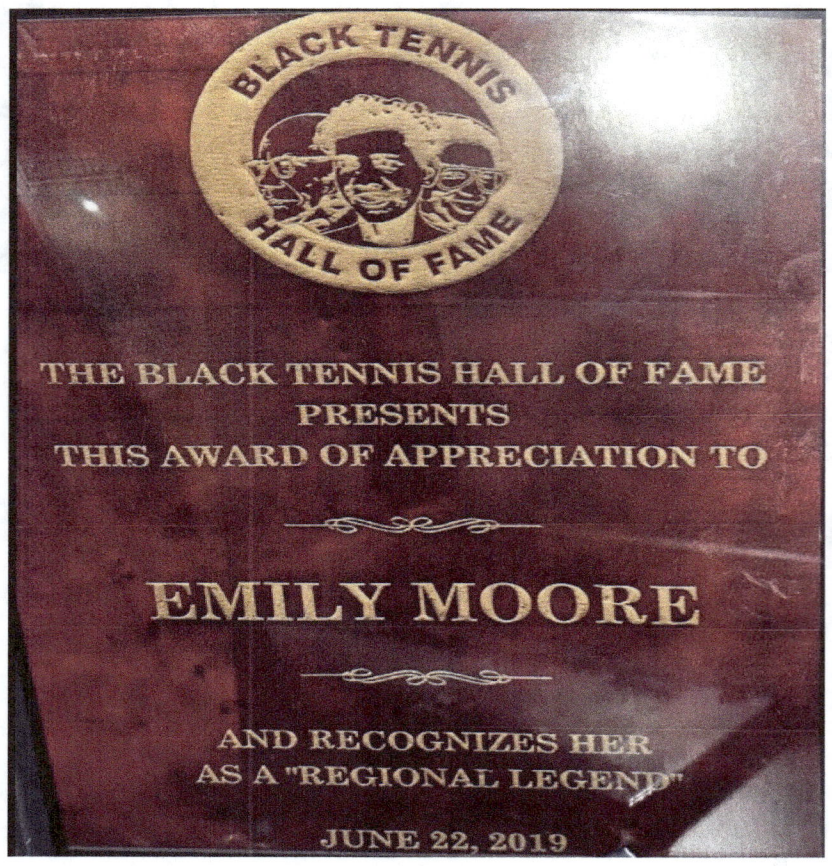

FIGURE 89 THE BLACK TENNIS HALL OF FAME AWARD. (COURTESY OF AYANNA MOORE)

FIGURE 88 FLYER SALUTING EMILY'S INDUCTION TO THE BLACK TENNIS HALL OF FAME. COURTESY OF SISTERS IN THE STRUGGLE

NAACP Freeport Roosevelt Branch #2147

Congratulates

Ms. Emily Moore

As you retire from The Roosevelt UFSD

The branch recognizes your many accomplishments and contributions as a Subscribing Lifetime member.

We thank you for your tireless commitment.

Best Wishes

Douglas Mayers, Branch President

Presented

January 30th, 2020

RETIREMENT OR NEW BEGINNINGS

PHOTO 85 EMILY ROOSEVELT SCHOOL DISTRICT PHOTO 2017. (COURTESY OF EMILY MOORE)

Emily as a Black-American woman, now in her 80s, have experienced and witnessed the changes, progressions, and retractions of society; the good, and the bad, but never did she let it stir her from providing fundamentals and education to the youth of the world. Emily has been a person who brings action and is very task orientated, hence the phrases "relax and take a break" are not in her vocabulary! For over 60 years, Emily has seen enough adventures for her lifetime, more than any of us may ever will. She has sat at the table, shook hands, hugged, and taught prominent Civil Rights activists, Clerical leaders, celebrities, and athletes of the world. Emily does hold more memories than what has been shared, with tons of opportunities presented to her, but for Emily, her participation, and accomplishments as a Civil Rights activist, and educator of her people as a coach and educator are what she values the most in this world.

Through all adversity, Emily Moore remained dedicated to her job as a physical educator, rarely missing any days of school as she took on chemo-radiation therapy. For Dr. Emily Moore, NOT showing up is not an option to her, for decades, children and adults relied on her presence to push the Roosevelt Community forward. Forever remembered, forever respected, and forever loved, Dr. Emily Moore, a champion of her people. A moment not spoken of often, but when Emily was diagnosed with breast cancer, she refrained from telling her peers and associates until she had to start Chemotherapy treatments, she continued to attend each meeting that she could, so she did not miss out on any disruptions or progress within in the school district and Board of Education. As a woman of strength, when Emily does anything, she does not do it for notoriety and attention. Emily did not want sympathy taken on her about her condition, therefore Emily did not reveal her health conditions to the Roosevelt School District and her peers for quite some time. Fortunately, and with God by her side, Emily fought through each treatment and entered remission before her retirement. In 2020, Emily finally retired from the Roosevelt School District as a physical education teacher at seventy-four years old, JUST to go back and run for president of the School Board! In response to why she decided to run, and whether would it tire her out:

> I 'm not going to be tired because I am at all the board meetings anyways! I might as well try to tell them the truth, and how to train against the devil that is taking away from the education of our youth. I do not care if only get two votes. I am standing on principle, I have a lot to do, and I am going to get it done!

During her battle with cancer, Emily won a seat on the Roosevelt Board of Education with unprecedented numbers of votes as a record of members young and old came out to support the educational veteran. What she finds the hardest about being a part of the board meetings before and during her occupancy are the educators and board members. She feels like they do not want to listen to Ms. Moore because she is older, and often labeled as "too old" to do the job. The truth in the matter is that there are generations of families from Roosevelt, who have always recognized that Emily should have been Board President at least once or twice over the past 40 years by now. Time and time again, Emily viewed that board selections and its legislature were disarrayed by ego and office politics that hindered the progression of Roosevelt's youth rather than advance, especially between the late 1990s and early 2000s. Emily also notices that the educators and committee do not even give the hired people in their positions to even get a foot out the door before they are bombarded with unrealistic notions and expectations, toppled with nonsense politics. As far as parental advisory, she feels like the effects of what racism, social and economic has done to families, the fight against it has worn down the fight of the later generations. Emily felt like the effects made Black people too satisfied because it took over four hundred years for basic liberties, and education was still a battle for the black community, often saying she feels like the people of Roosevelt have always been happy to get crumbs when they could have so much more." Like many educators, Emily hopes that what she has taught the people will come back and return to the community and rebuild Roosevelt to its glory.

> *New York is a place without a sense of its own past. Without a true sense of the past, it steams blindly toward the future without a rudder. It is a city with amnesia, like a person so afflicted; it does not know that anything is missing. I love New York City dearly; it just feels hollow to me sometimes. ..."* -Richard Pritchard (Prtichard, 2002, p. 19)

As New York is considered one of the most liberal states in the United States of America, the campaign for the presidency of former president Donald Trump, a New York Native in 2016. The age of social media, captured the true feelings of many white Americans about black Americans and other minority populations as displays of white pride ran rampant throughout America. The campaign displayed the depths of generationally taught racism that long lived in Long Island as the pride in the symbolism Donald Trump was represented and boasted along the main streets from Glen Cove to Merrick, to Oceanside well past his presidency. The atrocities committed by the Republican office during Trump's bid and active presidency showed the world that racism and gender discrimination were okay for the White American. The darkening of the doorways and minds of the new generations of children, the moment Dr. Moore has spoken of had finally come true.

As far as the social climate of the United States, racism continues to rear its head as most politicians try to avoid the uncomfortable conversations of the ugly truth. In recent times, the presidency of Donald Trump in 2016 had been viewed simply as a slap in the face of justice and equality, the fight Emily Moore has been combating on social, political, and educational scales for much of her lifetime. Most of the unjust actions against the black community continue to be upheld through law enforcement misconduct and brutalities, currently, it seems that the United States is split along the lines of "Black Lives Matter", "Blue Lives Matter" and "All Lives Matter" due to the high population of deaths due to the shooting of unarmed Black men and women during traffic cops, and no-knock warrants.

As Emily grows older, she has seen how the world has grown colder in the pursuits of humanity, as the American people of all creeds and religions have come together in the name of Civil Rights for Black people in 2021, STILL. As far as Voting rights go, the Republican party has relentlessly sought to find ways to restrict voter access to the black and brown minority communities since the election of President Barack Obama in 2008, but 2021 showed the most vigorous restriction of voter access after the United States had the first ever option to vote by mail due to the Coronavirus-19 that spread throughout the world.

> The numbers scare the republicans because it shows that everyone would vote if they had better access to the facilitation of active voting. We (Black and Brown) are the majority, and that is something the United States government has worked against before we were even determined a freed population, then actual American Citizens. Why do a population that has built the landscape of the United States and all over the world with their blood, sweat, tears, and life has to fight for a place in this society? There was a burial ground in Manhattan of our people, the archaeologist said half the people in the grave had been worked to death! Crushed spines carrying the loads of stone that build this land to be what it is today! If the black and Brown people were able to take back their voices, and implement them, the white Americans would have to fear repercussions and reparations for many families and politicians who still hold offices today. They would have to acknowledge and truly find a way to make up for what they have done to us as a people, just for the color of our skin. It is pathetic. They gave reparations to the Jewish, the Japanese, and other Asians for Vietnam and communism, where is the justice for Black folk?

> - *Emily Moore*

PHOTO 86 EMILY DURING FINAL DAY AS A PHYSICAL EDUCATION TEACHER FOR THE ROOSEVELT SCHOOL DISTRICT.(COURTESY OF EMILY MOORE)

The Roosevelt School District held a retirement ceremony for Dr. Emily Moore

On January 30, 2020.

FIGURE 90 WHISTLE PRESENTED TO INDICATE HER RETIREMENT AS A COACH.(COURTESY OF AYANNA MOORE)

PHOTO 87 SOME OF EMILY'S FIRST STUDNETS: L TO R: GARY BATTLE, SPENCER BELCHER, AND ROBERT MCFADDEN. (COURTESY OF EMILY MOORE)

PHOTO 88 L TO R: DR .MCKNIGHT, EMILY, AND MS. MCKNIGHT . (COURTESY OF EMILY MOORE)

PHOTO 89 DR. BARBRA SOLOMAN, AND EMILY

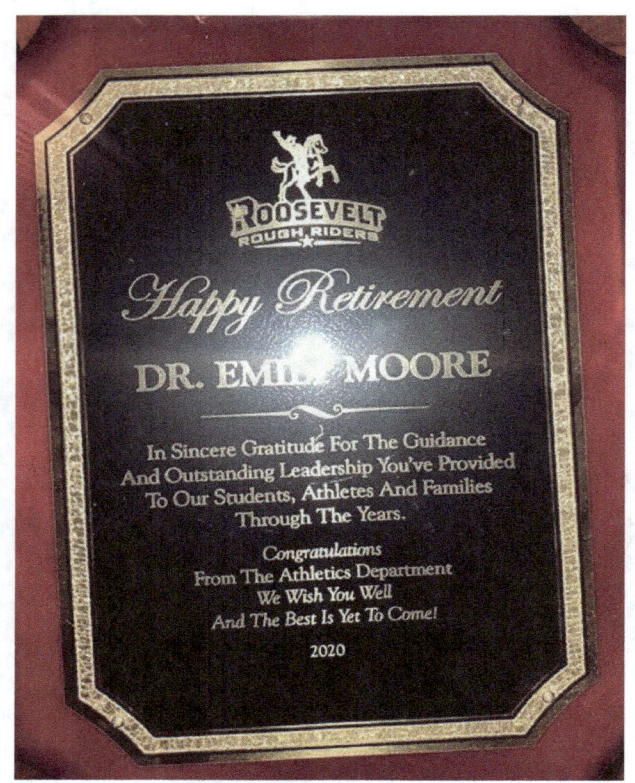

FIGURE 91 COURTESY OF AYANNA MOORE

Happy Retirement

Dr. Emily Moore

In Sincere Gratitude for The Guidance and Outstanding Leadership, you've provided To Our Students, Athletes, and Families through the Years.
Congratulations

From the Athletics Department

We Wish You Well

And the Best Is Yet to Come!

2020

Emily received a SCOPE Award for Community Service. SCOPE is a New York non-profit based program that offers professional development, conferences, training, childcare, preschool, elementary enrichment courses, outdoor education, summer environmental adventure programs and workshops/speakers bureau for parents and students.

New York State Assembly Citation

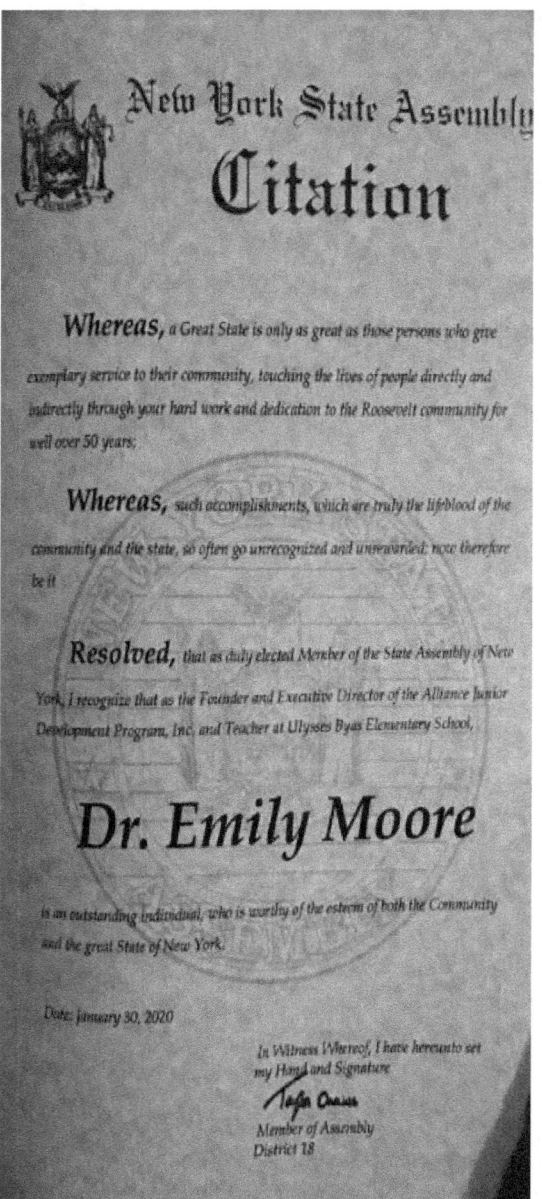

Whereas a Great State is only as great as those people who give exemplary service to their community, touching the life of people directly and indirectly through your hard work and dedication to the Roosevelt community for well over 50 years.

Whereas,
such accomplishments, which are truly the lifeblood of the community and the state, so often go unrecognized and unrewarded; now therefore be it.

Resolved, that as duly elected Member of the State Assembly of New York, I recognize that as the Founder and Executive Director of the Alliance Junior Development Program, Inc., and Teacher at Ulysses Byas Elementary School,

Dr. Emily Moore

is an outstanding individual, who is worthy of the esteem of both the community and the great of New York.

Date: January 30, 2020

Member of Assembly

District 18

FIGURE 92 CITATION. COURTESY OF
AYANNA MOORE

Top 100 Registry

Business Leaders & Professionals

2021 Woman of the Year

Presented to

Emily Moore

In recognition of your outstanding efforts and achievements in the field of education

FIGURE 94 (SODE, 2021 EASTERN HALL OF FAME: DR. EMILY MOORE, 2022)

Dr. Emily Moore has left an indelible mark on thousands of people in the Lon Island tennis community. Though many know her as the beloved director of tennis at the Alliance Junior Tennis Development Program, her incredible Story cannot be overlooked....

In 2021, Dr. Emily Moore was inducted into the 34th class of the Eastern Tennis Hall of Fame for her coaching career.

Dr. Moore was inducted into the Eastern Tennis Hall of Fame in 2021. Left to right: Ilana Kloss, Billie Jean King, Dr. Moore, Dr. Harold German.

USTA EASTERN

FIGURE 95 (SODE, 2021 EASTERN HALL OF FAME: DR. EMILY MOORE, 2022)

They honored me for my efforts, but I was just doing what I was supposed to for my community, and the future of it, training the youth to be productive in life. Independent thinkers, to not see failure and allow it to run their life. To show them that they are greater than what is expected of them. It is an award to me and those who came to learn from me.

- Emily Moore

FIGURE 96   USTA EASTERN HALL OF FAME AWARD SITIS
INBETWEEN A PHOTO OF BARACK OBAMA AND QUEEN
MOTHER MOORE. COURTESY OF AYANNA MOORE

PHOTO 91 FRIENDS, USTA TENNIS STAFF, COUNCIL WOMAN DORTHY GOSBY AND SIBLINGS OF EMILY MOORE DURING HER INDUCTION CEREMONY TO THE USTA . COURTESY OF EMILY MOORE

The Marquis Who's Who
Publications Board

Certifies that

Emily Moore

has hereby been approved as a subject
of biographical record in

Who's Who in the World

inclusion in which is limited to individuals who possess professional integrity,
demonstrate outstanding achievement in their respective fields and have made
innumerable contributions to society as a whole.

2022-2023

Erica Lee, President

The Marquise Who's Who Publications Board

Certifies that

Emily Moore

Has hereby been approved as a subject of biographical record in

Who's who in the World

Inclusion in which is limited to individuals who possess professional integrity, demonstrate outstanding achievement in their respective fields and have made innumerable contributions to society as a whole.

2022-2023

The Elder House: The Elder's Gift to the Children

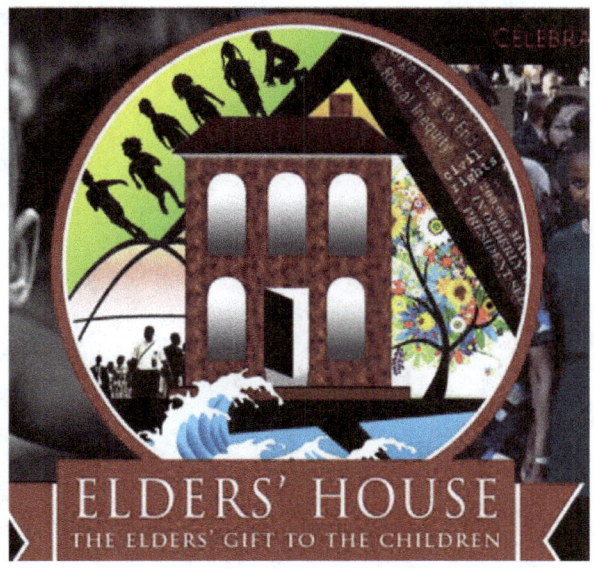

FIGURE 97 LOGO OF THE ELDERS' HOUSE COURTESY OF THE ELDERS' HOUSE

As a consistent contributor to the history of African, and Black Americans, Emily joined various activists to create The Elders' house to preserve the stories, accomplishments, and achievements of people of black and brown skin from all over the world. The Elders' House contains African art, books, family collections, films, oral histories, and personal papers that are published and unpublished material. The Elder's House is in Selma, Alabama. From inside the location, spectators can view the historic Edmund Pettus Bridge, The same bridge viewers all over the world watch

Black and white Americans of all ages receive uncompromising brutality at the hands of the Alabama State Police as they attempt to cross the bridge. This bridge is now named the John L. Lewis Bridge after the late congressperson. Emily Moore is on the wall of respect within the Museum for her civil rights activism and one of the founders.

Elders' House:

The Elders' Gift to the Children

1304 Water Avenue

Selma, Alabama 36703

info@EldersHouse.org

In addition to the elder house, Dr. Moore is trying to compile documents to submit to the State of New York Historical Preservation office with the pursuit of enlisting her home as a national relic. The residence is located near the tennis courts that are named after her at Roosevelt/ Arthur Mackey Park. Another reason is that, since 1963, the family house has been in her family, one of the first black families to reside in Roosevelt. It stands as one of the original buildings of the suburban home boom in the Long

Island Area of the 1950s. The home currently houses all of Dr. Moore's accolades and historic memorabilia.

If you want to help petition in support of a nomination to be added to the register, please send an email to almoore34@gmail.com

To be frank, to track down and list all the accolades that Dr. Emily Moore has received during her lifetime would truly take an unprecedented amount of time to collect. Just know that when Emily says that she will do something, she does it to the best of her abilities, until she has completed the task. A person of her word, someone who will not agree to things that she cannot, a rarity who reflects her time, and the world recognizes that.

American Tennis Association – National Board Member
New York Tennis Regional Organization (NYTRO) – president
National Educators Association
National Alliance of Black Educators
Lifetime member – National Council of Negro Women
Nassau Central Black Business and professional women
The national association for Female Executives
United States Tennis Association
National Action Network
Martin Luther King Jr annual honors and awards – outstanding citizen contribution to the improvement of Education and Community
MLK community service award and Teacher's award
Harlem Junior Tennis - presented in appreciation for your thoughtful and selfless dedication as a board member and friend to the kids and their tennis program.
Nassau County Legislature Citation

Trailblazer of the New Millennium from Patrick C Williams Sr, legislator of District #1

Arthur Ashe Multicultural Enhancement Award from the United States Tennis Association

Nassau County's 2015 Women of Distinction Award

Tennis Development Award from The Black Tennis & Sports Foundation

Outstanding Youth Advocate Award from the Eastern Section of the Long Island Youth Foundation

Rough Rider Remarks

I have known Dr. Emily Moore probably my whole life. My dad and her brothers were very close. My family and Dr. Moore have a long history before I was even born. I am so honored to share how she has impacted my life and the Roosevelt Community.

As a student athlete from Freeport, I used to ride my bike to Roosevelt to play basketball with her niece and other Roosevelt players at Roosevelt Park. I always admired how Dr. Moore cared for young people and made them feel important. She always had something positive and inspiring to say to us. I spent time at her home and noticed how young people felt safe and loved. One summer, while I was home from college, she gave me the opportunity to work for her. Her tennis camp was an opportunity to interact with younger children and teach them tennis. Working for Dr. Moore, I experienced first-hand, how she was and still is, invested in young people. She taught me how to be civic minded, initiative-taking, and supportive. She showed me the value of myself and helped cultivate my talents. She also introduced me to the true meaning of "it takes a village."

She has been an intricate part of my village, as she continues to serve as an inspiration of determination, dedication, compassion, and service for others. She is one of the reasons Roosevelt has become my second home and a place that I continue to give my time and effort to as I try to continue her work and the work of other elders in the community. I only pray that I can empower the young people in Roosevelt the positive and affirming love and knowledge she has instilled in me. I will forever be grateful for the lessons I learned from Dr. Moore. I SALUTE her for being a positive force in the community and always putting the youth first.

Thank You

Cassandra Jackson, Freeport Class of 1989

Educator and Assistant Principle for the Roosevelt School District

---

It is with gratitude that I share my thoughts and experiences about Dr. Emily Moore. Dr. Moore was my physical education teacher when I was in junior high school more than 45 years ago. She was energetic, conscious, and driven to nothing less than greatness and excellence for her students and humanity. Dr. Moore was my eldest niece's physical education teacher, whom she still loves and holds in high esteem. My other four nieces and nephews learned tennis in Dr. Moore's Junior Alliance tennis summer camp program, along with countless other youngsters in New York. At the end of one summer, Dr. Moore decided to obtain a bus and insisted that her students attend the U.S Open qualifying finals annually at the U.S Tennis center in Flushing, Queens, New York. As an adult chaperone, I hold this experience dear to my heart, and will cherish it for life.

Dr. Moore has raised generations of young people and used tennis as a vehicle of change for the youth and adults. She always made sure that young people are exposed to positive and unique life

experiences. During the summers, as requested by Dr. Moore, I graciously conducted a girl's empowerment group through the Junior Alliance program. Dr. Moore and I have been members of Sisters in the Struggle and National Action Network for decades together. I continue to learn valuable life lessons from Emily as we affectionately call her. Dr. Moore supports everyone she encounters, by always encouraging people to "pursue their dreams, do their best and write their stories because no one can tell your story better than you can."

Dr. Moore contributes money, time, and talents in her care for others, as she brings them along her life's journey. She reminds us about the values of home, school, church, and community working together are the essential foundations for success. Dr. Moore is 80 years old, serving as a trustee on the Roosevelt School board of education. My mom, family, and countless communities love Dr. Emily Moore, a Warrior woman of good character and integrity, who loves and takes care of the world.

Humbly,

Beverly Cunningham,

Roosevelt High School, Class of 1974

Lifetime Roosevelt resident, and retired School Counselor

A Woman of such honor, courageousness, strength, and high morals when it pertains to her integrity, wisdom, and intelligence. I have been in awe of Dr. Moore's work for as long as I can remember. The motivation she has given to me 100 % of the time and the stories she has talked about her travels are still things I cannot fathom. To people of Roosevelt, her efforts are unfathomable. This wonderful soul is a survivor and taught generations the abilities to play physically and mentally through her informative training. The training makes you pull yourself into a direction of possibilities and opportunities instead of destructive and statistical outcomes. I am a product of my environment, but I am still pure. Not steeped on, or cut, I show love even when it hurts. Now my heart is a divine power of my healing. I used to bust my brain to force myself to be as great as others, but now I know I am my own celebrity. A closed mouth will not get fed, and nobody owed me anything, but I really have the conviction in my spirit now that has been strategically magnified thanks to Dr. Moore on her own, she assisted this troubled soul. I was afraid of success and was not even aware, anxiety was not even the case. The way I had shaped my life then took a toll on me; she played a positive roll to help me gain back control. I create poetry and counsel. Honestly, I matured faster with her guiding me through reality, and of her just telling it like it is. My passion is solid, God bless the child that can hold their own and Dr. Emily Moore has accomplished all of that and then some. I know from her essence alone that Black people are chosen to do the most prolific things on earth, even though we go thorough the most. All is well, God Bless my brothers and sisters, let's assist on building out nation using our bright talents with our education and experiences for the future, utilize a great deal of basic common sense with positive energy.

Jerome Bryce, Roosevelt

Year of Birth 1992

At an age when our older generation should be considering retiring and slowing down, Dr. Moore took on one of the most challenging roles that one could imagine – School board Trustee for the Roosevelt School District. It was a position that I once held, and she defeated me earnestly. I can only admire her will and fight and as a member of Kappa Alpha Phi, Inc I show the utmost deference to a beautiful sister of Delta Sigma Theta, Inc, who was initiated at a time where there was great need for Black social organizations that were based upon survival and social advancement of our people. I am a direct product of her education, and witness to her willingness to teach others that went far above and beyond requirements and expectation. Dr. Moore may be seasoned, but I can attest that her backhand stroke on the Tennis court still has the velocity that comes with decades of practice, performance, and teaching.

Alfred Taylor,

Roosevelt High Class of 1995

Current Supervisor for Nassau County Sanitation District No. 2

Ms. Moore was my tennis coach high school, I really appreciated how she never made us feel like an anomaly doing tennis. Wherever we were, she made sure we felt like we belonged. She did not play! And would yell across the court BACKHAND! It was great, you could tell how much she really cared. Her being a coach was really a gem. I appreciated how she pushed us."

Tolitha Henry,
Roosevelt High School class of 2010

Thanks for being a positive light during my short time I spent teaching at Ulysses Byas!

Degoldyne Francois-Ulceus, Educator

To My Warrior Soror Dr. Emily Moore,

History is … CHANGE.

Which starts with the vision of one person.

Therefore, Black History cannot be confined to one month because Black History is made every single day by people like EMILY who remind the world how beautiful Black really is.

So, from Brownsville to Harlem, from Motown to Compton, From Freeport to Roosevelt,

This is merely a reminder that we are all Black History in the making, like EMILY MOORE

So, Emily, we thank you for making your mark in history!

Carol Gilliam

Black Heritage Librarian - Retired,

Roosevelt Public Library

PHOTO 92 FORMER PRESIDENT BARACK OBAMA, MARCIA HAZELTON, AND HER GRANDSON, A MOMENT THAT EMILY IS VERY PROUD OF.

We were Rough Riders when we met at Morgan because we did civil rights demonstrations together. We have been very close for years, from class to demonstrations, and to jail, we even had rough teachers! We were always doing or getting into something together. Emily is the godmother of my daughter, who served as superintendent in Freeport and Roosevelt Schools, she even lived with Emily at one point, so I frequent New York. When I come now, we go to church together at Donnie McClurkin Church, she helped him by giving him money to help establish his church there in Freeport. Emily really, really, loves the children and helped hundreds get scholarships and further in life because of Tennis.

Dr. Marsha Saxon-Hazelton

Retired Educator

Morgan State University, Class of 1965

BIBLIOGRAPHY

(n.d.). Retrieved from NYS Historic Newspapers: https://nyshistoricnewspapers.org/lccn/sn95071064/2018-03-01/ed-1/seq-2/#date1=01%2F01%2F1&index=0&date2=12%2F31%2F2020&words=Jarvis+Moses&to_year2=2020&searchType=advanced&sequence=0&from_year2=1&proxdistance=5&page=1&county=Nassau&rows=20&ortext=&proxte

(n.d.). Retrieved from http://www.speedwayandroadracehistory.com/freeport-stadium-ny.html

Allison Keyes. (2019, May 22). *The 'Clotilda,' the Last Known Slave Ship to Arrive in the U.S., Is Found*. Retrieved from The Smithsonian Magazine: https://www.smithsonianmag.com/smithsonian-institution/clotilda-last-known-slave-ship-arrive-us-found-180972177/

The Chicago Tribune. (1966, July 14). Riots in Chicago. *The Chicago Tribune*.

(PBS), P. B. (Director). (1990's). *The Murder of Emmett Till: Emmett's Mother Speaks* [Motion Picture].

(1998, September 3). *Long Island Newsday*, p. A6.

Afro-American, B. (1963, February 20). 274 Arrested, Crowd Grows in Northwood. *The Baltimore Afro-American*.

Afro-American, T. B. (1963, February 19). 218 Students Arrested. $90,000 Bail Set for 150 . *The Baltimore Afro-American*.

Alexander, M. (1972, May 18). Ousted' Firebrand' Striking Sparks. *Long Island's Newsday*.

Authority Acts to Clean Bennington Park. (1942, 01 22). *The Leader: Nassau County*.

authors, v. (n.d.). *Perspectives on History: In memoriam* . Retrieved from https://www.historians.org/research-and-publications/perspectives-on-history/april-1997/in-memoriam-april-1997

Barr, K. (2015, Novemeber 13). *List of KKK Members Reveals History of Racism on Long Island*. Retrieved from The Osprey: https://www.theosprey.info/culture/list-of-kkk-members-reveals-history-of-racism-on-long-island/

Beherens, D. (2009, July 11). The KKK Flares up in Long Island. *Long Island Newsday* .

Blain, K. N. (2018). "To Keep Alive the Teaching of Garvey and the Work of the UNIA" Audley Moore, Black Women's Activism, and Nationalist Politics during the Twentieth Century. New York , New York. Retrieved from https://muse.jhu.edu/pub/163/article/704643

Blain, K. N. (2018). To Keep Alive the Teaching of Garvey and the Work of the UNIA" Augley Moore, Black Women's Activism, and Nationalist Politics during the Twentieth Century. *Palimpset: A Journal on Women, Gender, and the Black International, Volume 7, Issue 2*, 83-107. Retrieved from www.

Bond, D. J. (2010, April 15). Race: Founder Julian Bond Remembers 50 Years of SNCC. (N. -N. Conan, Interviewer) Retrieved from https://www.npr.org/templates/story/story.php?storyId=126021836

Boyd, A. (2016, November 17). Despite Prejudice, Roosevelt Perserveres. *Freeport Leader*, p. 10.

Brady-Handy. (n.d.). Hiriam Rhdes Revels. *LC-DIG-cwpbh-00554.* Library of Congress.

Branham, R. J. (1995). " I was gone on debating": malcolm X's prison debates and public confrontations. *Argumentation and Advocacy.*

Brown, D. (2001). *Oral History: Emily Moore, Civil Rights Activist.*

Business: Cleveland Avenue Controversy Deepens. (2021, October 21). Retrieved may 2022, from LI HERALD.com: https://www.liherald.com/stories/cleveland-avenue-controversy-deepens,135604

Cadambi, A. (2011, september 13). *Baltimore students demonstrate to integrate Northwood Theater, 1963.* Retrieved from Global Non-Violent Action Database: https://nvdatabase.swarthmore.edu/content/baltimore-students-demonstrate-integrate-northwood-theater-1963

Christensen, S. (2007, December 7). *The Great Migration (1915-1960).* Retrieved february 2020, from The Black Past: https://www.blackpast.org/african-american-history/great-migration-1915-1960/

Cinema Treasures. (2011). *Northwood Theater: 1572 Havenwood Road Baltimore, MD 21218.* Retrieved 2019, from https://www.cinematreasures.org/theaters/27135/photos/23245

Civil Rights Digital Library. (1965). *Watts Riots.* Retrieved from Civil Rights Digital Library: https://crdl.usg.edu/events/watts_riots

Cleaveland Avenue School. (2017, 01 27). Retrieved 2019, from New York Heritage digital collections: https://cdm16694.contentdm.oclc.org/digital/collection/p15281col l12/id/16909/rec/1

Columbia university. (2012, August 15). *Ulysses Byas, a pioneering Black School Superintendent, is dead at 88*. Retrieved from TC People: https://www.tc.columbia.edu/articles/2012/august/ulysses-byas-a-pioneering-black-school-superintendent-is-d/

Comus Fanning, Dido and Julia Dyd Havens Johnson. (n.d.). Retrieved from Sylvester Manor: https://www.sylvestermanor.org/comus-julia-dido

Conneticut and parts adjacent. (n.d.). Retrieved 2022, from The New York Public Library Digital Collections: https://digitalcollections.nypl.org/items/b5868620-3273-0134-e06d-00505686a51c

Crew, T. f., Kreig, C., Feeney, R., & Rushton, D. (2018, March 1). Freeport's 19th Century notable African-Americans . *Freeport Herald Leader*, p. 2. Retrieved from https://nyshistoricnewspapers.org/lccn/sn95071064/2018-03-01/ed-1/seq-2/#date1=01%2F01%2F1&index=0&date2=12%2F31%2F2020&words=Jarvis+Moses&to_year2=2020&searchType=advanced&sequence=0&from_year2=1&proxdistance=5&page=1&county=Nassau&rows=20&ortext=&proxte

Crowe, K. L., & Lewis, T. (2021). *The 1921 Tulsa Massacre*. Retrieved from National Endowment for the Humanities: https://www.neh.gov/article/1921-tulsa-massacre

Crumell, D. (1964). *NAACP Ends Roosevelt School Boycott*.

Douglass, F. (1857, August 4). *No Progress without Struggle*. Retrieved from https://collectiveliberation.org/wp-content/uploads/2013/01/Douglass_No_Progress_Without_Struggle.pdf

Elite American Educators. (2014, October 16). *Emily Moore* . Retrieved 2020, from https:/eliteamericaneducators.com/so14/10/16/emily-moore/

falls, s. (n.d.).

Family, T. M. (2001). *The Moore Family History* .

Farmer, A. (2016 , July 3). *Black Women Organize for the Future of Pan-Africanism: The Sixth Pan-African Congress* . Retrieved from https://www.aaihs.org/queen-mother-moore-matriarch-of-the-captive-african-nation/

First Public Apperance of women of the K.K.K on Long Island. (1924). Retrieved from Library of Congress: https://www.loc.gov/resource/cph.3a5229/

Foner, E. (2020, February 16). *There Have Been 10 Black Senators Since Emanicipation*. Retrieved from New York Times: www.nytimes.com/2020/02/14/opinion/sunday/hiram-revels-reconstruction-150.html

Freeport. (1961). *Freeport High School Voyouger* . Freeport.

Freeport High School . (1961). Womens Varsity Basketball Team. *Freeport High School Vouyguer*. Freeport: Freeport High School.

Freeport High School. (1957). Freeport High School Voyuerger. *Freeport High School Voyuerger, 1957*. Freeport: Freeport High School.

Freeport High School. (1959). Freeport High Scool Voyeugor . freeport: Freeport High School.

Freeport Memorial Library. (1906). Property of Moses Jarvis 1906 Map. Freeport.

Gardner, B. (1990). Educational Changes: "The needs of the children," vital speeches of the day, vol 56.

Gary Richardson, Federal Reserve Bank of Richmond. (2013, Novemeber 22). *The Great Depression*. Retrieved from Federal Reserve History: https://www.federalreservehistory.org/essays/great-depression

George, N. (2020, October 19). *The Greats.* Retrieved from The New York Times : https://www.nytimes.com/interactive/2020/10/19/t-magazine/angela-davis.html

Gerry Butler. (2007, March 3). *Martin Robinson Delany (1812-1885)*. Retrieved from Black Past: https://www.blackpast.org/african-american-history/delany-major-martin-robison-1812-1885/

Gill, W. E. (1992). *The History of Maryland's Historically Black Colleges.* Washington D.C: U.S Department of Education .

Gill, W. E. (1992). *University History*. Retrieved from About MSU: http://www.morgan.edu/About_MSU/University_History.html

Graham Russell, G. H. (1994). In *" Pretends to Be Free": Runaway Slave Advertisements from Colonial and Revolutionary New York and New Jersey* (p. 297). New York: Garland Publishing.

Harlem Renaissance. (n.d.). Retrieved from National Gallery of Art: https://www.nga.gov/learn/teachers/lessons-activities/uncovering-america/harlem-renaissance.html

History.com Editors. (2009, October 29). *Sojourner Truth*. Retrieved march 2020, from HISTORY: https://www.history.com/topics/black-history/sojourner-truth

History.com Editors. (2020, July 7). *The Central Park Five*. Retrieved from HISTORY: https://www.history.com/topics/1980s/central-park-five

History: Famous Cases & Criminals: Mississippi Burning. (n.d.). Retrieved from FBI: https://www.fbi.gov/history/famous-cases/mississippi-burning

Hofstra University Library Special Collections Department. (unknown). *Slavery on Long Island*. Retrieved from https://www.hofstra.edu/pdf/library/libspc_soli.pdf

Jacobs, H. (2001). *Incidents In The Life of A Slave Girl* . Dover Thrift Editions .

James Farmer Part 4 of 7. (n.d.). Retrieved april 4, 2020, from FBI Records: The Vault: https://vault.fbi.gov/james-farmer/james-farmer-part-4-7/view

James, M. L., & LaGumina, S. J. (1980). The Blacks of Roosevelt. *Etnicity in suburbia: the Long Island experience*.

Jefferies, J. L. (2020). Malcolm X, the Omega Psi Phi Fraternity, Inc. and Morgan State College. *Spectrum: A Journal on Black Men*, 127-150.

Johnson, L. B. (1964). Public Papers of the presidents of the United States: Lyndon B. Johnson, 1963-65. In M. P. Johnson, *Reading the American Past: Selected Historical Documents: Vol. 2 from 1865* (pp. 251-254). Washington D.C: U.S Government Printing office.

Johnson, M. (2013, August 14). *Postman's 1963 Walk for Justice, Cut Short on An Alabama Road*. Retrieved from https://www.npr.org/2013/08/14/211711898/a-postmans-1963-walk-for-justice-cut-shirt-on-an-alabama-road

Kennedy, J. F. (1963, June 11). *Historic Speeches*. Retrieved april 2020, from John F. Kennedy Presidential Library and Museuem: https://www.jfklibrary.org/learn/about-jfk/historic-speeches/televised-address-to-the-nation-on-civil-rights

Kentake, M. (2016, July 27). *Mother Moore: 20th Century Woman Warrior.* Retrieved from Kentakepage: https://kentakepage.com/queen-mother-moore-20th-century-woman-warrior/

Krieg, Feeney, Rushton. (2018, February). *Freeport's 19th Century notable African Americans.* Retrieved from LIHERALD: https://www.liherald.com/stories/freeports-19th-century-notable-african-americans,100505

Landy, C. A. (n.d.). *When did slavery end in New York?* Retrieved may 6, 2021, from Hisotry Society of the New York Courts: https://history.nycourts.gov/when-did-slavery-end-in-new-york/

Landy, C. A. (n.d.). *When did Slavery End in New York?* Retrieved from Historical Society of the New York Courts: https://history.nycourts.gov/when-did-slavery-end-in-new-york/#:~:text=It%20was%20not%20until%20March,total%20abolition%20of%20legal%20slavery.

Lane, P. E. (1961). 11 Bennington Avenue. *11 Bennington Avenue.* Freeport Memorial Library, Freeport. Retrieved from New York Heritage digital collections: https://cm16694.contentdm.oclc.org/digital/collection/p15281coll12/1d/5379/rec/38

Law, D. K. (2020, October 26). *Queen Mother Moore and Reparative Histories by Dr. Hanna Ishmael.* Retrieved from Women's History Network: https://www.womenshistorynetwork.or/queen-mother-more-and-reparative-historie-by-dr-hanna-ishmael/

Lewis, D. L. (1, september 2003). *In Memorium: August A. Meier (1923-2003).* Retrieved from The Newsmagazine of the American Historical Association: Prospectives in History: https://www.historians.org/publications-and-directories/perspectives-on-history/september-2003/in-memoriam-august-a-meier

Lewis, D. L. (2003, septemeber 1). *In Memoriam: August A. Meier (1923-2003)*. Retrieved february 6, 2019, from American Histrorical Society: Perspectives On History: https://www.historians.org/reasearch-and-publications/perspectives-on-history/september-2003/in-memoriam-august-a-meier

Library, F. M. (2015, january 30). *Spring Dance*. Retrieved 2019, from New York Heritage Digital Library : http://cdm16694.contentdm.oclc.org/digital/collection/p15281coll12/id/7229/rec/1

Library, F. M. (2019). *Bethel African Methodist Episcopal Church*. Retrieved from New York Heritage: Digital Collection: https://cdm16694.contentdm.oclc.org/digital/collection/p15281coll12/id/3323

Lisa Black, James Hill, Laurie Cohen, Jerry Thomas. (1996, August 29). *Dellinger is Arrested, But World Not Watching* . Retrieved from Chicago Tribune: https://www.chicagotribune.com/news/ct-xpm-1996-08-29-9608290303-story.html

Longwood Central School District. (n.d.). *Women and Girls Parade with The Klan.* Retrieved 2020, from Longwood Central District: build.longwood.ix/12.ny.us/cms/one.aspx?partalId=2549374&pageId=5484967

markia. (n.d.).

Marrow, G. (2020). About Emily Moore at Morgan. (A. Moore, Interviewer)

Martin D. Jenkins, Educator Born. (2022, may 30). Retrieved from African American Registry: https://aaregistry.org/story/martin-d-jenkins-educator-and-more/

Martine, D. B. (1992). *Native Tribes of Long Island*. Retrieved from On This Site: https://eremynative.com/onthisite/wiki-tribes-of-long-island

Mastrovia, M. (2012, September 3). *The 196 Democratic National Convention and Missisippi Freedom Democratic Party*. Retrieved April 9, 2021, from The DLG B : Blog of the Digital Library of Gerogia: https://blog.dlg.galileo.usg.edu/?p=3793

McFadden, R. G. (2023, August). Robert McFAdden on Dr.Emily Moore. (A. L. Moore, Interviewer) Roosevelt.

McGovern, A. M. (n.d.). *Bennington Park for MAAP*. Retrieved from https://libguides.freeportlibrary.info/ld.php?content_id=21943651

Meier, A. (1992). *A White Scholar and the Black Community, 1945-1965: Essays and Reflections*. University of Massachussetts Press.

Meier, A. (n.d.). August Meier Papers. NY.

Moore, E. (2018). My life . (A. Moore, Interviewer)

Moore, E. (2021). Awards. Roosevelt.

Moore, E. (2023). Awards . Rooseevelt: Emily Moore.

Moore, M. (2020, august). Ancestors of Emily and Marion Moore. (A. L. Moore, Interviewer)

Moore, R. (1940, January 12). (R. Moore, Ed.) *Unknown:A weekly Newspaper for Colored Citizens of Broward County*.

Moore, R. F. (1940, January 12). The Whole Trouble Today. *Fort Lauderdale Colored Bulletin*. Fort Lauderdale.

Morgan Magazine. (2011). *1*.

Morgan State University. (1965). Promethlone Class of 1965. Baltimore.

Morgan, J. (199*). Where others Failed, Dropout Class Succeeds. *Newsday Long Island*. Hempstead.

Movement, T. E. (n.d.). *Abolitionism: European and American social movement*. Retrieved from Britannica: https://www.britannica.com/topic/abolitionism-European-and-American-social-movement/Southern-defense-of-the-peculiar-institution

Nassau County Review, 2 February 1917. (1917, February 2). Retrieved from NYS Historic Newspapers: https://nyshistoricnewspapers.org/?a=d&d=nscr19170202-01.1.1&e=-------en-20--1--txt-txIN----------

National Park Services. (n.d.). *Person: Harriet Tubman* . Retrieved july 19, 2021, from National Park Service: https://nps.gov/people/harriet-tubman.htm

New York Almanack. (2020, june 23). 1926 KKK rally at the Mineola Fair Grounds . *News Day Long Island*. Long Island: Newsday Long Island . Retrieved feb 5, 2021, from The New York Almanack: newyorkalmancak.com/2020/06/when-the-klan-ruled-in-freeport-long-island/

New York Heritage: Digital Collections. (1956). *Freeport High School Yearbook, 1956.* Retrieved from New York Heritage: Digital Collections: http://www.nyheritage.contentdm.oclc.org/digital/collection/p15281coll12/id/28192/rec/69

New York Law School . (2018, Fenruary 27). *Moxey Alexander Rigby, Class of 1925, First African American Judge Elected in Nassau County.*

Retrieved 2019, from Digital Commons: https://digitalcommons.nyls.edu/firsts/13/

Newsday Long Island. (1972). Mock Trial Convicts Patrolman. *Newsday Long Island*.

Noelle Trent. (unknown). *Frederick Douglass: United States Official and Diplomat*. Retrieved from Britannica: https://www.britannica.com/biography/Frederick-Douglass

NY TIMES. (1925, August 2). Patchogue Klan Parades: Elks clear way for Gowned Marchers - Legion has concert. *New York Times*.

Office of the Historian, Foreign Service Institute. (n.d.). *Milestones 1961-1968: The Bay of Pigs invasion and its Aftermath, April 1961-October 1962*. Retrieved from Office of the Historian: https://history.state.gov/milestones/1961-1968/bay-of-pigs

Office of the Mayor for the City of Fort Lauderdale. (2006, July 5). Procalamation . *Raliegh Moore Day*. Ft. Lauderdale.

Olly, J. M. (2021). *Long Road to Freedom: Surviving Slavery on Long Island*.

Olly, J. (unkown). *Long Island during Prohibition (1920-1933)*. Retrieved from Long Island History Journal: http://lihj.cc.stonybrook.edu/2017/articles/long-island-during-prohibition-1920-1933/

Olsen, E. (1944, April). The Slave Code in Colonial New York . *The Journal of Negro History, 29*(2), 147-165.

Pace, E. (1997, may 7). Queen Mother Moore, 98, Harlem Rights Leader, Dies. *The New York Times*.

Pace, E. (2003, March 25). *August Meier,79,Authority on Black American History*. Retrieved 2 13, 2019, from The New York Times:

http://www.nytimes.com/2003/03/25/us/august-meier-79-authority-on-black-american-history.html

Papers of John F. Kennedy. (1961, 03 01). *Archives*. Retrieved 04 02, 2019, from John F. Kennedy Predidential Library and Musuem: jfklibraru.org/asset-viewer/archives/JFKPOF/054-007

Paquette, C. (1996, November 17). Book Details Klan Role in Smithtowns Past. *The New York Times* .

Parish, J. (2007, Summer). *Archives of Maryand (Biographical Series) Verda Freedom Welcome (1907-1990)*. Retrieved from https://mas.maryland.gov/megafile/msa/speccol/sc3500/sc3520/0 12300/012344/html/12344extbio.html

Parrish, S. (2009). Stars and Stories: Emily Moore. In S. Parrish, *One Square Mile: The History of Roosevelt, NY from an Autobiographical Perspective*. USA: Sheldon Parrish.

Paul Cuffee (1759-1817). (n.d.). Retrieved from Paul Cuffee School: A maritime charter school for Providence Youth: https://www.paulcuffee.org/about/mission-history/paul-cuffee/

Policeman cleared in LI Youth's death. (1971). Retrieved from https://www.nytimes.com/1971/12/16/archives/policeman-cleared-in-li-youths-death.html

Powell, M. (2002, April 21). Separate and Unequal In Roosevelt, Long Island: A New York Town's Schools Struggle Against the Toll of Segregation. *The Washington Post*.

President John F. Kennedy's Inaugural Address (1961). (1961). Retrieved from National Archives: https://www.archives.gov/milestone-documents/president-john-f-kenndeys-inaugural-address

Priester, D. R. (1987). *The Moore Family History*.

Prtichard, E. T. (2002). *Native New Yorkers: The Legacy of the Algonquin People of New York.* Council Oak Books.

queen. (n.d.).

Redlining. (n.d.).

Ritchie, E. (1883, Novemeber 10). Freeport. *The Signal : A Long Island Representative Paper.*

rosenthal. (1975).

Samuel Momodu. (2020, october 10). *Prathia Hall Wynn (1940 - 2002) .* Retrieved from Black Past: https://www.blackpast.org/african-american-history/prathia-hall-wynn-1940-2002/

Sandler, G. (1992, December 1). Malcolm Stirred the Pot. *The Baltimore Sun.*

School, F. H. (2010, October 15). *Senior Class, 1913, Freeport High School .* Retrieved june 7, 2019, from New York Heritage digital collection: https://cdm1664.contentdm.oclc.org/digital/collection/p15281coll 12

School, L. (2019, January 15). *Queen Mother Audley Moore Pt. 2: Harlem, the black struggle, and the CPUSA.* Retrieved from Liberation School: https://www.liberationschool.org/queen-mother-audley-moore-2

Seidman, S. (2012). Tricontinental Routes of Solidaritty: Stokely in Cuba. *Journal of Transnational American Studies.* Retrieved from https://doi.org/10.5070.t842015751

(1914).Senior Class, 1913, Freeport High School . *New York Digital Library: Senior Class, 1913, Freeport High School.* Freeport Memorial Library, Freeport.

Shane, H. G. (1990). Educational Foresight for the 1990's. *The education Digest*, 3-5.

Sharpton, R. A. (2023, September 22). (A. L. Moore, Interviewer)

Silver, R. R. (1971, december 3). Suspension of Policeman Saught in slaying of Black Youth on L.I. *The New York Times*.

Smithsonian: National Museum of African American History and Culture. (unknown). *The Black Panther Party: Challenging Police and Promoting Social Change*. (National Musuem of African American History and Culture) Retrieved from https://nmaahc.si.edu/explore/stories/black-panther-party-challenging-police-and-promoting-social-change#:~:text=breadcrumb&text=Founded%20in%20Oakland,protected%20black%20citizens%20from%20brutality.

Sode, S. (2022, February 14). *2021 Eastern Hall of Fame: Dr. Emily Moore*. Retrieved from USTA: https://www.usta.com/en/home/stay-current/eastern/2021-eastern-hall-of-fame--emily-moore.html

Sode, S. (2022, 02 14). *Eastern: 2021 Eastern Hall of Fame: Dr. Emily Moore*. Retrieved 2022, from United States Tennis Association: usta.com/en-home/home/stary-current/eastern/2021-eastern-hall-of-fam-emily-moore.html

The '60s at 50. (2019, 5). Retrieved 2019, from https://americanhistorysi.edu/sites/defaults/files/a200%20%20flyer%252C%201957%20Prayer%20Pilgrimage%20LC%20loan.jpg

The Associated Press. (19, July 2021). *Gloria Richardson, An Influential Yet Largely Unsung Civil Right Pioneer, Has Died*. Retrieved from NPR: Obituraries: https://www.npr.org/2021/07/19/1017820962/gloria-richardson-civvil-rights-pioneer-dies

The Editors of Enclyclopedia Britannica. (2022, April 19). *Juneteenth*. Retrieved from Britannica: https://www.britannica.com/topic/Juneteenth

The Editors of Encyclopedia Britannica. (2014, May 8). *"Dutch West Company"*. Retrieved from Encylopedia Britannica: https:britannica.com/money/topic/Dutch-West-India-Company

The Leader. (1960). Emily Moore FHS "Red Devil". *The Leader*.

The Leader. (1961). The Yatch Club Sponsers FHS Library Club Tea. *The Leader*.

The Leader: Freeport's official Newspaper. (1949, April 24). F.H.S Gets Field of Nine Acres for Its Exclusive Use. *The Leader* , pp. 1, 120.

The National Archives. (n.d.). *The Amistad Case*. Retrieved from National Archives: https://www.archives.gov/education/lessons/amistad

The Peace Corps . (1967).

Toomey, P. (2000, August 31). *Arthur Ashe Statue Unveiled by USTA at Flushing Meadows*. Retrieved from Queens Chronicle: https://www.qchron.com/editions/queenswide/arthur-ashe-statue-unveiled-by-usta-at-flushing-meadows/article_eafc23bf-2d73-55f2-bcc8-7b5f9be78c41.html

Truth, S. (1851). *Ain't I a Woman?* (S. Truth, Performer) Women's Convention, Akron, Ohio, USA.

undisclosed. (1963, February). 26 Are Arrested in theater case.

unknown. (1883, Novemeber 2). Long Island Notes. *The Long-Islander*.

Unknown. (1914, February 27). Demand Property Back . *The Brooklyn Daily Eagle*.

Unknown. (1922, May 4). Decribes Freeport Election as Crude. *The Brooklyn Daily Eagle* .

unknown. (1950, Decemeber 30). Aged Freeport Mother Triumphed Against the Odds. *Nassau Daily Review-Star*.

unknown. (1972, November 8). Outlook is Bleak in Roosevelt. *The New York Times*.

unknown. (n.d.). *The History of Roosevelt.* Retrieved from Roosevelt UFSD: https://www.rooseveltufsd.org/domain/113

ushistory.org. (https://www.history.org/us/27.asp, january 21). *The Peculiar Insitution*. Retrieved from U.S History Online Textbook: 2021

Victor G. Becker. (2022, 8 7). *The Tribes of Long Island: designed, compiled and lithographed by Victor G. Becker; Map Collection.* Retrieved from Brooklyn Historical Society: https://mapcollections.brooklynhistory.org/map/the-indian-tribes-of-long-island-designed-compiled-and-lithographed-by-victor-g-becker/

Vigeant, F. (2022, February 16). *Programs: Fannie Lou Hamer's America*. Retrieved February 2023, from https://www.witf.org/2022/02/16/198359

Vise, D. d. (2011, novemeber 11). Morgan State Honors its Sit in Pioneers. *The Washington Post*.

Wayne Coffey. (2007, August). *The Queen and her Court*. Retrieved from The Daily News.

William G. Pomeroy Foundation. (2016). *Historical Marker: Bennington Park.* Retrieved 2019, from https://www.wgpfoundation.org/historic-markers/bennington-park

William G. Pomeroy Foundation. (n.d.). *Historical Marker: Bennington Park.* Retrieved 2019, from Historical Marker: wpgpfpundation.org/historic-markers/bennington-park-park/

Zizori, W. F. (2020, July 9). *Baltimore's Northwood: Remembrance of Desegregation Past.* Retrieved from Maryland Matters: https://www.marylandmatters.org/2020/07/09/baltimores-northwood-remembrance-of-desegregation-past/